ROUTLEDGE LIBRARY EDITIONS:
ACCOUNTING HISTORY

Volume 24

FINANCIAL ACCOUNTING MILESTONES IN THE ANNUAL REPORTS OF UNITED STATES STEEL CORPORATION

FINANCIAL ACCOUNTING MILESTONES IN THE ANNUAL REPORTS OF UNITED STATES STEEL CORPORATION

The First Seven Decades

Edited by
RICHARD VANGERMEERSCH

Routledge
Taylor & Francis Group

LONDON AND NEW YORK

First published in 1986 by Garland Publishing, Inc.

This edition first published in 2021
by Routledge
2 Park Square, Milton Park, Abingdon, Oxon OX14 4RN

and by Routledge
52 Vanderbilt Avenue, New York, NY 10017

Routledge is an imprint of the Taylor & Francis Group, an informa business

British Library Cataloguing in Publication Data
A catalogue record for this book is available from the British Library

ISBN: 978-0-367-33564-9 (Set)
ISBN: 978-1-00-304636-3 (Set) (ebk)
ISBN: 978-0-367-52236-0 (Volume 24) (hbk)
ISBN: 978-0-367-52239-1 (Volume 24) (pbk)
ISBN: 978-1-00-305709-3 (Volume 24) (ebk)

Publisher's Note
The publisher has gone to great lengths to ensure the quality of this reprint but points out that some imperfections in the original copies may be apparent.

Disclaimer
The publisher has made every effort to trace copyright holders and would welcome correspondence from those they have been unable to trace.

FINANCIAL ACCOUNTING MILESTONES IN THE ANNUAL REPORTS OF UNITED STATES STEEL CORPORATION
The First Seven Decades

Richard Vangermeersch, editor

Garland Publishing, Inc.
New York and London
1986

For a complete list of Garland's publications in accounting,
please see the final pages of this volume.

Library of Congress Cataloging-in-Publication Data

Annual report of the United States Steel Corporation
for the fiscal year ended . . . . Selections.
Financial accounting milestones in the annual
reports of United States Steel Corporation.

(Accounting thought and practice through the years)
"Selections from the annual reports of U.S. Steel
Corporation over the period 1902–1963"—P.
Includes index.
1. United States Steel Corporation—Accounting—
History.   2. Steel industry and trade—Accounting—
History.   3. Corporation reports—History.   4. Financial
statements—History.   I. Vangermeersch, Richard G. J.
II. United States Steel Corporation.   III. Title.
IV. Series.
HV5686.S75A55 1986   338.7'669142'0973   86-10000
ISBN 0-8240-7874-8

Design by Bonnie Goldsmith

The volumes in this series are printed on acid-free, 250-year-life paper.

Printed in the United States of America

CONTENTS

Introduction

Living in 1939; About Our Financial Affairs; Inventories;
Consolidated General Balance Sheet.

INTRODUCTION

This book extracts sections from the annual reports of United States Steel Corporation over the period 1902–1968. These extracts are milestones in the history of financial reporting in the United States. Historians and others interested in the evolution of accounting practice should find these documents of interest.

United States Steel was founded on April 1, 1901, during the trust movement. The company was one of the first major industrial corporations in the United States to publish a lengthy annual report to its shareholders, and May called its first report a "landmark for financial accounting in this country" [1943, p. 54]. Since the company continued this reporting policy in the years that followed, a study of U. S. Steel's annual reports is, in effect, a study of the best of financial reporting in the United States.

Considering the importance of U. S. Steel and its early and continued policy of detailed reporting, it is not surprising that these reports have been reviewed elsewhere. The first study was by Clair [1945], who reviewed nine aspects of the annual reports from 1902 to 1943. Clair found that U. S. Steel's reporting format changed in 1939: "The language of the 1939 report was conspicuous for its clarity and the statistics were presented in a much less formidable and more understandable fashion" [1945, p. 41]. However, he also noted that "on the score of disclosure some may say that the recent financial statements are weaker than those of prior years because of the reduction in the amount of detail" [1945, p. 51].

A second study was a detailed examination of the annual reports by Vangermeersch [1970], who also analyzed depreciation policies [1971]. He concluded that the management of U. S. Steel has been a positive force in terms of disclosure to stockholders and has generally tended to choose accounting methods that lowered net income in the year of the change [1970, p. 257]. These findings were similar to those in his study of the depreciation policies of U. S. Steel [1971, p. 69].

Schiff [1978] published an article that contrasted the 1902 and 1974 reports in order to shed further light on Benston's assertions about the efficacy of the Securities and Exchange Commission requirements for public reporting. His research demonstrated that the 1902 annual report compared very favorably with that of 1974, which is consistent with Benston's conclusion that SEC efforts did not pass a cost/benefit analysis [1978, p. 282].

Another study by Vangermeersch [1978] included U. S. Steel as one of the twenty companies whose annual reports were reviewed. That study selected items from Vangermeersch [1979], which analyzed sixty-three aspects of the annual reports of twenty companies from 1861 through 1969. He found that U. S. Steel did not abuse the freedom given to companies on the use of Earned Surplus and extraordinary items on the Income Statement [1978, pp. 654 and 657]. He also noted that U. S. Steel was not unusual in its maintaining the same audit firm [1979, p. 59].

The latest study by Younkins, Flesher, and Flesher [1984] analyzed sixteen topics from the annual reports of U. S. Steel from 1902 through 1951. They noted that U. S. Steel was the first company to publish consolidated statements in the contemporary format [1984, p. 249] and that it "was a leader in the development of financial reporting during the first half of the twentieth century" [1984, p. 246].

The 1902 report was greatly influenced by Arthur Lowes Dickinson, senior partner of Price Waterhouse & Company in the United States, and William Jay Filbert, Comptroller of U. S. Steel, and "did present some very relevant information on interim results at a level superior to current practice" [Schiff, 1978, pp. 280–281]. For instance, quarterly profits were disclosed. The positioning of the Income Account as the first item illustrated the importance of reporting net income [Vangermeersch, 1970, pp. 21–26]. U. S. Steel deducted dividends from net income, and this policy, which continued through the years, was not uncommon: "It is evident that many managements have perceived dividends to be a component of the yearly addition to retained earnings than to be a distribution from the retained earnings account" [Vangermeersch, 1979, p. 13].

Among other points of significance were the $25 million working capital contribution, which was included as a part of Undivided Surplus, and the charges to the Undivided Surplus account. There was also a detailed schedule of Maintenance, Renewals, and Extraordinary Replacements. It appears that depreciation was funded. Detailed disclosures of production, inventories, capital stock, long-term debt, property expenditures, and mergers were given. Information about employees was noted. Management took the opportunity to state its operating philosophies. The Balance Sheet was listed in reverse order of liquidity. The Income Account was supplemented by a General Profit and Loss Account. A funds statement was presented. Younkins, Flesher, and Flesher found this surprising [1984, p. 255]. Monthly earnings were disclosed. There were seven pages devoted to a Summary of Manufacturing Plants and twenty-two pages to Views of Representative Properties. Vangermeersch concluded that U. S. Steel could only be commended for the very informative data it presented to the stockholders [1970, p. 55].

In 1903 comparative reporting was extended to the Income Account. The 1903 Annual Report also featured "conservative" steps taken by U. S. Steel's management in appropriations from net earnings and in inventory valuation. This conservative policy, which was more conservative than a policy recommended by Montgomery [Vangermeersch, 1970, pp. 67–68], was extended to the valuation of intercompany inventories in 1904.

Price Waterhouse noted in the 1908 Annual Report that the lower level of operations had led, in effect, to a lower depreciation charge. With 13 million ingots produced in 1907, U. S. Steel had a depreciation charge of $25.7 million. In 1908, 7.8 million ingots resulted in a $15.4 million charge [Vangermeersch, 1971, p. 72]. Vangermeersch noted that the relationship between depreciation and production had been stressed by such accounting writers as Matheson and Pixley [1971, p. 57]. He quoted Filbert, who stated, "Depreciation is not the same amount year by year, you know. If you don't run your plants, your depreciation is not as great" [1971, p. 57].

A significant reclassification of depreciation funds from the liability section to the asset section, as a contra asset, occurred in the Balance Sheet in the 1910 Annual Report. Vangermeersch found that the reclassification was related to the Corporate Excise Tax of 1909 [1971, pp. 77–80]. Another significant reclassification occurred in 1911, when the intercompany profit in ending inventory was deducted from the total of Inventories, rather than being a component of Undivided Surplus.

There was also a $.7 million charge for appropriation for permanent pension fund in the Account. "Conservatism" was once again discussed in the Inventories section.

A version of the base stock inventory valuation approach was adopted in 1916. U. S. Steel made significant accounting adaptations because of the entry of the United States into World War I. $55 million was appropriated in the Income Account for additional property, new plants, and construction. The base stock approach was continued, and a special Allowance for Estimated Proportion of Extraordinary Cost of Facilities Installed by Reason of War Requirements and Conditions was established. In 1918 war efforts were summarized, and the excess cost paid for war facilities was analyzed. The policies for inventory and new facilities were continued in 1918, 1919, and 1920. Vangermeersch considered these accounting policy changes as price justification maneuvers by U. S. Steel [1970, pp. 89–94]. The economic downturn of 1921 led to a dramatic decrease in net earnings. This occurred even though the inventory reserve decreased by $29.2 million. U. S. Steel and Price Waterhouse felt compelled to explain the situation. A further decrease occurred in 1922. By 1923 the downturn had ended, and $40 million was set aside for additions, improvements, or betterments.

There was a gale of accounting activity in 1929, almost as if U. S. Steel were able to predict the Great Depression that followed the Great Crash. There was a housecleaning of accounts closed to Surplus. Vangermeersch commented on the freedom U. S. Steel's management had to affect these changes through Surplus [1970, p. 99]. The downturn in business was discussed. Earnings Per Share was disclosed for the first time in the Annual Report for 1930. This disclosure policy was discontinued in 1931 and not resumed until 1949. The continued downturn in business was reported in 1930. There would have been a net loss for 1931, except for profits on the sales of fixed property. A reclassification from General Condensed Profit and Loss Account to the Consolidated Income Account of $13.9 million of overhead expenses and taxes occurred in 1932 and was discussed in the Operations for the Year section. In 1933 the Surplus account was increased by a refund from past years and a reversal of a reserve totalling $25 million and then decreased by appropriations totalling $22 million. Some business improvement was reported, and a schedule of working capital was included in the 1933 Annual Report. The reclassification of overhead and taxes continued in 1934.

In 1935 it was reported that the company had performed a detailed study of its investment in depreciable property, and this led to writedowns and reclassifications. By 1936 disclosure was made of intangibles. In 1937 it was proposed that intangibles be written down to $1 in the following year. U. S. Steel also discussed its activities on behalf of the health and welfare of its workers. In 1938 the writedown of intangibles occurred as a part of a recapitalization. Vangermeersch concluded that U. S. Steel wrote down fixed assets in 1935 in order to reduce depreciation charges [1970, pp. 128–131]. He believed that the policies of segregating and writing down intangible assets were the culmination of the "de-watering" of the original valuation of U. S. Steel [1970, pp. 135–139 and 37–46].

The 1939 Annual Report ushered in a new public relations orientation. This annual report was much more colorful and much easier to read [Clair, 1945, p. 427]. The section How the Corporation Earned its Living in 1939 was a good example of this change. The Consolidated Balance Sheet was changed to the order-of-liquidity format, and there was a change in the method of classifying supplies. Vangermeersch attributed the format change to a study done by the National Association of Manufacturers, which recommended the annual report be a forum for industry opinion and for showing that the chief business function was the service performed for the nation [1970, pp. 142–143]. Younkins, Flesher, and Flesher commented that it was not until 1939 that a large firm like U. S. Steel dropped "cents" from the amounts appearing in its financial statements [1984, p. 254].

U. S. Steel adopted the life inventory method in 1941 and also started its wartime accounting era with the amortization of emergency facilities account and with the special provision for contingencies account. There was an explanation of U. S. Steel's changed pension policies in 1942. Since pension accounting issues were to become very significant, this discussion has important historical significance. The Notes to Accounts section was placed under the Consolidated General Balance Sheet and included discussions of many wartime accounting issues. The Reserve for Estimated Additional Costs Arising Out of War continued to increase in 1943. Treasury stock was reclassified in the equity section. The 1945 Annual Report included a $35.6 million writedown to the Reserve for Estimated Additional Costs . . . for additional amortization due to the ending of the emergency period. The Balance Sheet was in the working capital format. Vangermeersch considered U. S. Steel's wartime reserve to be in accordance with the promulgations of the American Institute of Accountants [1970, p. 157].

Peacetime did not mean labor peace for U. S. Steel or for the United States. U. S. Steel used two sections, Coal Strikes of 1946 and Steel Labor Situation, in its 1946 Annual Report to express its views on this matter. Financial matters were discussed in Profit and Loss Facts and Factors. $27.6 million of strike costs were charged to the Reserve for the Estimated Additional Costs Arising Out of the War account. Vangermeersch noted that this charge for strike costs to a wartime reserve was not in accord with Accounting Research Bulletin #26 [1970, pp. 185–186]. The 1947 Annual Report was utilized to explain U. S. Steel's struggle with inflation. Management went so far as to institute a version of replacement cost depreciation, and this led to a disagreement with its auditors. A new policy for deprecation was adopted in 1948 and received the approval of Price Waterhouse. An interesting discussion of deprecation and replacement cost appeared in 1949. Vangermeersch viewed the replacement cost depreciation fight as a trailblazing stance by U. S. Steel against the forces of the American Institute of Accountants (now the AICPA), the SEC, and Price Waterhouse [1971, pp. 63–64]. He noted that DuPont also adopted a replacement cost approach in 1947 [1978, pp. 657–658].

U. S. Steel disclosed its new policy of expensing $50 million of past service pension costs in 1950. In 1954 the topic of depreciation once again surfaced with a compelling appeal for plant modernization. The 1955 Annual Report contained the first disclosure of U. S. Steel's Combined Pension Trusts. Dramatic changes in pension funding policy and in the expensing of pensions occurred in 1958. Price Waterhouse noted the lack of comparability between 1957 and 1958 in its report. Vangermeersch considered the 1958 change as a "utilization of a discretionary accounting procedure to improve the net income figure . . ." [1970, p. 235]. A rather elaborate defense and explanation of "profits" was presented in 1958. The 1965 Annual Report contained discussions of U. S. Steel's accounting policies for investment credits and pension funding. In 1968 U. S. Steel switched its depreciation policy to the straight-line method. Vangermeersch considered that switch not uncommon during that period, and it was probably discounted by the market [1971, p. 69]. U. S. Steel also revised its policy of accounting for the investment credit in 1968.

The extracts from U. S. Steel's annual reports highlighted here are presented as they originally appeared. These documents capture many historical events and management's reaction to them. This information is, as Goldberg [1965] put it, part of "a vast reservoir of information which has been tapped only to a slight extent to date" [p. 79].

REFERENCES

Clair, R. S., "Evolution of Corporate Reports: Observations on the Annual Reports of the United States Steel Corporation," *The Journal of Accountancy*, [January, 1945], pp. 39–51.

Goldberg, L., *An Inquiry into the Nature of Accounting*, (American Accounting Association, 1965).

May, G. O., *Financial Accounting: A Distillation of Experience*, (The Macmillan Company, 1943).

Schiff, A., "Annual Reports in the United States: A Historical Perspective," *Accounting and Business Research*, [Autumn, 1978], pp. 279–284.

Vangermeersch, R., *A Study of Institutional Forces Concerned with Financial Accounting in the United States, Utilizing the Annual Reports of the United States Steel Corporation as Reference Points*, (University Microfilms, 1970).

———, "A Historical Overview of Depreciation: U. S. Steel, 1902–1970," *Mississippi Valley Journal of Business and Economics*, (Winter, 1971–72), pp. 56–74.

———, "Implications from an Analysis of Financial Accounting Events from the Annual Reports of 20 Industrial Companies Starting from 1861 through 1912 and Ending in 1969," *Collected Papers of the American Accounting Association's Annual Meeting, 1978*, pp. 648–670.

———, *Financial Reporting Techniques in 20 Industrial Companies Since 1861*, (University Presses of Florida, 1979).

Younkins, E., D. L. Flesher, and T. K. Flesher, "The Financial Statements of U. S. Steel, 1902–1951: A Half Century of Leadership in Reporting," Working Paper No. 58, Volume 3, *The Academy of Accounting Historians Working Paper Series*, co-edited by Ashton C. Bishop and Don-Rice Richards, (The Academy of Accounting Historians, 1984), pp. 246–259.

1902 ANNUAL REPORT

Income Account Shown First

Dividends Subtracted from Net Earnings

Working Capital Provided in Organization in Surplus Account

Quarterly Profits Given

Expenditures for Maintenance Detailed

Disclosure of Various Funds

Production Data and Finished Products Shown

Inventories in Significant Detail

Capital Stock and Debt Described

Property Account Analyzed

Merger of Union-Sharon Discussed

Employee and Stockholder Data Given

Orders on Hand Shown

Organizational Philosophy Explained

Price Waterhouse the External Auditors

Detailed Balance Sheet and General Profit and Loss Account

Funds Statement Portrayed

Bonds in Even Greater Detail

Monthly Earnings on a Comparative Schedule

Manufacturing Plants Catalogued

Pictures of Plants Shown

FIRST ANNUAL REPORT

TO STOCKHOLDERS OF

United States Steel Corporation

OFFICE OF UNITED STATES STEEL CORPORATION,
51 Newark Street, Hoboken, New Jersey.
April 6, 1903.

To the Stockholders:

The Board of Directors submits herewith a combined report of the operations and affairs of the United States Steel Corporation and its Subsidiary Companies for the fiscal year which ended December 31st, 1902, together with the condition of the finances and property at the close of that year.

INCOME ACCOUNT FOR THE YEAR.

The total net earnings of all properties after deducting expenditures for ordinary repairs and maintenance (approximately $21,000,000*), also interest on Bonds and fixed charges of the subsidiary companies, amounted to $133,308,763.72

Less, Appropriations for the following purposes, viz.:

Sinking Funds on Bonds of Subsidiary Companies	$624,064.43
Depreciation and Extinguishment Funds (regular provisions for the year)	4,834,710.28
Extraordinary Replacement Funds (regular provisions for the year)	9,315,614.76
Special Fund for Depreciation and Improvements	10,000,000.00

24,774,389.47

Balance of Net Earnings for the year $108,534,374.25

* The actual expenditures for ordinary repairs and maintenance, as see table on page 7, were $21,230,218.13. It cannot be stated, however, that this specific sum was taken out of the net earnings for the year, because in the manufacturing and producing properties the expenses for repairs and maintenance enter into and form a part of production cost. And as the net earnings of such properties are stated on the basis of gross receipts for product shipped, less the production cost thereof, the income for the year is charged with outlays for repairs and maintenance only to the extent that the production during such period was actually shipped. But as the shipments in 1902 equaled practically the year's production, approximately the entire amount of the expenditures in question has been deducted before stating the net earnings as above.

Balance of Net Earnings for the year, brought forward............................. $108,534,374.25

Deduct:

Interest on U. S. Steel Corporation Bonds for the year $15,187,850.00

Sinking Fund on U. S. Steel Corporation Bonds for the year............. 3,040,000.00

                                                         18,227,850.00

Balance $90,306,524.25

Dividends for the year on U. S. Steel Corporation Stocks, viz.:

Preferred, 7 per cent... $35,720,177.50

Common, 4 per cent... 20,332,690.00

4

                                             56,052,867.50

Undivided Profits or Surplus for the year....................................... $34,253,656.75

UNDIVIDED SURPLUS OF U. S. STEEL CORPORATION AND ITS SUBSIDIARY COMPANIES.

(Since Organization of U. S. Steel Corporation, April 1, 1901.)

Surplus or Working Capital provided in organization....................................... $25,000,000.00

The Surplus arising from operations for the nine months ended December 31, 1901,

as reported was... $19,828,827.14

Add, Profits during this period of properties owned but not heretofore included.... 375,627.86

                                  $20,204,455.00

Less, Written off in 1902 to Cost of Property and for adjustment of sundry contracts

and accounts.. 1,583,514.70

                                        18,620,940.30

Surplus for the year 1902, as above... 34,253,656.75

Total Surplus, December 31, 1902.. $77,874,597.05

NET PROFITS AND SURPLUS OF UNITED STATES STEEL CORPORATION AND SUBSIDIARY COMPANIES AT CLOSE OF EACH OF THE QUARTERS NAMED.

(INCLUDES ONLY SURPLUS RECEIVED OR EARNED ON OR SUBSEQUENT TO APRIL 1ST, 1901.)

Quarter Ending	Net Profits for Quarter Available for Dividends.	Surplus at Close of Quarter before Declaration of Dividends *	Dividends on U. S. Steel Corporation Stock for Respective Quarters.	Balance of Surplus.
June 30th, 1901	$19,907,277.28	$44,907,277.28	$13,957,028.25	$30,950,249.03
September 30th, 1901	20,063,626.25	51,013,875.28	14,010,277 75	37,003,597.53
December 31st, 1901	20,629,205.52	57,632,803.05	14,011,862.75	43,620,940.30
March 31st, 1902	16,700,221.26	60,321,161.56	14 013,434.25	46,307,727.31
June 30th, 1902	26,742,277.86	73,050,005.17	14,013,542.75	59,036 462.42
September 30th, 1902	25,849,817.58	84,886,280.00	14,012 946.25	70,873,333.75
December 31st, 1902	21,014,207.55	91 887,541.30	14,012,944.25	77 874 597.05

5.

* Includes Capital Surplus of $25,000 00, provided at date of organization.

NOTE.—Special Depreciation and Improvement Fund of $10 000,000, set aside from 1902 Net Earnings, is distributed in above table, $2,500,000 to each quarter of 1902.

MAINTENANCE, RENEWALS AND EXTRAORDINARY REPLACEMENTS.

The physical condition of the properties has been fully maintained during the year, the cost of which has been charged to current operations. The amount expended by all properties during the year for maintenance, renewals and extraordinary replacements aggregated $29,157,010.73.

This total is apportioned as follows:

Expended on	Ordinary Maintenance and Repairs.*	Extraordinary Replacements.†	Total.
Manufacturing Properties	$16,099,217.94	$6,978,230.48	$23,077,448.42
Coal and Coke Properties	881,804.77	94,664.39	976,469.16
Iron Ore Properties	355,220.12	....	355,220.12
Transportation Properties:			
Railroads	3,544,654.27	607,967.88	4,152,622.15
Steamships and Docks	313,801.37	192,317.80	506,119.17
Miscellaneous Properties	35,519.66	53,612.05	89,131.71
Total	$21,230,218.13	$7,926,792.60	$29,157,010.73

* See explanatory footnote on page 5.
† These expenditures were paid from funds provided from earnings to cover requirements of the character included herein, as more fully explained on page 8.

SINKING, DEPRECIATION AND EXTRAORDINARY REPLACEMENT FUNDS.

Provisional charges are made monthly to operations for Bond Sinking Funds and to establish funds for Depreciation, and for reserves for Extraordinary Replacements. The purposes for which these funds are particularly designed are as follows:

BOND SINKING FUNDS.—These are the funds required by the respective mortgages to be set aside annually for retirement of the bonds issued thereunder.

DEPRECIATION AND EXTINGUISHMENT FUNDS.—The appropriations for these purposes have been made with the idea that thus aided the bond sinking funds will liquidate the capital investment in the properties at the expiration of their life. These moneys are used not for current operating expenses, but to offset consumption and depreciation by the provision of new property or of reserve funds.

EXTRAORDINARY REPLACEMENT FUNDS.—These are designed to be used to improve, modernize and strengthen the properties. They are not used for ordinary maintenance, repairs and renewals (such expenses are included in current operating costs), but for the substitution of improved and modern machinery, plants, facilities, equipment, etc.

During the year ended December 31, 1902, the appropriations made for the foregoing funds, together with the payments therefrom, and the balances in the funds at the close of the year, were as follows:

FUNDS.	CREDITS TO FUNDS.			PAYMENTS FROM AND CHARGES TO FUNDS.		Balances to Credit of Funds Dec. 31, 1902.
	Balance December 31, 1901.	Set Aside from Earnings during 1902	Total.	Payments to Trustees of Sinking Funds.	Other Payments and Charges.	
Sinking Fund on United States Steel Corporation Bonds	$1,773,333.33	$3,040,000.00	$4,813,333.33	$3,040,000.00	......	$1,773,333.33
Sinking Funds on Bonds of Subsidiary Companies	157,344.36	624,064.43	781,408.79	564,064.43	......	217,344.36
Total Bond Sinking Funds	$1,930,677.69	$3,664,064.43	$5,594,742.12	$3,604,064.43	......	$1,990,677.69
Depreciation and Extinguishment	8,884,756.84	4,834,710.28	13,719,467.12	......	$12,011,856.53 (a)	1,707,610.59
Extraordinary Replacement	5,052,388.74	9,315,614.76	14,368,003.50	......	7,801,812.60 (b)	6,566,190.90
Special Depreciation and Improvement	......	10,000,000.00	10,000,000.00	......	......	10,000,000.00
Total	$15,867,823.27	$27,814,389.47	$43,682,212.74	$3,604,064.43	$19,813,669.13	$20,264,479.18

(a) Construction Expenditures charged off to Depreciation and Extinguishment Funds.
(b) Expended for Extraordinary Replacements.. $7,926,792.60
    Less Miscellaneous Receipts credited to Extraordinary Replacement Fund...................... 124,930.00

    Net $7,801,862.60

The balances to the credit of the several funds on December 31, 1902, per the preceding table, are included in the current assets of the organization, viz.:

In General Cash.. $1,773,333.33
In Current Assets—Cash, Marketable Securities, Inventories, etc........................ 18,491,145.85

Total $20,264,479.18

7

PRODUCTION.

The production of the several properties for the year 1902 was as follows:

IRON ORE MINED:

		Tons.	Tons.
From Marquette Range............	....	1,487,370	
From Menominee Range..........	....	2,675,754	
From Gogebic Range............	....	2,064,492	
From Vermillion Range..........	....	2,057,537	
From Mesaba Range.............	....	7,778,026	
			16,063,179
COKE MANUFACTURED...........	....		9,521,567
COAL MINED, not including that used in making coke...................................			709,367

BLAST FURNACE PRODUCTS:

		Tons.	Tons.
Pig Iron.......................	....	7,802,812	
Spiegel	....	128,265	
Ferro-Manganese and Silicon......	....	44,453	
			7,975,530

STEEL INGOT PRODUCTION:

		Tons.	Tons.
Bessemer Ingots..................	....	6,759,210	
Open Hearth Ingots...............	....	2,984,708	
			9,743,918

ROLLED AND OTHER FINISHED PRODUCTS FOR SALE.

	Tons.
Steel Rails..........	1,920,786
Blooms, Billets, Slabs, Sheet and Tin Plate Bars	782,637
Plates	649,541
Merchant Steel, Skelp, Shapes, Hoops, Bands and Cotton Ties...........	1,254,560
Tubing and Pipe.......	744,062
Rods	109,330
Wire and Products of Wire...........	1,122,809
Sheets—Black, Galvanized and Tin Plates	783,576
Finished Structural Work...........	481,029
Angle and Splice Bars and Joints...........	139,954
Spikes, Bolts, Nuts and Rivets...........	42,984
Axles	136,787
Sundry Iron and Steel Products...........	29,177
Total	8,197,232
Spelter	23,982
Copperas	14,224
	Bbls.
Cement	486,357

INVENTORIES.

The aggregate inventories of all properties on December 31, 1902, equaled the total sum of $104,390,844. About one-third of this sum is represented by the value of iron ore on hand. It is necessary to accumulate large tonnages of ore during the summer and fall months for conversion during the period extending from December 1 to April 15 when, owing to the close of navigation on the Great Lakes, the mining of ore is reduced and shipment from the mines entirely stopped.

The quantities of partly finished materials (Blooms, Billets, Bars, etc.), also of finished products, are somewhat above the normal average, owing largely to the railroad congestion at principal producing centres, which prevented prompt deliveries from the mills.

Inventories are taken on basis of actual cost of the materials and products at the several departments of the companies holding the same.

The following is a general classification of the inventories on December 31:

Ores	$34,072,939
Pig Iron, Scrap, Spiegel and Ferro	6,294,358
Coal and Coke	858,820
Pig Tin, Lead and Spelter	1,362,466
Limestone, Fluxes and Refractories	969,203
Rolls and Molds and Stools	2,359,505
Manufacturing Supplies, Stores and Miscellaneous items not otherwise classified	10,299,689
Ingots, Blooms, Billets, Sheet and Tin Plate Bars, Skelp, Rods, etc	12,824,909
Finished Products	18,968,396
Mining Supplies and Stores	1,866,125
Railroad Supplies and Stores	1,165,374
Material, labor and expense locked up in bridge and structural contracts, including estimated profit thereon $27,443,409	
Less bills rendered on account 17,447,810	
	9,995,599
Material in transit and on consignment	3,353,461
Total	**$104,390,844**

CAPITAL STOCK.

The outstanding capital stock of the United States Steel Corporation was increased during the year by the issues of the following amounts for the acquisition of additional shares of capital stock of the subsidiary companies surrendered for exchange, viz.:

Common Stock issued.. $75,200

Preferred Stock issued.. 75,500

The total capital stock of the United States Steel Corporation issued and outstanding on December 31, 1902, was as follows:

Common Stock.. $508,302,500

Preferred Stock.. 510,281,100

BONDED, DEBENTURE AND MORTGAGE DEBT.

At the beginning of the year the bonded and mortgage debt of the United States Steel Corporation
and Subsidiary Companies in the hands of the public was............................. $366,097,697.82

Issues were made during the year by the several companies, as follows, viz.:

Bessemer & Lake Erie R.R. Co., Erie Equipment Trust Bonds.............	$1,220,000.00	
Pittsburg, Bessemer & Lake Erie R.R. Co. Debenture Gold Bonds, total issue		
$500,000 (Carnegie Company proportion)................................	260,895.00	
Elgin, Joliet & Eastern Ry. Co. First Mortgage Bonds	648,000.00	
Duluth, Missabe & Northern Ry. Co. Con. Second Mortgage Bonds..........	75,000.00	
Sundry Real Estate Mortgages assumed by Coke Companies	166,443.35	
		2,370,338.35
		$368,468,036.17

Less, retired or acquired during the year, viz.:

The Johnson Co. (of Pa.) First Mortgage Bonds............................	$95,000.00	
National Steel Co.'s issues:		
Ohio Steel Co., First Mortgage Bonds................................	80,000.00	
Junction Iron & Steel Co., Mortgage Bonds..........................	35,000.00	
Shenango Valley Steel Co., Mortgage Bonds..........................	150,000.00	
Raney & Berger Iron Co., Mortgage Bonds...........................	80,000.00	

American Tin Plate Co. issues:

U. S. Iron & Tin Plate Mfg. Co., Mortgage Bonds.....................	$55,000.00
American Bridge Co., Purchase Money Mortgage Bonds...................	100,000.00
South-West Connellsville Coke Co., Mortgage Bonds.......................	36,000.00
Continental Coke Co., Purchase Money Mortgage Bonds..................	37,000.00
H. C. Frick Coke Co., First Mortgage Bonds............................	91,000.00
H. C. Frick Coke Co., Purchase Money Mortgage Bonds..................	150,000.00
Hostetter-Connellsville Coke Co., Purchase Money Mortgage Bonds (H. C. Frick Coke Co. proportion)..	12,500.00

11

Pittsburg, Bessemer & Lake Erie R. R. Co. Bonds (Carnegie Company proportion):

Car Trust Warrants...	17,639.40
Conneaut Equipment Trust..	26,089.50
Bessemer Equipment Trust..	39,134.25
Illinois Steel Co., Debenture Scrip................................	1,418.55
Sundry real estate mortgages of various companies..........................	691,795.63
Total Bonds and Mortgages paid and canceled.....................	$1,697,577.33

Bonds purchased by Trustees of Sinking Funds for investment therein, viz.:

U. S. Steel Corporation, 50 Year Gold Bonds................	$2,698,000.00	
Duluth, Missabe & Northern Ry. Con. First Mortgage..........	83,000.00	
Duluth, Missabe & Northern Ry. Con. Second Mortgage.......	151,000.00	
American Steamship Co., First Mortgage....................	183,000.00	
		3,115,000.00
		4,812,577.33

Bonded, Debenture and Mortgage Debt in hands of Public, December 31, 1902.........	$363,655,458.84
Net Decrease during the year..	$2,442,238.98

In addition to the foregoing transactions in bonds there were surrendered for exchange $207,000 of

13

The Carnegie Company Collateral Trust Bonds, and in lieu of which an equal amount of United States Steel Corporation 5 per cent. Fifty Year Gold Bonds was issued.

The amount of bonds and mortgages retired, $4,812,577.33, was paid from sinking and depreciation fund provisions and surplus earnings. Since the organization of the United States Steel Corporation, April 1, 1901, to January 1, 1903, the amount of bonds and mortgages paid and retired by all properties, including bonds purchased for sinking funds, was $6,384,758.75. There were issued during this same period bonds and mortgages for new property acquired to the amount of $3,456,659.76, a net decrease of $2,928,098.99.

A detailed schedule of the bonds of the several properties issued and outstanding in hands of public on December 31, 1902, will be found on page 27.

12

PROPERTY ACCOUNT.

The expenditures made during the year by all the properties and charged to Property Account equaled, less credits for property sold, the total sum of $16,586,531.77. These outlays were made for the completion of construction work at manufacturing properties under way when the U. S. Steel Corporation was organized, also for necessary additions and extensions authorized since its organization, for the acquirement of additional ore and coal property, the opening and development of new mines and plants, for additional equipment and facilities demanded by the growing requirements of the business of the transportation properties, to secure material reduction in cost of manufacture, transportation of raw and unfinished materials, and distribution of finished products, etc. As stated in the certificate of the chartered accountants (see page 24), "during the year only actual additions and extensions have been charged Property Account." The outlays as above are classified by properties as follows:

Expended by

United States Steel Corporation, on account of acquirement of stocks of subsidiary companies..	$258,473.31
Manufacturing Properties..	9,743,125.78
Ore Properties...	1,971,547.08
Coal and Coke Properties...	2,043,168.51
Transportation Properties..	2,741,652.51
Miscellaneous Properties...*Cr.*	171,430.52
Total	$16,586,531.77

Some of the principal additions to the properties of the subsidiary companies on account of which the above expenditures were made during the year are as follows:

MANUFACTURING PROPERTIES.

CARNEGIE STEEL CO.:

	Expenditures in 1902.
Two New Blast Furnaces, Edgar Thomson Works...	$793,041
Fourteen inch Billet and ten inch and thirteen inch Bar Mills, Duquesne Works.................	186,489
Two New O. H. Furnaces, Duquesne Works...	249,794
Additional Blowing Engines, Duquesne Works...	84,035
Extension Armor Plate Plant, Homestead Works...	1,192,48<
Two New O. H. Furnaces, Homestead Works..	162,371
One New Blast Furnace, Carrie Plant..	375,158

ILLINOIS STEEL CO.:

Two New Blast Furnaces and Ore Unloading Equipment, South Works.......................	245,818
Addition to Cement Plant, South Works..	70,843
Ingot Heating Furnace, Slab Mill, South Works...	79,999

13

15

AMERICAN STEEL AND WIRE CO.:

Expenditures
in 1902.

Oxide Plant, Worcester..	$87,062
Rail Bond Drop Forging Plant, Worcester...	60,518
Extension of three track Steel Trestle, Central Furnaces..............................	87,223
New Mixer and Blooming Mill, Newburgh Works.......................................	120,604
New Tinning Department, Newburgh Works..	29,041
New Copperas Plant, Rockdale Works...	22,432
Real Estate, New Works, Equipment and Warehouse, Pacific Works, San Francisco............	242,687

NATIONAL TUBE CO.:

New Blast Furnace, Riverside Department..	414,542
Real Estate, McKeesport...	90,288

NATIONAL STEEL CO.:

Eighteen inch Continuous Mill, Mingo Works...	210,277
New Shear Building, Mingo Works..	22,971
Enlargement Blooming Mill, Mingo Works...	22,293
New Blast Furnaces and Condenser Plant, Mingo Works	53,887
Addition to Converting Works, New Castle Works......................................	145,835
Additional Blowing Engines, Furnaces, New Castle Works	64,839
Additional Real Estate, Ohio Works..	21,000

AMERICAN STEEL HOOP CO.:

Enlargement and Improvement of Blast Furnaces, Isabella Furnaces.........................	915,236
Sixteen inch Mill and Equipment, McCutcheon Mills.......................................	39,688

AMERICAN TIN PLATE CO.:

Eight Additional Tin Mills, Extension to Specialty Tin House, Additional Warehouse and other Additions at Laughlin Works..	54,783
Construction of New Works and Sundry Additions at Chester Works.........................	67,177
Twelve Additional Tin Mills at Monessen Works..	518,099
Continuous Mill and Sundry Additions at Monongahela Works..............................	155,041

AMERICAN SHEET STEEL CO.:

New Jobbing Mill, Aetna Works..	$53,179
Sixteen Annealing Furnaces, Aetna Works...	55,506
Extension to Boiler Plant, Machine and Roll Shop, Aetna Works............................	28,064
Eight New Sheet Mills, Vandergrift Works..	131,827
Two New O. H. Furnaces, Vandergrift Works...	81,157
Extension of Natural Gas Line, Vandergrift Works..	130,714
Five Annealing Furnaces, Dover Works...	33,348
Electrical Equipment, Houk Mine, Dover Works...	13,905
Additions to Plant, Wellsville Works...	193,008
Two Jump Mills and other Additions at Scottdale Works...................................	36,921
Four Annealing Furnaces, Struthers Works...	43,854
Two Cold Mills, Struthers Works..	11,625
New Thirty Ton Electric Crane, Struthers Works...	25,332
Additions to Sheet Mill and two Additional Boilers, Struthers Works....................	34,601
Two New Sheet Mills, Wood Works...	41,986
Extension to Buildings, Wood Works..	28,431

15

AMERICAN BRIDGE CO.:

New Plant at Economy, Pa., Ambridge Plant...	683,494
Additions to the Trenton Plant...	154,861
Additions to the Toledo Plant..	43,970
Additions to the Brooklyn Plant..	110,864
New Machine Shop and accessory Buildings and Machinery, Pencoyd Plant..................	158,710

ORE PROPERTIES.

Additional Fee properties, leases, etc., acquired....................................	$985,322
Purchase of Additional Real Estate, and Timber Lands to provide Mining Timber.........	565,659
For construction at Savoy and Sibley mines of two new Steel Shaft Houses, new Engine, Power and Hoisting Plant, Compressors, Equipment, etc....................................	162,119
Additional Equipment and Additions to the Mining Plants at Fayal, Stephens and Adams mines..........	145,813
General Additions to Mining Plants and Equipment at various mines of a total expenditure, less credits for property sold and transferred, to amount of................................	112,629

17

		Expenditures in 1902.

COAL AND COKE PROPERTIES.

Additional coking and steam coal lands.. $258,480

Development of new coking coal properties in the Connellsville and Lower Connellsville districts, viz.:

Development and opening of mines... $498,854

Coke ovens... 284,596

Mine and oven equipment... 146,704

Dwellings 101,473

1,031,627

Development of coking coal property in the Pocahontas district in West Virginia..................... 585,885

This is the property referred to in the preliminary report to stockholders submitted at the annual meeting, February 17, 1902. Fifty thousand acres of coking coal are held under lease on a royalty basis, and on terms favorable for production and transportation.

Development of steam coal property in Washington and Allegheny counties, Pa...................... 198,058

16

TRANSPORTATION PROPERTIES.

Additional Equipment—16 Locomotives, 1,050 Steel Gondola and Hopper cars, 400 Steel Coal cars, 150 Box cars, 8 Caboose and 5 Passenger cars... $1,763,158

Union R.R.—Construction retaining wall along Monongahela River.................................. 151,202

Bessemer and Lake Erie RR.:

New line, Kremis to Osgood.. 196,367

New Shops and Office Building at Greenville... 72,472

New Hotel, Exposition Park... 25,575

General Construction by all railroads, including additional right of way, buildings, mine and logging spurs, sidings, etc.. 532,878

MISCELLANEOUS PROPERTIES.

Carnegie Natural Gas Co.—New gas lines and pumping station.................................... $293,698

Carnegie Land Co.—Credit for property sold, less cost of additional land and improvements acquired..Cr. 582,155

Additional property, real estate and improvements acquired by sundry Water and Supply Companies.... 117,027

PROPERTY ACCOUNT EXPENDITURES SINCE ORGANIZATION U. S. STEEL CORPORATION.

The total amount of expenditures for property account by all properties, from April 1, 1901, to December 31, 1902, was as follows:

During the nine months ending December 31, 1901...................................... $16,956,868.63

During the fiscal year ending December 31, 1902, as hereinbefore shown..................... 16,586,531.77

Total $33,543,400.40

On account of the expenditures as above, funds have been provided by issue of bonds and mortgages by the Subsidiary Companies (chiefly securities of railroads) to amount of....... 3,456,659.76

Balance of outlays for Property Account from April 1, 1901, to December 31, 1902, paid in Cash from depreciation accounts and surplus earnings.................................. $30,086,740.64

18

UNION-SHARON PURCHASE.

In December, 1902, the Corporation acquired the entire issue of Capital Stock of the Union Steel Company, which latter company had absorbed the Sharon Steel Company and had acquired the entire issues of Capital Stock of the Sharon Ore Company, the Sharon Coke Company, the Sharon Sheet Steel Company, the Donora Mining Company, the Republic Coke Company, the River Coal Company, and a controlling interest in the Capital Stock of the Sharon Tin Plate Company and the Sharon Coal and Limestone Company. Such acquisition was effected by direct negotiation with the owners, on the basis of actual cost of the properties to the vendors, except as to certain ore and coal property and other lands, and as to them on a basis not exceeding actual present value.

In consideration of the transfer of the Union Steel Company's stock the Steel Corporation guaranteed the principal and interest of the Union Steel Company's Fifty Year First Mortgage and Collateral Trust Five per Cent. Gold Bonds issued and to be issued to the aggregate principal sum of $45,000,000. The amount of these bonds which were outstanding at the time the stock was formally turned over to the Steel Corporation was............... $29,114,000

The balance of the issue of the above bonds is reserved for the following purposes:

Sold for cash at par to be taken in monthly instalments during 1903 by the vendors of Union Steel
Company stock, in accordance with agreement with them.................................... 8,512,000

> The cash received from the sale of these bonds is to be used for completing furnaces, mills, additions and extensions to the property under way on December 1, 1902, and to provide working capital.

Reserved to retire outstanding bonds of the Sharon Steel properties at their maturity................. 3,500,000
Reserved for future use for additions, construction and improvements............................ 3,874,000

Total authorized issue... $45,000,000

The property acquired through the capital stock of the Union Steel Company, completed and under construction, is as follows:

Manufacturing Plants at Donora and Sharon, Pa.—5 Blast Furnaces, 24 O. H. Furnaces, 2 Blooming, Slabbing and Sheet Bar Mills, 4 Rod Mills, 2 Wire and Nail Mills, 1 Skelp Works, 1 Tube Works, 1 Plate Mill, 1 Tin Plate Plant, 1 Sheet Plant, By-Product Coke Plant, 212 ovens.

Coking coal property in Lower Connellsville district, 4,740 acres of coal and 810 acres of surface.

Steam coal property on Monongahela River, 1,524 acres of coal and 179 acres of surface.

The Sharon and Penobscot mines (in fee) and Donora and Sweeny mines (leases) on the Mesaba Range, containing approximately 40,000,000 tons of iron ore.

Two modern steel ore steamers.

The negotiations preliminary to the transfer of the above properties were completed and the properties formally turned over to this organization after January 1, 1903. Therefore the earnings of such properties for December, 1902, and the assets, liabilities and bonded debt thereof at the close of the year are not included in the statements and balance sheet embraced in this report.

It is believed the earnings of the above properties will be sufficient to provide at least the interest on the bonds and a sinking fund which will eventually pay and retire the bonds.

EMPLOYES AND PAY ROLLS.

The average number of employés in the service of all properties during the entire year was....... 168,127

The aggregate amount paid during the year for salaries and wages of employés was........... $120,528.343

The following shows the classification of the number of employés between the several departments named:

Employés of	Number.
Manufacturing Properties...................................	125,326
Coal and Coke Properties...................................	16,519
Iron Mining Properties....................................	13,465
Transportation Properties..................................	11,160
Miscellaneous Properties...................................	1,657
Total................................	168,127

EMPLOYES' SUBSCRIPTIONS TO PREFERRED STOCK.

On December 31, 1902, the Board of Directors submitted to the employés of the Corporation and its Subsidiary Companies a plan whereby every employé was granted the opportunity to participate in the profits of the organization through the purchase of Preferred Stock of the Corporation. Copy of the circular setting forth the plan in detail was sent to each stockholder of record.

The plan was most favorably received by the employés, the subscriptions exceeding by about one hundred per cent. the amount it was anticipated would be taken. Allotments of stock were made to subscribers on the following basis:

To Class "A" employés, 50 per cent. of their subscription.
To Class "B" employés, 60 per cent. of their subscription.
To Class "C" employés, 70 per cent. of their subscription.
To Class "D" employés, 80 per cent. of their subscription.

To Class "E" employés, 90 per cent. of their subscription.

To Class "F" employés, 100 per cent. of their subscription.

The total number of employés who subscribed for stock was 27,379 and the number of shares allotted them 48,983.

As indicated in the circular above referred to it is the intention of the Corporation, if the plan meets with continued success, to annually make a similar offer to employés, excepting, of course, that the price at which the stock then will be offered cannot now be determined. At the date of submitting this report every indication points to the complete success of the plan.

To provide for the offer for sale of Preferred Stock to employés under the above plan, the Corporation purchased the necessary shares of its Preferred Stock. The investment in this stock is included in the General Balance Sheet, in the item of "Sundry Marketable Stocks and Bonds." The amount paid for purchase of this stock will be collected in cash from employés in monthly instalments during 1903 and subsequent years, together with 5 per cent. interest on the deferred payments.

NUMBER OF STOCKHOLDERS.

The following shows the number of stockholders in the United States Steel Corporation in March, 1903, in comparison with the number at corresponding date in preceding year:

	1902.	1903.	Increase.
Preferred	25,296	31,799	6,503
Common	17,723	26,830	9,107
Total	43,019	58,629	15,610

The foregoing does not include the subscriptions for preferred stock by the 27,379 employés referred to in the preceding section.

ORDERS ON HAND.

The tonnage of unfilled orders on the books at the close of 1902 equaled 5,347,253 tons of all kinds of manufactured products. At the corresponding date in preceding year the orders booked equaled 4,497,749 tons. In many of the classes of heavier products, like rails, plates and structural material, practically the entire capacity of the mills is sold up until nearly the end of the year 1903.

ORGANIZATION.

In the Preliminary Report submitted to stockholders at the first annual meeting, February 17, 1902, reference was made to what had been accomplished to that time in bringing into harmonious co-operation the various companies and departments within the organization. During the year further advances have been made in this direction and the beneficial results anticipated therefrom, as was indicated in the report above referred to, have been fully realized.

The policy and business of this Corporation, and the companies in which it is interested, are to a large extent considered and determined by the regular committees, or their sub-committees, or special committees consisting of the presidents or other officers of subsidiary companies or some of them, thus deriving the benefit which necessarily results from deliberate and combined action of all.

Direct control and active management of the subsidiary companies are in charge of their respective officials. Each company has a complete organization, consisting of a president, vice-president, general manager, superintendents, etc., etc. The presidents of the subsidiary companies are as follows:

W. E. Corey.............................. { Carnegie Steel Company, National Steel Company, American Steel Hoop Company.

James H. Reed.......................... { Bessemer & Lake Erie Railroad Company, Union Railroad Company.

Thomas Lynch........................... { H. C. Frick Coke Company, and other Coal and Coke Companies.

Thomas F. Cole.......................... { Minnesota Iron Company, Oliver Iron Mining Company, and other Mining Companies.

D. M. Clemson............................Pittsburg Steamship Company.

William P. Palmer..........................American Steel and Wire Company.

William B. Schiller........................ { National Tube Company, Shelby Steel Tube Company.

W. T. Graham..............................American Tin Plate Company.

E. J. Buffington...........................Illinois Steel Company.

George G. McMurtry.........................American Sheet Steel Company.

Alfred J. Major............................American Bridge Company.

Joshua A. Hatfield...........................American Bridge Company of New York.

Daniel Coolidge...........................Lorain Steel Company.

A. F. Banks................................ { Elgin, Joliet & Eastern Railway Company, Chicago, Lake Shore & Eastern Railway Company.

F. E. House................................Duluth & Iron Range Railroad Company.

W. J. Olcott................................Duluth, Missabe & Northern Railway Company.

Each subsidiary company is fully equipped for success independently of any other company or corporation, but the association and connection with the officers of other companies in which this Corporation is interested, and with the officers and committees of this Corporation, results in great benefit to each subsidiary company, and to this Corporation. It is believed the officials of subsidiary companies represent the very best talent that can be secured.

These presidents are in constant communication with each other, and with the officials and members of the committees of this Corporation. The officers and committees of this Corporation are also in daily communication with each other. The Executive Committee and the Finance Committee of this Corporation meet regularly each week, and frequently in special session; and sub-committees for special work are appointed from time to time.

As an illustration of the method of transacting business, suppose one of the subsidiary companies is desirous of making a substantial expenditure for improvements, or of entering into a contract of sale or purchase involving a large sum of money, or of making some important change in policy, the superintendent or manager who first suggests the proposed action will make recommendation to his superior officer, giving reasons in detail. This will reach the president of the particular company, and be considered by him and his committee. After decision the subject is submitted to the president, or other officer, of this Corporation, and is brought before the Executive Committee of this Corporation for consideration. As the presidents of subsidiary companies meet monthly for consultation, many, if not most, important questions are also considered at these meetings, and recommendations then made for consideration by the officials and committees of this Corporation. After the question has been considered by the Executive Committee of this Corporation, if a question of money is involved (and frequently if a question of policy is involved) the subject is then considered by the Finance Committee.

The Board takes pleasure in acknowledging the loyal and efficient services of the officers and employés of the Corporation and the several Subsidiary Companies.

BY ORDER OF THE BOARD OF DIRECTORS.

CHARLES M. SCHWAB,
President.

21

CERTIFICATE OF CHARTERED ACCOUNTANTS.

NEW YORK, March 12, 1903.

To the Stockholders of the United States Steel Corporation:

We have examined the books of the U. S. Steel Corporation and its Subsidiary Companies for the year ending December 31, 1902, and certify that the Balance Sheet at that date and the Relative Income Account are correctly prepared therefrom.

We have satisfied ourselves that during the year only actual additions and extensions have been charged to Property Account; that ample provision has been made for Depreciation and Extinguishment, and that the item of "Deferred Charges" represents expenditures reasonably and properly carried forward to operations of subsequent years.

We are satisfied that the valuations of the inventories of stocks on hand as certified by the responsible officials have been carefully and accurately made at approximate cost; also that the cost of material and labor on contracts in progress has been carefully ascertained, and that the profit taken on these contracts is fair and reasonable.

Full provision has been made for bad and doubtful accounts receivable and for all ascertainable liabilities.

We have verified the cash and securities by actual inspection or by certificates from the Depositories, and are of opinion that the Stocks and Bonds are fully worth the value at which they are stated in the Balance Sheet.

And we certify that in our opinion the Balance Sheet is properly drawn up so as to show the true financial position of the Corporation and its Subsidiary Companies, and that the Relative Income Account is a fair and correct statement of the net earnings for the fiscal year ending at that date.

PRICE, WATERHOUSE & CO.

ASSETS.

PROPERTY ACCOUNT:

Properties owned and operated by the several companies	$1,453,635,551.37	
Less Surplus of Subsidiary Companies at date of acquirement of their Stocks by U. S. Steel Corporation, April 1, 1901 .... $116,356,111.41		
Charged off to Depreciation and Extinguishment Funds 12,011,856.53		
	128,367,967.94	**$1,325,267,583.43**

DEFERRED CHARGES TO OPERATIONS:

Expenditures for Improvements, Explorations, Stripping and Development at Mines, and for Advanced Mining Royalties, chargeable to future operations of the properties **3,178,759.67**

TRUSTEES OF SINKING FUNDS:

Cash held by Trustees on account of Bond Sinking Funds **459,246.14**
($4,022,000 par value of Redeemed bonds held by Trustees not treated as an asset.)

INVESTMENTS:

Outside Real Estate and Other Property	$1,874,872.39	
Insurance Fund Assets	929,615.84	**2,804,488.23**

CURRENT ASSETS:

Inventories	$104,390,844.74	
Accounts Receivable	48,944,189.68	
Bills Receivable	4,153,291.13	
Agents' Balances	1,091,318.99	
Sundry Marketable Stocks and Bonds	6,091,340.16	
Cash	50,163,172.48	**214,834,157.18**

$1,546,544,234.65

Audited and found correct.
PRICE, WATERHOUSE & CO.,
Auditors.

24

LIABILITIES.

CAPITAL STOCK OF U. S. STEEL CORPORATION:
Common	$508,302,500.00	
Preferred	510,281,100.00	**$1,018,583,600.00**

CAPITAL STOCKS OF SUBSIDIARY COMPANIES NOT HELD BY U. S.
STEEL CORPORATION (*Par Value*):
Common Stocks..	$44,400.00	
Preferred Stocks..	72,800.00	
Lake Superior Consolidated Iron Mines, Subsidiary Companies.............	98,714.38	**215,914.38**

BONDED AND DEBENTURE DEBT:
United States Steel Corporation Bonds..	$303,757,000.00	
Less, Redeemed and held by Trustee of Sinking Fund..................	2,698,000.00	
Balance held by the Public...............................	$301,059,000.00	
Subsidiary Companies' Bonds..................................... $60,978,900.75		
Less, Redeemed and held by Trustees of Sinking Funds... 1,324,000.00		
Balance held by the Public.................................	59,654,900.75	
Debenture Scrip, Illinois Steel Company......................................	40,426.02	**360,754,326.77**

MORTGAGES AND PURCHASE MONEY OBLIGATIONS OF SUBSIDIARY
COMPANIES:
Mortgages	$2,901,132.07	
Purchase Money Obligations...	6,689,418.53	**9,590,550.60**

CURRENT LIABILITIES:
Current Accounts Payable and Pay Rolls...................................	$18,675,080.13	
Bills and Loans Payable...	6,202,502.44	
Special Deposits due Employés and others.............................	4,485,546.58	
Accrued Taxes not yet due..	1,051,605.42	
Accrued Interest and Unpresented Coupons..............................	5,398,572.96	
Preferred Stock Dividend No. 7, payable February 16, 1903..................	8,929,919.25	
Common Stock Dividend No. 7, payable March 30, 1903....................	5,083,025.00	**49,826,251.78**
Total Capital and Current Liabilities...		**$1,438,970,643.53**

SINKING AND RESERVE FUNDS:
Sinking Fund on U. S. Steel Corporation Bonds...............................	$1,773,333.33	
Sinking Funds on Bonds of Subsidiary Companies...........................	217,344.36	
Depreciation and Extinguishment Funds......................................	1,707,610.59	
Improvement and Replacement Funds..	16,566,190.90	
Contingent and Miscellaneous Operating Funds.............................	3,413,783.50	
Insurance Fund..	1,539,485.25	**25,217,747.93**

BOND SINKING FUNDS WITH ACCRETIONS...   **4,481,246.14**
Represented by Cash, and by redeemed bonds not treated as assets (see contra).

UNDIVIDED SURPLUS OF U. S. STEEL CORPORATION AND SUB-
SIDIARY COMPANIES:
Capital Surplus provided in organization of U. S. Steel Corporation............	$25,000,000.00	
Surplus accumulated by all companies since organization of U. S. Steel Corporation	52,874,597.05	**77,874,597.05***
		$1,546 544,234.65

25

* *NOTE.*—In preliminary Report submitted to stockholders at the First Annual Meeting, February 17, 1902, the accumulated surplus of all subsidiary companies to November 30, 1901, was shown as $174,344,229.32. This total, however, included the surplus of the subsidiary companies at time of the original acquisition of their stocks by United States Steel Corporation in 1901, which surplus in this balance sheet is stated in diminution of Property Account.

United States Steel Corporation and Subsidiary Companies.

GENERAL PROFIT AND LOSS ACCOUNT

Year Ending December 31, 1902.

GROSS RECEIPTS.

Gross Sales and Earnings..	$560,510,479.39

MANUFACTURING AND OPERATING EXPENSES.

Manufacturing and Producing Cost and Operating Expenses.................................		411,408,818.36*
Balance		$149,101,661.03
Miscellaneous Manufacturing and Operating Gains and Losses (Net)..........	$2,654,189.22	
Rentals received...	474,781.49	
		3,128,970.71
Total Net Manufacturing, Producing and Operating Income...........................		$152,230,631.74

OTHER INCOME.

Proportion of Net Profits of properties owned but whose operations (gross revenue, cost of product, expenses, etc.) are not included in this statement....	$1,972,316.45	
Interest and Dividends on Investments and on Deposits, etc....................	3,454,135.50	
		5,426,451.95
Total Income...		$157,657,083.69

GENERAL EXPENSES.

Administrative, Selling and General Expenses (not including General Expenses of Transportation Companies)...	$13,202,398.89	
Taxes	2,391,465.74	
Commercial Discounts and Interest.......................................	1,908,027.90	
		17,501,892.53
Balance of Income...		$140,155,191.16

INTEREST CHARGES, ETC.

Interest on Bonds and Mortgages of the Subsidiary Companies..............	$3,879,439.91	
Interest on Bills Payable and Purchase Money Obligations of Subsidiary Companies and Miscellaneous Interest.....................................	2,234,144.43	
Rentals paid...	732,843.10	
		6,846,427.44
Net Earnings for the Year, see page 5..		$133,308,763.72

27

* Includes charges for ordinary maintenance and repairs, see footnote on page 5.

25

United States Steel Corporation and Subsidiary Companies.

SUMMARY OF FINANCIAL OPERATIONS OF ALL PROPERTIES.

Year Ending December 31, 1902.

Showing the Net Resources for the Year and Disposition Thereof.

RESOURCES.

Profit and Loss Surplus for the year, per Income Account. page 6			$34,253,656.75
Net Receipts appropriated from Earnings for Bond Sinking, Depreciation and Improvement Funds (See Income Account, page 8)		$27,814,389.47	
Less, Payments therefrom to Trustees of Bond Sinking Funds	$3,604,064.43		
Expended for Extraordinary Replacements	7,926,792.60		
		11,530,857.03	
		$16,283,532.44	
Net Receipts account Insurance and Contingent Funds during the year		804,319.35	
Balance of Receipts for Year included in Fund accounts			17,087,851.79
Bonds and Mortgages issued			2,370,338.35
Sundry Miscellaneous Receipts			5,920.98
Total Net Resources			$53,717,767.87

PAYMENTS MADE FROM ABOVE.

Expended for Additional Property and Construction, per page 15	$16,586,531.77	
Bonds and Mortgages paid (not including bonds redeemed with sinking funds)	1,697,577.33	
Purchase Money Obligations, Bills Payable and Special Deposits paid off	13,652,367.94	
		31,936,477.04
Balance of Net Resources for the year, accounted for as below		$21,781,290.83

INCREASE IN CURRENT ASSETS, VIZ.:

In Sundry Securities and Investments	$3,193,604.83	
In Accounts and Bills Receivable in excess of increase in Accounts Payable.	9,595,635.15	
In Inventories and Miscellaneous Accounts	12,625,946.02	
	$25,415,186.00	
Less, Decrease in Cash on hand December 31, 1902, as compared with preceding year	3,633,895.17	
Balance as above	$21,781,290.83	

26

BONDED AND DEBENTURE DEBT OUTSTANDING, DECEMBER 31, 1902.

	Total Bonds.	Held by Trustees Skg. Funds.	Balance in Hands of Public.	Maturity.	Rate.	Payable.
U. S. Steel Corporation 50 Year Gold Bonds	$303,737,000.00	$2,698,000.00	$301,059,000.00	April 1, 1951.	5	½₂ Monthly
The Carnegie Co., Collateral Trust........	243,000.00	....	243,000.00	April 1, 2000.	5	
Illinois Steel Co., Conv. Debentures......	2,872,000.00	....	2,872,000.00	January 1, 1910.	5	Jan. and July
Illinois Steel Co., Non-Conv. Debentures...	6,900,000.00		6,900,000.00	April 1, 1913.	5	April and Oct.
The Johnson Co. (now Lorain Steel Co.), 1st Mortgage............	1,208,000.00	....	1,208,000.00	$100,000 each Sept. 1.	6	Mar. and Sept.
Am. S. & W. Co., Allegheny Furnace Mtge.	78,000.00	....	78,000.00	August 1, 1911.	5	Feb. and Aug.
National Steel Co. Bonds, viz.:						
Ohio Steel Co., 1st Mortgage..........	845,000.00	....	845,000.00	{ Various amts. on } { June 1, to 1908. }	6	June and Dec.
Bellaire Steel Co., 1st Mortgage.....	301,000.00	....	301,000.00	March 2, 1906	6	Mar. and Sept.
Rosena Furnace Co., 1st Mortgage.....	250,000.00	....	250,000.00	December 1, 1912.	5	June and Dec.
Buhl Steel Co., 1st Mortgage.........	200,000.00	....	200,000.00	November 1, 1903.	6	May and Nov.
King, Gilbert & Warner, 1st Mortgage.	100,000.00	....	100,000.00	May 1, 1905.	6	May and Nov.
American Tin Plate Co. Bonds, viz.:						
New Castle Steel and Tin Plate Co.....	75,000.00	....	75,000.00	March 1, 1906.	6	Mar. and Sept.
American Sheet Steel Co. Bonds, viz.:						
W. Dewees Wood Co., 1st Mortgage...	2,000,000.00	....	2,000,000.00	May 1, 1910.	5	May and Nov.
Total....................	....	....	$316,131,000.00			
COAL AND COKE COMPANIES.						
H. C. Frick Coke Co., 1st Mortgage......	1,600,000.00	....	$1,600,000.00	$100,000 each July 1.	5	Jan. and July
H. C. Frick Coke Co., Pur. Money Mtge..	300,000.00	....	300,000.00	$150,000 each Jan. 1.	5	Jan. and July
Host.-Conn. Coke Co., Pur. Money Mtge..	1,000,000.00	....	*1,000,000.00	February 1, 1942.	6	Feb. and Aug.
Hostetter Coke Co., 1st Mortgage........	175,000.00	....	*175,000.00	$25,000 each August 1.	6	Feb. and Aug.
Continental Coke Co., Pur. Money Mtge...	900,000.00	....	900,000.00	$100,000 each Feb. 1.	6	Feb. and Aug.
Continental Coke Co., Pur. Money Mtge...	629,000.00	....	629,000.00	$37,000 each April 27.	4½	April 27
*Less, half of these bonds outstanding account stock of Host.-Conn. Co. not owned by Frick Coke Co	....	....	4,604,000.00 587,500.00			
Balance of Coal & Coke Co.'s Bonds...	....	....	$4,016,500.00			
TRANSPORTATION COMPANIES.						
Union Railroad Co., 1st Mortgage........	2,000,000.00	....	$2,000,000.00	September 1, 1946.	5	Mar. and Sept.
*Pitts., Bess. & Lake Erie R. R. Co. Bonds :						
1st Mortgage Consolidated............	6,342,000.00	....	6,342,000.00	January 1, 1947.	5	Jan. and July
Debenture Gold Bonds................	2,000,000.00	....	2,000,000.00	June 1, 1919.	5	June and Dec.
Pittsburg, Shenango & Lake Erie Ry :						
1st Mortgage	3,000,000.00	....	3,000,000.00	October 1, 1940.	5	April and Oct.
1st Mortgage Consolidated	658,000.00	....	658,000.00	July 1, 1943.	5	Jan. and July
Bessemer Equipment Trust............	300,000.00	....	300,000.00	$75,000 each July 1.	6	Jan. and July
Conneaut Equipment Trust............	350,000.00	....	350,000.00	See Note " A."	6	Mar. and Sept.
Shenango Equipment Trust............	725,000.00	....	725,000.00	See Note " B."	5	April and Oct.
Greenville Equipment Trust...........	1,000,000.00	....	1,000,000.00	See Note " C."	5	May and Nov.
Butler Equipment Trust..............	2,050,000.00	....	2,050,000.00	April 1, 1921.	5	April and Oct.
Note " A." $50,000 1903 and $60,000 each March 1 thereafter. Note "B " $72,000 April 1, 1904 to 1908, $73,000 each April 1 thereafter. Note " C." $100,000 May 1, 1911 to 1920.						
Bessemer & Lake Erie R. R. Co.:						
Erie Equipment Trust	1,220,000.00	....	1,220,000.00	March 1, 1922.	5	Mar. and Sept.
Elgin, Jol. & East. Ry. Co., 1st Mortgage.	8,500,000.00	....	8,500,000.00	May 1, 1941.	5	May and Nov.
Duluth & Iron Range R. R. Co. Bonds:						
1st Mortgage......................	6,732,000.00	....	6,732,000.00	Oct. 1, 1937.	5	April and Oct.
2d Mortgage.....................	1,000,000.00	....	1,000,000.00	Jan. 1, 1916.	6	Jan. and July
Duluth, Missabe & No. Ry. Co. Bonds:						
First Division, 1st Mortgage..........	1,174,000.00	....	1,174,000.00	Jan. 1, 1922.	6	Jan. and July
Consolidated, 1st Mortgage...........	2,326,000.00	555,000.00	1,771,000.00	Jan. 1, 1923.	6	Jan. and July
Consolidated, 2d Mortgage...........	2,621,000.00	408,000.00	2,213,000.00	Jan. 1, 1918.	5	Jan. and July
Pittsburg Steamship Co. Bonds:						
1st Mortgage (P. S. S)	2,437,000.00	....	2,437,000.00	Jan. 1, 1915.	5	Jan. and July
No. Lakes S. S. Co., Mortgage........	60,000.00	....	60,000.00	$10,000 each Sept. 1.	5	Mar. and Sept.
American S. S Co., 1st Mortgage......	5,280,000.00	361,000.00	4,889,000.00	Nov. 1, 1920.	5	May and Nov.
*Less, proportion of P., B. & L. E. R. R. Bonds outstanding account stock not owned by Carnegie Co................	....	....	$48,421,000.00 7,854,599.25			
			$40,566,400.75			
Total Bonds.......................	....	....	$360,713,900.75			
Debenture Scrip, Illinois Steel Co. (Payable April 1, 1913)................	40,426.02	....	40,426.02			
Grand Total.....................	....	....	*360,754,326.77			

29

United States Steel Corporation and Subsidiary Companies.

MONTHLY EARNINGS FROM APRIL 1, 1901, TO DECEMBER 31, 1902.

	1901.	1902.
January	....	$8,901,015.72
February	....	7,678,583. 47
March	....	10,135,858.40
April	$7,356,744.32	12,320,765.87
May	9,612,349.23	13,120,930.23
June	9,394,747.72	12,220,361.97
July	9,580,151.46	12,041,913.53
August	9,810,880.60	12,972,728.87
September	9,272,811.38	11,930,846.47
October	12,205,773.73	12,652,706.97
November	9,795,840.34	10,686,905.74
December	7,758,297.73	8,646,146.48
Total Nine Months 1901	$84,787,596.51	....
Total Year 1902	....	$133,308,763.72

Total Nine Months 1901 .... $84,787,596.51

Total for same period 1902 .... 106,593,306.13

SUMMARY OF MANUFACTURING PLANTS
OWNED BY SUBSIDIARY COMPANIES OF
UNITED STATES STEEL CORPORATION

Name of Operating Company	Blast Furnaces: Number of	Bessemer Steel Works: Number of Works	Bessemer Steel Works: Number of Converters	Open Hearth Steel Works: Number of Works	Open Hearth Steel Works: Number of Furnaces	Blooming, Slabbing, Billet and Sheet Bar Mills: Number of Works	Blooming Mills: Number of Mills in Works	Number of Rail Mills	Plate Mills: Number of Works	Plate Mills: Number of Mills in Works	Puddling Mills: Number of Works	Puddling Mills: Number of Puddling Furs.	Puddling Mills: Number of Rock Rolls	Skelp Mills: Number of Works	Skelp Mills: Number of Mills in Works	Merchant, Bar, Hoop and Cotton Tie Mills: Number of Works	Merchant etc.: Number of Mills in Works	Structural Shape Mills: Number of Works	Structural Shape Mills: Number of Mills in Works	Rod Mills: Number of Works	Rod Mills: Number of Mills in Works	Wire Mills: Number of Works	Wire Mills: Departments for (Galvanizing)	Wire Mills: Departments for (Tinning)	Sheet Mills etc.: Number of Works	Sheet Mills etc.: Number of Mills in Works	Sheet Mills etc.: Tinning Departments for	Sheet Mills etc.: (Galvanizing) Departments for	Number of Tube Mills	Number of Bridge and Structural Plants	Number of Foundries	Miscellaneous Works
Carnegie Steel Co.	21	8	8	4	60	8	11	2	3	7						8	6	2	8												2	1-Axle Works, 2-Armor Plant, 2-Bolt and Rivet Depts.
National Steel Co.	17	5	10	1	6	6	14	1																							1	
Am. Steel Hoop Co.	3	2				2	6		1	2	8	164	8			11	42													1	2	2-Cement Plants, 1-Spike, Bolt and Nut Factory
Illinois Steel Co.	10	1	5	1	10	1	2	2								2	8			2	2										1	
Lorain Steel Co.	2	8	2			4	6	1	1	3																						1-Frog and Switch Works
Am. Steel & Wire Co.	12	2	6	3	15	2	2				4	121	5	5	22	3	8			18	21	22	17	6	2	2		5			5	2-Zinc Smelting Works
National Tube Co.	5		4			9	12				1	19	1	5	19														16		4	
Shelby Steel Tube Co.														1	1							1	1						7		1	2-Cut Nail Mills, 1-Galvanizing Works
Am. Sheet Steel Co.					10	1	1																		20	164					1	
Am. Tin Plate Co.				1	11	1	1																		23	250	21					
American Bridge Co.				1		1	1																							26		1-Axle Works
Union Steel Co.	5			2	24	2	5		1	1				1	3			1	3	2	4	2	2		2	30	1	1	1		5	
Grand Total	84	16	35	14	130	31	60	6	6	13	13	304	14	12	45	19	64	3	11	16	27	24	19	6	47	446	22	6	24	27	22	13-Miscellaneous

29

South Works, American Steel & Wire Company, Worcester, Mass.

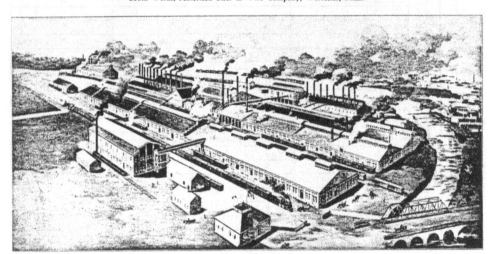

Allentown Works, American Steel & Wire Company, Allentown, Penna.

Shoenberger Works, American Steel & Wire Company, Pittsburg, Penna.

1903 ANNUAL REPORT

Appropriations from Net Earnings
Writedowns of Inventory
Comparative Income Figures Given
Use of Undivided Surplus
Conservative Treatment of New Property
Conservatism Mentioned in Inventories

INCOME ACCOUNT FOR THE YEAR 1903.

The total net earnings of all properties after deducting expenditures for ordinary repairs and maintenance (approximately $22,000,000), also interest on bonds and fixed charges of the subsidiary companies, amounted to.. $109,171,152.35

Less Appropriations for the following purposes, viz.:

Sinking Funds on Bonds of Subsidiary Companies.........................	$1,598,012.48	
Depreciation and Extinguishment Funds (regular provisions for the year)...	4,599,822.47	
Extraordinary Replacement Funds (regular provisions for the year)........	9,297,530.89	
Special Fund for Depreciation, Improvements and Construction	10,000,000.00	
		25,495,365.84

Balance of Net Earnings in the year 1903... $83,675,786.51

Deduct:

Interest on U. S. Steel Corporation 50 Year 5 per cent. Gold Bonds..........	$15,195,850.00	
Interest on U. S. Steel Corporation 10-60 Year 5 per cent. Gold Bonds.......	3,886,946.38	
Sinking Fund on U. S. Steel Corporation 50 Year 5 per cent. Gold Bonds.....	3,040,000.00	
Sinking Fund on U. S. Steel Corporation 10-60 Year 5 per cent. Gold Bonds..	757,500.00	
		22,880,296.38

Balance, carried forward... $60,795,490.13

5

Balance, brought forward.. $60,795,490.13

Less: Charged off for depreciation in Inventory valuations and for the adjustment of sundry

accounts 5,378,837.63

Balance $55,416,652.50

Dividends for the year 1903 on U. S. Steel Corporation Stocks, viz.:

Preferred, 7 per cent.. $30,404,173.41

Common, 2¼ per cent.*.. 12,707,562.50

43,111,735.91

Undivided Profits or Surplus for the year.. $12,304,916.59

* Dividends of 3½ per cent. on Common Stock were actually paid in 1903, but the dividend of 1 per cent. paid March 30, 1903, was charged to the Income Account for 1902.

COMPARATIVE INCOME ACCOUNT

FOR THE FISCAL YEARS ENDING DECEMBER 31, 1903 AND 1902.

	1903	1902	Increase or Decrease.
NET EARNINGS..	$109,171,152.35	$133,308,763.72	$24,137,611.37 Dec.
Less, Appropriations for the following purposes, viz:			
Sinking Funds on Bonds of Subsidiary Companies......	1,598,012.48	624 064.43	973,948.05 Inc.
Depreciation and Extinguishment, Extraordinary Replacement, Improvement and Construction Funds.........	23,897,353.36	24,150,325.04	252,971.68 Dec.
Balance of Net Earnings for the year....................	$83,675,786.51	$108,534,374 25	$24,858,587.74 Dec.
Deduct:			
Interest on U. S. Steel Corporation Bonds...............	19,082,796.38	15,187,850.00	3,894,946.38 Inc.*
Sinking Funds on U. S. Steel Corporation Bonds........	3,797,500.00	3,040,000.00	757,500.00 Inc.*
Less: Charged off for depreciation in inventory valuations and for the adjustment of sundry accounts..............	$60,795,490.13	$90,306,524.25	$29 511,034.12 Dec.
	5 378,837.63	....	5,378,837.63 Inc.
Balance..	$55,416,652 50	$90,306 524.25	$34,889,871.75 Dec.
Dividends on U. S. Steel Corporation stocks, viz:			
Preferred, 7 %..	30,404,173.41	35,720,177.50	5,316,004.09 Dec.*
Common, 2½ % in 1903, 4 % in 1902....................	12,707 562 50	20,382,690.00	7,625,127.50 Dec.
Undivided Profits or Surplus for the year.................	$12,304,916.59	$34,253,636.75	$21,948,740.16 Dec.

* Increase in Interest and Sinking Fund charges due to issue of bonds in conversion of Preferred Stock during the year, the dividends on which latter show a decrease.

6

UNDIVIDED SURPLUS OF U. S. STEEL CORPORATION AND ITS SUBSIDIARY COMPANIES.

(Since April 1, 1901.)

Surplus or Working Capital provided in organization...		$25,000,000.00
Surplus accumulated by all companies from April 1. 1901, to December 31, 1902,		
per Annual Report for 1902..	$52,874.597.05	
Less: Adjustments in sundry accounts in 1903...........................	48.702.70	
		52,825,894.35
Surplus of all companies for the year 1903...		12,304,916.59
		$90,130.810.94
LESS: Expense conversion Preferred Stock and sale of 10-60 Year Bonds ($783,560 not yet paid)..	$6,800,000.00	
Charged off on December 31, 1903, by authority of the Board of Directors, for expenditures made from Surplus since April 1, 1901, for Construction and for payment of Capital Liabilities (see page 17).	17.234.128.58	
		24,034,128.58
Balance of Undivided Surplus, December 31, 1903...........................		$66,096,682.36

SUMMARY OF EXPENDITURES FOR CONSTRUCTION AND ADDITIONAL PROPERTY AND FOR PAYMENT OF CAPITAL LIABILITIES.

From April 1, 1901, to December 31, 1903.

As shown in tables on preceding pages of this report, the amounts expended for the above purposes were as follows:

For Construction and Additional Property (page 15) $64,585,536.37

For Bonds and Mortgages discharged, exclusive of bonds redeemed with Sinking Fund
moneys (page 14)... 4,599,655.49

For Purchase Money Obligations paid off, originally issued for account acquirement of property (page 15)... 25,007,729.55

Total... $94,192,921.41

Of the foregoing there has been financed by issue and sale of securities the following amounts, viz.:

By Union Steel Co.'s Mortgage and Collateral Trust Bonds, $8,512,500 issued,
less $2,855,772.21 proceeds therefrom used to pay off Bills Payable out-
standing December 1, 1902, leaving for account of Construction expenditures $5,656,727.79

By Bonds and Mortgages of Sundry Subsidiary Companies (principally railroads) 4,606,060.13

By Purchase Money Obligations issued................................. 1,100,000.00

            11,362,787.92

Leaving Balance paid from Depreciation and Improvement Funds and Surplus Accounts. $82,830,133.49

This Balance is represented by the following items, viz.:

Expenditures for construction and additional property, and for payment of purchase obligations,
for which the treasury may be reimbursed from proceeds of sale of Ten-Sixty Year 5%
Bonds, as indicated in circular to Stockholders dated April 17, 1902................. $25,028,527.76

Payments made for discharge of certain bonds, mortgages and purchase obligations, in lieu of
which securities of subsidiary companies may be issued, for benefit of the U. S. Steel Corporation, thus replacing capital liabilities existing when the Corporation was organized.. 11,423,112.48

Expenditures for construction of new plant at Lorain, Ohio; for additional real estate for manufacturing site at McKeesport, Pa.; for new coking plants in the Pocahontas field, W.
Va.; and for purchase of the Aragon Mine, which may be paid for from future depreciation funds or covered by securities of subsidiary companies to be provided............ 8,414,749.47

Expended in 1903 for construction, account Union Steel Company properties, in excess of
amount financed (additional Union Steel Co. bonds being issuable for this item)....... 2,764,461.25

Sundry credits to be left in construction account.....................................Cr. 101,778.30

Total carried forward.. $47,529,072.66

Total brought forward... $47,529,072.66

Construction expenditures and capital liabilities paid from Depreciation and Improvement
    Funds, and formally written off to such funds (these funds being reserved from earnings
    and properly applicable for the expenditures included herein)....................... 18,066,932.25

Construction expenditures and payment of capital liabilities, paid from Surplus and charged off
    December 31, 1903, by authority of Board of Directors, to Undivided Surplus; the Prop-
    erty Account being correspondingly credited.................................... 17,234,128.58

    Total... $82,830,133.49

The item of $18,066,932.25 charged off to Depreciation and Improvement Funds includes $14,296,895.58 expended for new property and construction, and $3,770,036.67 paid in discharge of capital liabilities. The total as above
was written off to the Funds, and Property Account correspondingly credited, as follows:

Written off on December 31, 1902.. $6,091,088.34
Written off on December 31, 1903:
    To Depreciation and Extinguishment Funds.......................... 3,972,833.90
    To Bond Sinking Funds... 15,000.00
    To Improvement and Replacement Funds............................ 7,988,010.01
                                 ———————— $18,066,932.25

The amount written off to Undivided Surplus covers $4,096,266.75 of payments for discharging capital liabilities,
and $13,137,861.83 of expenditures for construction and new property. The additions, betterments and new property
covered by this last named item are such as were rendered imperative by the business needs of the organization.
Though these expenditures were for purposes which would permit of their being financed by issues of securities, nevertheless it was considered undesirable for such purposes to increase the outstanding capital or debt. This
was the case also as to the capital liabilities paid off from surplus. Accordingly by resolution of the Finance Committee, approved by the Board of Directors, the sum of $17,234,128.58 has been transferred from Undivided Surplus to
liquidate the expenditures referred to, the Property Account being correspondingly reduced.

INVENTORIES.

The total inventories of all properties on December 31, 1903, amounted to $107,976,523, in comparison with an aggregate of $104,390,844 on December 31, 1902, an increase of $3,585,679. This increase is more than accounted for in the item of ore alone, which shows an increase over last year of $7,946,049, or 23 per cent., in inventory valuation, and an increase of 31 per cent., in quantity on hand. This increase in the quantity of ore on hand is due partly to the fact that inventories this year include the stocks of the Union Steel Company (not embraced last year), and partly owing to the diminution of ore conversions during the last quarter. As explained in previous reports, it is necessary (owing to close of navigation on the Great Lakes during the winter) to mine and to ship to furnaces and to storage docks, during the summer and fall, sufficient quantities of ore to insure a supply for the furnaces up to the early summer of the succeeding year. The inventories of commodities other than ore are also increased by reason of including the stocks of Union Steel Company, to which reference is made above.

Inventory valuations are conservative. They were taken on the basis of actual purchase or production cost of materials to the respective companies holding the same, unless (as happened in some instances) such cost was above the market value on December 31, 1903, in which cases the market price was used. The aggregate inventory valuation of all raw, partly finished and finished materials produced within the organization is very largely below the market prices on December 31, 1903. No profit is taken up by any one subsidiary company on materials and products of its own production until the same have been shipped to customers. The estimated profits carried as an asset in inventories for gains on uncompleted bridge and structural contracts equal only about one-half of the profit which it is expected will be realized thereon when completed.

The following is a general classification of inventory valuations on December 31:

Ores	$42,018,988
Pig Iron, Scrap, Ferro and Spiegel	5,885,039
Coal and Coke	1,871,404
Copper, Nickel, Aluminum and Alloys	346,798
Pig Tin, Lead, Zinc, Spelter, Dross and Skimmings	1,454,308
Limestone, Fluxes and Refractories	1,210,915
Rolls, Molds and Stools	2,553,260
Manufacturing Supplies, Stores and Miscellaneous Items not otherwise classified	7,837,113
Ingots, Steel and Nickel	881,979
Blooms, Billets, Slabs, Sheet and Tin Bars, etc.	5,321,339
Wire Rods	540,516
Skelp	1,152,572
Finished Products	21,564,586
Mining Supplies and Stores (for ore and coal)	1,983,046
Railroad Supplies and Stores	1,368,697
Merchandise of Supply Companies	614,520
Material, labor and expense locked up in bridge and structural contracts, including estimated profit thereon ... $23,468,732	
Less, Bills rendered on account ... 16,028,984	
	7,439,748
Stocks abroad and on consignment	1,347,165
Material in Transit	2,584,530
Total	$107,976,523

1904 ANNUAL REPORT

Intercompany Profit in Inventory No Longer in Net Earnings

Conservatism Rules Again

UNDIVIDED SURPLUS OF U. S. STEEL CORPORATION AND SUBSIDIARY COMPANIES.

(Since April 1, 1901.)

Surplus or Working Capital provided in organization..		$25,000,000.00
Balance of Surplus accumulated by all companies from April 1, 1901, to December 31, 1903, per Annual Report for Year 1903, exclusive of amount of $10,371,803.25, transferred January 1, 1904, in connection with inauguration of new accounting plan adopted as of that date, to separate surplus account as shown below...	$30,724,879.11	
Less: Adjustments in sundry accounts in 1904.............................	31,516.80	
		30,693,362.31
Undivided Profits of all companies for the year 1904..		5,047,852.19
		$60,741,214.50
Less: Charged off on December 31, 1904, by authority of the Board of Directors, for expenditures made from Surplus for construction and payment of capital liabilities (see page 21), viz.:		
Expenditures made during year 1904............................	$5,563,985.61	
Expenditures made during previous years.........................	2,929,249.97	
		8,493,235.58
Balance of Undivided Surplus, December 31, 1904, exclusive of subsidiary companies' Inter-Company profits in Inventories..		$52,247,978.92
Undivided Surplus of subsidiary companies representing profits accrued on sales of materials to other subsidiary companies, and on hand in latter's inventories, viz.:		
Balance on December 31, 1903, transferred as above	$10,371,803.25	
Less: Decrease during the year 1904...............................	1,254,336.48	
Balance, December 31, 1904...................................		9,117,466.77
Total Undivided Surplus, December 31, 1904..		$61,365,445.69

6

In the Annual Report for 1903 reference was made to the fact that it had been decided, commencing with January, 1904, to take over into the aggregate earnings reported currently for all companies the profits arising to one subsidiary company from sale of materials to another, only 'when such profits shall have been actually realized by the conversion of the materials involved into finished products, and the sale and delivery of the same to customers outside of the organization. Prior to January, 1904. the profits in question had been reported in the combined earnings of all companies concurrently with the delivery of the materials by one company to another, and without reference to whether the receiving company had at that time converted and shipped the material, or continued to carry it in its inventory. In order to inaugurate this new method of accounting it was necessary to segregate and carry in a separate surplus account the amount of such Inter-Company profit which was included in the Undivided Surplus reported on December 31, 1903. Accordingly the amount of $10,371,803.25 was transferred as at January 1, 1904, and, as shown in the preceding statement of Undivided Surplus, is separately reported. At the close of the year 1904 the amount of such Inter-Company profits had been reduced to $9,117,466.77, owing principally to the diminution of quantities of Inter-Company materials on hand in inventories in comparison with December 31, 1903.

Under the plan of accounting now in vogue these intermediate Inter-Company profits are, in effect, carried into the combined accounts for all companies, first, to the specific surplus account representing such profits, not being included or reported, however, in statements of net earnings of all properties as from time to time published, *except* when and as they are transferred from said specific surplus account as hereinafter stated. When materials carrying such Inter-Company profits are worked up into finished products and are shipped to customers outside of the organization, and thus converted from an inventory asset into cash or accounts receivable, the Inter-Company profits previously accrued on such materials and carried theretofore in the specific surplus account referred to, are transferred to and reported in the current earnings statements. Therefore, the net earnings reported under this plan for all companies represent practically cash earnings to the organization. This method of accounting is conservative and assures greater uniformity from month to month with reference to the net earnings reported in comparison with the cash income of the organization as a whole, and any possible adjustment at close of year in the inventory valuation of Inter-Company materials on hand will be made without affecting in any way the current year's earnings and income as previously reported. Any such adjustments would be made against the specific or suspended surplus :account. The plan also permits the ascertainment of operating and production expense statistics on a more uniform basis from month to month.

1908 ANNUAL REPORT

Curtailment of Operations and Depreciation

CERTIFICATE OF CHARTERED ACCOUNTANTS

NEW YORK, March 8, 1909.

To the Stockholders of the United States Steel Corporation:

We have examined the books of the U. S. Steel Corporation and Subsidiary Companies for the year ending December 31, 1908, and certify that the Balance Sheet at that date and the Relative Income Account are correctly prepared therefrom.

During the year only actual additions and extensions have been charged to Property Account; having regard to the curtailment of operations throughout the year, sufficient provision has been made for Depreciation and Extinguishment; and the item of "Deferred Charges" represents expenditures reasonably and properly carried forward to operations of subsequent years.

The valuations of the inventories of stocks on hand as certified by the responsible officials have been carefully and accurately made at approximate cost; and the cost of material and labor on contracts in progress has been properly ascertained.

Full provision has been made for bad and doubtful accounts receivable and for all ascertainable liabilities.

We have verified the cash and securities by actual inspection or by certificates from the Depositories, and are of opinion that the marketable Stocks and Bonds included in Current Assets are worth the value at which they are stated in the Balance Sheet.

And we certify that in our opinion the Balance Sheet is properly drawn up so as to show the true financial position of the Corporation and Subsidiary Companies on December 31, 1908, and that the Relative Income Account is a fair and correct statement of the net earnings for the fiscal year ending at that date.

PRICE, WATERHOUSE & CO.

1910 ANNUAL REPORT

Reclassification of Depreciation Funds
Appropriated Surplus Established

ASSETS

PROPERTY ACCOUNT
   Properties Owned and Operated by the Several Companies
   Balance of this account as of December 31, 1910, per details on page 32...................... $1,547,884,381.23

   Less, Balances at December 31, 1910, to credit of:
      Accrued Bond Sinking, Depreciation and Replacement Funds, per table on
         page 10... $65,802,823.77
      Bond Sinking Funds with Accretions, being income appropriated for gen-
         eral depreciation and invested in redeemed bonds not treated as assets
         (but interest on which is currently added to the sinking funds) and
         in cash as below... 51,868,696.70
                                                                                              117,671,520.47
                                                                                              $1,430,212,860.76

DEFERRED CHARGES TO OPERATIONS
   Payments for Advanced Mining Royalties, Exploration expenses and Miscel-
      laneous charges, chargeable to future operations of the properties......... $15,331,704.91
      Less, Fund reserved from Surplus to cover possible failure to real-
      ize Advanced Mining Royalties.. 7,000,000.00
                                                                                              8,331,704.91

INVESTMENTS
   Outside Real Estate and Investments in sundry securities, including Real Estate Mortgages and
      Land Sales Contracts..
                                                                                              2,369,394.04

SINKING AND RESERVE FUND ASSETS
   Cash resources held by Trustees account of Bond Sinking Funds.............. $856,519.00
         (In addition Trustees hold $51,641,500 of redeemed bonds, which are
         not treated as an asset.)
   Contingent Fund and Miscellaneous Assets................................... 3,295,464.79
   Insurance and Depreciation Funds' Assets (Securities at cost, and
      Cash) $21,668,921.45
      Less, Amount of foregoing represented by Capital Obliga-
         tions of Subsidiary Companies authorized or created
         for capital expenditures made (see contra).......... 9,753,000.00
                                                                           11,915,921.45
                                                                                              16,067,905.24

CURRENT ASSETS
   Inventories* $176,537,823.71
   Accounts Receivable... 44,603,273.53
   Bills Receivable.. 5,540,180.77
   Agents' Balances.. 696,833.76
   Sundry Marketable Bonds and Stocks.. 4,410,793.61
   Cash (in hand and on deposit with Banks, Bankers and Trust Companies sub-
      ject to cheque).. 56,953,514.16
                                                                                              288,742,419.54

* Inventory valuations include profits accrued to subsidiary companies on materials and products sold to other subsidiary companies and undisposed of by the latter
—see contra specific surplus account for these profits. The total valuations of all
inventories are below the actual current market prices.

We have audited the above Balance Sheet, and certify that in
our opinion it is properly drawn up so as to show the true financial position of the United States Steel Corporation and Subsidiary Companies on December 31, 1910.
                  PRICE, WATERHOUSE & CO.,
                                 Auditors.
New York, March 10, 1911. $1,745,724,284.49

50

LIABILITIES

CAPITAL STOCK OF U. S. STEEL CORPORATION
Common $508,302,500.00
Preferred 360,281,100.00 **$868,583,600.00**

CAPITAL STOCKS OF SUBSIDIARY COMPANIES NOT HELD BY U. S.
STEEL CORPORATION (*Par Value*)... **620,352.50**

BONDED AND DEBENTURE DEBT OUTSTANDING
(For detailed statement see pages 15 and 36.)
United States Steel Corporation 50 Year 5% Bonds......................... $274,412,000.00
United States Steel Corporation 10-60 Year 5% Bonds..................... 190,777,500.00

$465,189,500.00
Subsidiary Companies' Bonds, guaranteed by U. S. Steel Corporation........... 52,774,000.00
Subsidiary Companies' Bonds, not guaranteed by U. S. Steel Corporation...... 78,356,661.51
Debenture Scrip, Illinois Steel Co.. 31,705.19 **596,351,866.70**

CAPITAL OBLIGATIONS OF SUBSIDIARY COMPANIES AUTHORIZED
OR CREATED FOR CAPITAL EXPENDITURES MADE (HELD IN
THE TREASURY SUBJECT TO SALE, BUT NOT INCLUDED IN ASSETS OR LIABILI-
TIES—See page 15)... $11,900,000.00

MORTGAGES AND PURCHASE MONEY OBLIGATIONS OF SUBSIDIARY
COMPANIES
Mortgages $784,792.38
Purchase Money Obligations.. 2,313,000.00 **3,097,792.38**

CURRENT LIABILITIES
Current Accounts Payable and Pay Rolls.................................... $23,695,264.04
Bills Payable... 813,500.00
Special Deposits or Loans due employes and others........................ 886,122.16
Accrued Taxes not yet due, including provision for corporation excise tax...... 6,789,827.16
Accrued Interest and Unpresented Coupons................................. 7,991,373.15
Preferred Stock Dividend No. 39, payable February 27, 1911................. 6,304,919.25
Common Stock Dividend No. 29, payable March 30, 1911.................... 6,353,781.25 **52,834,787.01**

Total Capital and Current Liabilities.. **$1,521,488,398.59**

SUNDRY RESERVE FUNDS
Contingent and Miscellaneous Operating Funds.............................. $11,689,728.70
Insurance Funds.. 8,402,999.21 **20,092,727.91**

APPROPRIATED SURPLUS TO COVER CAPITAL EXPENDITURES
(See statement on page 32.)
Invested in Property Account—Additions and Construction..................... $35,203,189.22
Reserved for account future construction at Gary, Indiana, Plant............. 4,796,810.78 **40,000,000.00**

UNDIVIDED SURPLUS OF U. S. STEEL CORPORATION AND SUB-
SIDIARY COMPANIES
Capital Surplus provided in organization.................................... $25,000,000.00
Balance of Surplus accumulated by all companies from April 1, 1901, to Decem-
ber 31, 1910, per table on page 6.. 105,438,718.67
Total Surplus exclusive of Subsidiary Companies' Inter-Company
Profits in Inventories... $130,438,718.67

Undivided Surplus of Subsidiary Companies, representing Profits accrued on
sales of materials and products to other subsidiary companies and on hand
in latter's Inventories.. 33,704,439.32 **104,143,157.99**

$1,745,724,284.49

51

1911 ANNUAL REPORT

Intercompany Profit in Inventory Removed from Undivided Surplus

Pension Fund Appropriated

"Conservatism" Stressed Again

UNDIVIDED SURPLUS OF U. S. STEEL CORPORATION AND SUBSIDIARY COMPANIES

(Since April 1, 1901)

Surplus or Working Capital provided in organization................................. $25,000,000.00

Balance of Surplus accumulated by all companies from April 1, 1901, to
December 31, 1910, exclusive of subsidiary companies' inter-com-
pany profits in inventories, per Annual Report for year 1910...... $105,438,718.67
Less, Charges to and Appropriations from the foregoing balance dur-
ing the year 1911, viz.:
Discount in sale of subsidiary companies' bonds $750,000.00
Appropriation for permanent Pension Fund............ 663,018.37
————— 1,413,018.37

$104,025,700.30
Surplus Net Income for the year 1911, as above.................... 4,665,494.78
————— 108,691,195.08

Total Undivided Surplus, December 31, 1911, exclusive of Profits earned by subsidiary companies on inter-company sales of products on hand in inventories
(see note below)... $133,691,195.08

NOTE.—The Surplus of Subsidiary Companies representing Profits accrued on sales of materials and products to other
subsidiary companies and on hand in latter's Inventories, which in previous years was carried as a part of the Surplus,
is now stated as a deduction from the amount of Inventories included under Current Assets—See Consolidated General
Balance Sheet, page 32.

6

INVENTORIES

OF

MANUFACTURING AND OPERATING MATERIALS AND SUPPLIES AND SEMI-FINISHED AND FINISHED PRODUCTS,
INCLUDING NET ADVANCES ON CONTRACT WORK, ETC.

The total book valuation of the inventories of the above classes of assets for all of the properties, equaled at December 31, 1911, the sum of $176,067,189, a decrease in comparison with the total at the close of the preceding year of $470,635.

Inventory valuations as above stated are on the basis of the actual purchase or production cost of the materials to the respective subsidiary companies holding the same, unless such cost was above the market value on December 31, 1911, in which case the market price was used. But as stated in previous annual reports the valuations on the basis indicated include, in respect of such commodities in stock at the close of the year as had been purchased by one subsidiary company from another, an amount of profits accrued thereon to the subsidiaries selling the same or furnishing service in connection therewith. These profits are not, however, carried into the currently reported earnings of the entire organization until converted into cash or a cash asset to it, being meanwhile segregated and carried in a specific surplus account which is practically a guarantee fund for these profits so locked up in inventories pending their realization in cash. In order to present the accounts on even a more conservative basis than heretofore observed, it was decided in this year's Consolidated General Balance Sheet to state the amount of the specific surplus account referred to as a reduction in the total valuation at which all inventories are carried in current assets (see Balance Sheet, page 32). Accordingly in the subjoined table the surplus account in question is likewise shown. This plan results in there being carried in the combined assets for all of the companies, the inventories of those materials and products on hand which have been transferred and sold from one subsidiary company to another, at net values which are substantially the production cost to the respective subsidiary companies furnishing the same. The net valuation thus obtained and shown for the total inventories of all materials and products is largely below the market value of the same.

The following is a general classification of the inventory valuations at December 31, 1911, in comparison with the valuations at the close of the preceding year:

	Dec. 31, 1911	Dec. 31, 1910
Ores	$73,642,448	$80,345,434
Pig Iron, Scrap, Ferro and Spiegel...........................	6,998,670	7,348,570
Coal, Coke and Other Fuel...................................	3,728,595	4,282,791
Pig Tin, Spelter, Copper, Nickel, Aluminum and Dross and Skimmings......	6,536,069	5,385,399
Limestone, Fluxes and Refractories...........................	2,000,130	2,281,845
Rolls, Molds, Stools, Annealing Boxes, etc...................	6,101,885	5,776,398
Manufacturing Supplies, Stores and Sundry Items not otherwise classified...	13,682,475	13,467,993
Ingots—Steel	1,278,318	1,001,785
Blooms, Billets, Slabs, Sheet and Tin Plate Bars, etc..........	7,756,691	7,755,479
Wire Rods..	829,461	941,101
Skelp	968,516	910,598
Finished Products...	32,737,559	31,913,767
Mining Supplies and Stores (for ore and coal properties)	3,163,242	3,183,109
Railroad Supplies and Stores................................	3,350,134	3,631,629
Merchandise of Supply Companies............................	748,004	771,429
Material, labor and expense locked up in Bridge and Structural Contracts $19,989,678		
Less, Bills rendered on account........................ 14,588,385		
	5,401,293	2,649,990
Stocks abroad and on consignment...........................	5,351,377	3,957,616
Material in Transit..	1,792,322	1,390,365
Bills rendered account work done on Sundry Material in Process of Manufacture	....	Cr. 457,474
Total Inventory valuations to subsidiary companies............	$176,067,189	$176,537,824
Amount included therein representing profits of subsidiary companies on Inter-Company sales of materials and products on hand......	22,583,600	33,704,439
Valuation exclusive of Inter-Company Profits..................	$153,483,589	$142,833,385

16

1916 ANNUAL REPORT

Normal Prices for Inventory
Inventory Reserve

INVENTORIES

OF

MANUFACTURING AND OPERATING MATERIALS AND SUPPLIES AND SEMI-FINISHED AND FINISHED PRODUCTS, INCLUDING NET ADVANCES ON CONTRACT WORK, ETC.

The book valuation of the inventories of the above classes of assets for all the subsidiary companies, after allowing credit for reserve of $13,524,794 for amount of actual cost or market value of inventory stocks in excess of normal prices therefor, equalled at December 31, 1916, the sum of $181,901,004, an increase of $20,787,104, in comparison with the total at close of preceding year.

Inventory values before allowing for credit for the reserve above mentioned, are on the basis of the actual purchase or production cost of the materials to the respective subsidiary companies holding the same (unless such cost was above the market value on December 31, 1916, in which case the market price was used) except that in respect of such commodities in stock at the close of the year as had been purchased by one subsidiary company from another there has been excluded the approximate amount of profits in such sales price which had accrued to the subsidiaries selling the same or furnishing service in connection therewith. These profits are not carried into the currently reported earnings of the entire organization until converted into cash or a cash asset to it. Accordingly, in the combined assets for all of the companies, the inventories of those materials and products on hand which have been transferred and sold from one subsidiary company to another, are carried at net values which are substantially the production cost to the respective subsidiary companies furnishing the same. The net valuation thus obtained and stated for the total inventories of all materials and products is largely below the market value of the same.

The following is a general classification of the inventory valuations at December 31, 1916, in comparison with the valuations at the close of the preceding year:

	Dec. 31, 1916	Dec. 31, 1915
Ores—Iron, Manganese and Zinc	$50 021 287	$45 532 472
Pig Iron, Scrap, Ferro and Spiegel	18 581 072	9 075 586
Coal, Coke and Other Fuel	4 168 595	4 925 090
Pig Tin, Lead, Spelter, Copper, Nickel, Aluminum and Dross and Skimmings	10 415 759	7 866 748
Limestone, Fluxes and Refractories	3 904 814	3 011 134
Rolls, Molds, Stools, Annealing Boxes, etc.	7 814 775	6 638 562
Manufacturing Supplies, Stores and Sundry Items not otherwise classified	23 908 526	17 343 454
Ingots—Steel	1 930 101	1 790 298
Blooms, Billets, Slabs, Sheet and Tin Plate Bars, etc.	11 659 281	11 658 042
Wire Rods	893 491	953 535
Skelp	1 566 349	1 824 779
Finished Products	30 612 642	31 091 145
Mining Supplies and Stores (for ore and coal properties)	4 083 029	2 851 564
Railroad Supplies and Stores	5 941 113	3 767 177
Merchandise of Supply Companies	962 945	674 527
Material, labor and expense locked up in Bridge and Structural Contracts $41 939 697		
Less, Bills rendered on account 37 673 716		
	4 265 981	1 996 438
Stocks abroad and on consignment	9 738 287	6 857 423
Material in transit	4 957 751	3 255 926
Total	$195 425 798	$161 113 900
Less, Reserve for amount of actual cost or market value of stocks in excess of normal prices therefor	13 524 794	....
Balance	$181 901 004	$161 113 900

16

58

UNITED STATES STEEL CORPORATION AND SUBSIDIARY COMPANIES

CONDENSED GENERAL PROFIT AND LOSS ACCOUNT

For year ending December 31, 1916

GROSS RECEIPTS—Gross Sales and Earnings (see page 23)			$1,231,473,779.47
OPERATING CHARGES, VIZ.:			
Manufacturing and Producing Cost and Operating Expenses, including ordinary maintenance and repairs and provisional charges by subsidiary companies for depreciation..	$843,263,542.07		
Administrative, Selling and General Expenses, employes' compensation under merit plan and Pension payments (not including general expenses of transportation companies)......	24,458,377.08		
Taxes (including allowance for accrued Federal taxes, payable in 1917)...............	26,599,720.90		
Commercial Discounts and Interest...	6,202,650.47		
	$900,524,290.52		
Less, Amount included in the above charges for provisional allowances for depreciation here deducted for purpose of showing the same in separate item of charge, as see below..	32,762,072.38		
		867,762,218.14	
Balance...		$363,711,561.33	
Sundry Net Manufacturing and Operating Gains and Losses, including idle plant expenses, Royalties received, adjustments in inventory valuations, etc...............................	$4,566,576.97		
Rentals received	163,569.62		
		4,730,146.59	
Total Net Manufacturing, Producing and Operating Income before deducting provisional charges for depreciation..		$368,441,707.92	
OTHER INCOME			
Net Profits of properties owned, but whose operations (gross revenue, cost of product, expenses, etc.) are not classified in this statement..	$512,311.69		
Income from sundry investments and interest on deposits, etc................................	5,922,147.80		
		6,434,459.49	
Total...		$374,876,167.41	
Less the following adjustments and charges, viz.:			
Reserved for amount of actual cost or market value in excess of normal prices of inventory stocks on hand at close of year and for other contingent reserves.........	$15,624,794.09		
Net Balance of Profits earned by subsidiary companies on sales made and service rendered account of materials on hand at close of year in purchasing companies' inventories, and which profits have not yet been realized in cash from the standpoint of a combined statement of the business of the U. S. Steel Corporation and subsidiary companies	15,825,711.13		
Interest charges of subsidiary companies on their securities held as investments for combined insurance funds of all subsidiary companies, this interest being taken up as direct credits thereto...	428,569.75		
		31,879,074.97	
Total Earnings in the year 1916 per Income Account, page 33		$342,997,092.44	
INTEREST CHARGES OF SUBSIDIARY COMPANIES			
On Bonds and Mortgages...	$9,384,568.56		
On Purchase Money Obligations and Special Deposits or Loans...............................	38,346.38		
		9,422,914.94	
Balance of Earnings of the several companies for the year before deducting provisional charges for depreciation..		$333,574,177.50	
LESS, CHARGES AND ALLOWANCES FOR DEPRECIATION, VIZ.:			
By Subsidiary Companies..	$32,762,072.38		
By U. S. Steel Corporation..	6,785,540.27		
		39,547,612.65	
Net Income in the year 1916...		$294,026,564.85	

1917 ANNUAL REPORT

Appropriation for Additional Property, New Plants and Construction, $55 Million

Normal Prices Inventory Allowance Continued

Normal Prices Philosophy Extended to Facilities

Price Waterhouse Endorses this Philosophy

SIXTEENTH ANNUAL REPORT

TO STOCKHOLDERS OF

United States Steel Corporation

OFFICE OF UNITED STATES STEEL CORPORATION,
51 Newark Street, Hoboken, New Jersey,
March 19, 1918.

To the Stockholders:

The Board of Directors submits herewith a combined report of the operations and affairs of the United States Steel Corporation and Subsidiary Companies for the fiscal year which ended December 31, 1917, together with a statement of the condition of the finances and property at the close of that year.

INCOME ACCOUNT FOR THE YEAR 1917

The total earnings of all properties after deducting all expenses incident to operations, including those for ordinary repairs and maintenance (approximately $85,000,000), employes' compensation under merit plan, allowances for estimated proportion of extraordinary cost of facilities installed by reason of war requirements and conditions, also taxes (including an estimate of $233,465,435 for account of Federal income, war income and war excess profits taxes payable in 1918), but exclusive of charge for interest on outstanding bonds, mortgages and purchase obligations of the subsidiary companies, amounted to............................ $304,161,471.53*

Less, Interest on outstanding bonds, mortgages and purchase money obligations of the subsidiary companies.. 8,869,291.50

Balance of Earnings in the year 1917.. $295,292,180.03

Less, Charges and Allowances for Depreciation applied as follows, viz.:
To Depreciation and Extraordinary Replacement Funds and Sinking
Funds on Bonds of Subsidiary Companies..................... $43,296,038.26
To Sinking Funds on Bonds of U. S. Steel Corporation 7,257,233.41

50,553,271.67

Net Income in the year 1917... $244,738,908.36

Deduct:
Interest on U. S. Steel Corporation Bonds outstanding, viz.:
Fifty Year 5 per cent. Gold Bonds............................... $12,227,119.83
Ten-Sixty Year 5 per cent. Gold Bonds........................... 9,029,183.34

$21,256,303.17

Premium paid on Bonds redeemed, viz.:
On Subsidiary Companies' Bonds................... $117,914.50
On U. S. Steel Corporation Bonds................. 745,933.69

863,848.19

22,120,151.36

Balance carried forward.. $222,618,757.00

* Amount for the year as adjusted by apportioning to Earnings reported for each of the first three quarters the charges made to the Net Income at close of subsequent quarters for net additional allowances for war income and war excess profits taxes account of the earlier quarters. The adjusted monthly earnings for the year reflecting these additional charges for taxes are shown in table on page 38.

5

Balance brought forward.. $222,618,757.00

Add: Net Balance of sundry charges and credits, including adjustments of various accounts 1,600,807.54

Balance $224,219,564.54

Dividends for the year 1917 on U. S. Steel Corporation Stocks, viz.:

Preferred, 7 per cent... $25,219,677.00

Common, { Regular, 5 per cent.................................. 25,415,125.00
Extra, 12 per cent................................... 60,996,300.00
Extra, 1 per cent (Red Cross Dividend)............... 5,083,025.00

116,714,127.00

Net Income in the year 1917.. $107,505,437.54

Less, Appropriated from Net Income on account of expenditures made and to be made on authorized appropriations for additional property, new plants and construction, as shown in last quarterly report.................................. 55,000,000.00

Balance carried forward to Undivided Surplus.................................. $52,505,437.54

63

United States Steel Corporation and Subsidiary Companies

CONDENSED GENERAL PROFIT AND LOSS ACCOUNT

For year ending December 31, 1917

GROSS RECEIPTS—Gross Sales and Earnings (see page 24).............................			$1,683,962,552.21
OPERATING CHARGES, VIZ.:			
Manufacturing and Producing Cost and Operating Expenses, including ordinary maintenance and repairs and provisional charges by subsidiary companies for depreciation..	$1,089,672,606.33		
Administrative, Selling and General Expenses, employes' compensation under merit plan and pension payments (not including general expenses of transportation companies)......	26,336,813.09		
Taxes (except as included in following item)..	18,800,259.98		
Allowance for estimated amount of Federal income, war income and war excess profits taxes	233,465,434.97		
Commercial Discounts and Interest...	9,332,460.31		
	$1,377,607,574.68		
Less, Amount included in the above charges for provisional allowances for depreciation here deducted for purpose of showing the same in separate item of charge, as see below..	43,296,038.26		
		1,334,311,536.42	
Balance..			$349,651,015.79
Sundry Net Manufacturing and Operating Gains and Losses, including idle plant expenses, Royalties received, adjustments in inventory valuations, etc................................	$16,530,959.27		
Rentals received	222,617.28		
		16,753,576.55	
Total Net Manufacturing, Producing and Operating Income before deducting provisional charges for depreciation...			$366,404,592.34
OTHER INCOME			
Net Profits of properties owned, but whose operations (gross revenue, cost of product, expenses, etc.) are not classified in this statement...	$489,566.20		
Income from sundry investments and interest on deposits, etc..................................	11,305,300.95		
		11,794,867.15	
Total..			$378,199,459.49
Less the following adjustments and charges, viz.:			
Reserved for amount of actual cost or market value in excess of normal prices of inventory stocks on hand at close of year and for other contingent reserves	$29,748,302.39		
Allowance for estimated proportion of extraordinary cost of facilities installed by reason of war requirements and conditions...	29,785,000.00		
Net Balance of Profits earned by subsidiary companies on sales made and service rendered account of materials on hand at close of year in purchasing companies' inventories, and which profits have not yet been realized in cash from the standpoint of a combined statement of the business of all companies.................................	14,118,890.42		
Interest charges of subsidiary companies on their securities held as investments for combined insurance funds, this interest being taken up as direct credits thereto......	385,795.15		
		74,037,987.96	
Total Earnings in the year 1917 per Income Account, page 33			$304,161,471.53
Less, Interest Charges on Subsidiary Companies' Bonds, Mortgages and Purchase Money Obligations.........			8,869,291.50
Balance of Earnings for the year before deducting provisional charges for depreciation...............			$295,292,180.03
LESS, CHARGES AND ALLOWANCES FOR DEPRECIATION, VIZ.:			
By Subsidiary Companies..	$43,296,038.26		
By U. S. Steel Corporation..	7,257,233.41		
		50,553,271.67	
Net Income in the year 1917...			$244,738,908.36

CERTIFICATE OF INDEPENDENT AUDITORS

NEW YORK, March 12, 1918.

To the Stockholders of the United States Steel Corporation:

We have examined the books of the U. S. Steel Corporation and Subsidiary Companies for the year ending December 31, 1917, and certify that the Balance Sheet at that date and the Relative Income Account are correctly prepared therefrom.

During the year only actual additions and extensions have been charged to Property Account, and a substantial provision for the extraordinary cost of facilities and additions installed by reason of war requirements and conditions has been charged to operations. The provision made for depreciation and extinguishment is, in our opinion, fair and reasonable. The item of Deferred Charges represents expenditures reasonably and properly carried forward to operations in subsequent years.

The valuations of the stocks on hand, as shown by inventories certified by the responsible officials, have been carefully and accurately made at approximate cost, and an adequate reserve has been made in respect of all abnormal values. Full provision has been made for bad and doubtful accounts receivable and for all ascertainable liabilities. In our opinion, based on the information now available, sufficient provision has also been made for excess profits and income taxes.

We have verified the cash and securities by actual inspection or by certificates from the Depositaries, and are of opinion that the Marketable Bonds and Stocks included in Current Assets are worth the value at which they are stated in the Balance Sheet, and

We certify that in our opinion the Balance Sheet is properly drawn up so as to show the financial position of the Corporation and Subsidiary Companies on December 31, 1917, and the Relative Income Account is a fair and correct statement of the net earnings for the fiscal year ending at that date.

PRICE, WATERHOUSE & CO.

1918 ANNUAL REPORT

U. S. Steel—The Good Citizen

Willing to Bear the Excess Cost of New Facilities

Helping Win the War in France

Employees Furloughed

Liberty Loan Bonds Purchased

Employees Help Out

Reserves for Inventory Continues

So does Allowance for Excess Cost of New Facilities

ACTIVITIES OF THE UNITED STATES STEEL CORPORATION IN THE WAR

It was realized immediately following the entrance of the United States into the war with Germany that the supply of steel, both for direct consumption and use at the front and for the multitude of industrial activities upon which the production of war materials was dependent, was of paramount importance. The President of the American Iron and Steel Institute was in writing requested by the Secretary of War and the Secretary of the Navy to form a committee to mobilize the iron and steel industry and to take general charge of the supplying of steel necessary for war purposes, which was done, and the United States Steel Corporation in common with other iron and steel producers at once placed at the disposal of the Government its full and unrestricted services and resources in assisting to meet the military demands of the United States and its associates in the war. It is believed the efforts of the Government were never to an important extent lessened or delayed by lack of a proper supply of steel. During the entire period following the declaration of war and until the armistice was signed the committee referred to and representatives of the Corporation, together with other iron and steel manufacturers, were in constant touch and association with the various Governmental departments, commissions and agencies, and devoted much time in assisting and co-operating with the view of obtaining the maximum production of steel and of the various classes of raw materials required for its manufacture. Prior to the entrance of the United States into the war the Corporation had likewise taken a large part in supplying materials to the Allies for their requirements.

Except for the existence of highly integrated units, with large capacity for the production and transportation of steel products, and their perfection of organization, system, improvements and methods, together with the incidental working capital which permitted immediate extensions, additions and diversifications whenever requested or evidently desirable, the military necessities of the United States and its associates in the war could not have been adequately provided.

In connection with the above statement the following details are given:

TONNAGE OF STEEL (ALL KINDS) FURNISHED BY THE CORPORATION FOR WAR PURPOSES

(Includes only tonnage which from available records it is known was applied for war purposes. Unquestionably a large amount of tonnage was in addition shipped to customers and by them used for such purposes.)

Shipped to	Shipped from August 1, 1914 to April 1, 1917 Tons	Shipped from April 1, 1917 to December 31, 1918 Tons	Total August 1, 1914 to December 31, 1918 Tons
The United States Government and other customers in United States	1,434,530	7,669,910	9,104,440
The Allies (exported)	4,623,110	2,669,840	7,292,950
The United States Railroad Administration (during year 1918 only)	....	2,042,070	2,042,070
Total	6,057,640	12,381,820	18,439,460
PRODUCTS OTHER THAN STEEL			
Toluol and Benzol Products.............(Gallons)	11,802,651	16,067,310	27,869,961
Ammonium Sulphate and Liquor...........(Pounds)	234,016	21,095,638	21,329,654
Spelter ....(Tons)	26,890	13,517	40,407
Cement ....(Barrels)	46,725	556,742	603,467

In order to increase the productive capacity of the properties to meet the greater demands for steel necessitated by war conditions, both in respect of volume of tonnage and for new or modified forms of steel, also for sundry auxiliary products and by-products urgently required for war purposes, there has been appropriated and expended since August 1, 1914, for additions, extensions and betterments the sum of $302,776,000. This covers expenditures both at and for manufacturing plants and by the raw material departments—ore, coal, lime-stone and natural gas—also by the subsidiary transportation interests, the major part of whose operations relate to the carriage from mines to mills of raw materials for iron and steel making. Large outlays were also made for construction of houses and dwellings necessary for employes at various places adjacent to the plants, and for the development of townsites. These additions and improvements, particularly those made since the United States entered the war, have been made at a greatly increased cost compared with what their installation would have cost under pre-war conditions; but they were made ,at the request of representatives of the Government and were required for the pressing necessities of the war. The following is a condensed summary of these expenditures:

Properties	Expended August 1, 1914 to April 1, 1917	Excess Cost over Estimated Pre-war Cost	Expended April 1, 1917 to December 31, 1918	Excess Cost over Estimated Pre-war Cost
Manufacturing Plants, except shipbuilding...........	$69,675,082	$10,672,374	$127,144,626	$52,571,085
Shipbuilding Plants	....	....	20,963,305	10,206,827
Coal Properties	3,401,808	502,266	16,723,848	7,655,370
Iron Ore Properties	706,209	78,784	3,429,239	1,378,149
Limestone and Gas Properties......................	506,848	88,473	2,241,080	1,021,964
Transportation Properties	25,747,606	5,150,102	21,356,533	8,621,837
Housing Facilities for Employes, etc................	76,741	15,191	10,803,274	5,338,449
Totals	$100,114,294	$16,507,190	$202,661,905	$86,793,681

69

The foregoing aggregate expenditures covered a wide range of additions and improvements, all serving to increase the productive capacity of steel and other products for use in directions contributing to the prosecution of the war. Some of the principal extensions made and facilities installed for the production of strictly war materials and for war purposes are stated below. In conjunction with the installations named, there were also necessitated expansions in facilities for production of the raw materials required, including their transportation, together with necessary anterior and auxiliary departments such as blast furnaces, steel works, rolling mills, power plants, shops, yards, cranes, and all other facilities and equipment forming integral parts of steel manufacturing plants. The list follows:

Shipbuilding plants at Kearny, N. J., and on the Chickasaw River, near Mobile, Ala. These plants have a total of 20 ways, and an annual capacity of 40 completed 10,000 ton ocean-going steamers. The plants are fully equipped for the complete construction of steamships. The Kearny plant is self-contained in respect of the construction of all ship parts, and the Chickasaw plant will be similarly equipped except as to supplying engines. After conferences with Governmental agencies these plants were conceived and undertaken solely as war measures and to their erection and the construction of ships the full resources of the United States Steel Corporation have been devoted.

Equipment and facilities were installed at nine of the American Bridge Company's bridge and structural shops, also at the Fairfield works of T. C., I. & R. R. Co., for the production of fabricated ship work. The Corporation was the pioneer in work of this kind. Orders were undertaken for the fabrication of ship steel for 131 hulls. Of these the steel for 70 complete hulls had been shipped to the close of the year.

Plate Mills particularly designed for rolling ship plates were constructed as follows:

Homestead, Pa.	110″ Mill	South Chicago, Ill.	90″ Mill
Gary, Ind.	160″ Mill	Fairfield, Ala.	110″ Mill

At Shoenberger plant, the 127″ plate mill was rehabilitated, and at Lorain, O., Works, changes were made and equipment installed to enable the large skelp mill to roll ship plates. These new mills and improvements to existing mills resulted in increasing the productive capacity of plates approximately 923,000 tons per annum.

At Gary, Ind., a gun forging plant was built for the production of rough-turned gun forgings for 155 mm. field guns and 240 mm. howitzers. Work was commenced on this plant in November, 1917, and the first forgings were made on May 6, 1918, for the Ordnance Department of the United States.

New mills for rolling Projectile steel were installed as follows: At Gary, Ind., a 40″ 2 high blooming mill; at Donora, Pa., a 3 high mill; and at a number of plants the existing rolling mills were modified, improved and extended and special facilities installed to permit them to roll Projectile steel. The capacity of the large new Duluth, Minn., plant was devoted to the production of this class of steel. During the period of the war the subsidiary companies shipped a total of 1,733,618 gross tons of Projectile steel to the United States and its Allies.

At the South Chicago works of Illinois Steel Company a plant, consisting of 4 large electric furnaces, was installed to produce high grade steel for gun forgings and other special military purposes. At these furnaces there was also installed a large amount of auxiliary equipment for casting, specially treating and handling the steels produced.

At the Homestead, Pa., works, the armor plate department was enlarged and special equipment and facilities installed to manufacture forgings for carriages for 155 mm. and 9.5″ guns. There were shipped during the period of the war 69,795 gross tons of Armor Plate and products of the Armor Plate Department.

Complete plants and equipment for the manufacture of Shell forgings of various sizes and types were constructed at the Homestead and Schoen plants of Carnegie Steel Co., and the Ellwood and Christy Park plants of National Tube Co., having an annual capacity of about 4,000,000 shells. An aggregate of 703,827 gross tons of Shell forgings were shipped during the period of the war.

At Christy Park plant of National Tube Co. there was installed equipment for the production of torpedo and submarine air flasks, steam pipe for war vessels, gas bombs, trench mortars, and airplane motor cylinder forgings. At the Ellwood works, facilities and equipment were provided for the production of small diameter tubing for torpedo boat destroyers and for airplanes.

At various mills of the American Steel & Wire Co., 375 machines were installed to make special forms of barbed wire for military uses. The several wire rope producing plants of this company were extended and much equipment added for the manufacture of wire rope and cable of various types, including special forms for submarine nets and mines, required by the naval and military establishments, the Emergency Fleet Corporation, other shipbuilders, and by other interests engaged on work incident to the war program.

At the several wire plants special machinery was added to make springs for Browning and Lewis machine guns; for pistols; hand grenades; gas masks; artillery casings and draft gear; Liberty Motor springs; stream-line shapes for stays for aircraft. Equipment was also added to make special electrical wires and cables for military uses.

By-Product Coke Plants, with auxiliary toluol and benzol recovery departments, were constructed and extensions made to existing plants, as stated below. The construction of these plants during the period of the war was undertaken principally to meet the requirements of the Government for toluol, benzol and sulphate of ammonia needed in connection with the manufacture of explosives. The plants also increased the production of coke, of which there was a marked shortage throughout the country. The plants were as follows:

New Plants			Additions to Plants		
Clairton, Pa.	768	ovens;	Gary, Ind.	140	ovens;
Cleveland, O.	180	"	Fairfield, Ala.	154	"
Lorain, O.	208	"	At Joliet, Ill., Farrell, Pa., and Duluth, Minn., benzol recovery plants were added to the existing coke plants.		

In the Pennsylvania, West Virginia, Kentucky, Alabama and Southern Illinois coal districts, the Corporation's subsidiaries made large expenditures for opening new coal mines and expanding existing operations and mobilizing and handling the product so as to obtain the maximum possible output of coal under the conditions prevailing. The most important single new development of this kind was the opening of new workings at Lynch, Harlan County, Kentucky, at an expenditure of over $4,000,000. Coal was first shipped from these operations on October 31, 1917, and an output of about 3,500 tons per day was reached by July 1, 1918.

In many lines the subsidiary companies, at the request of the War and Navy Departments, undertook special research work in their laboratories with the view of developing new forms of materials desired for war purposes, and processes for obtaining quantity production. Some of the directions in which this research work developed practical results were the following:

Immediately upon the declaration of war the American Sheet and Tin Plate Company undertook the study of chemicals for gas masks and it is understood the Government's first specifications for chemicals were based on data furnished by this company. The chief of the American Sheet and Tin Plate Company's Research Laboratory was transferred to the service of the Government and was placed in direct charge of the designing and manufacturing of all gas masks and the chemicals therefor. Four other employes of the Laboratory also entered the department in charge of gas mask manufacture.

The American Sheet and Tin Plate Company furnished substantially all of the steel sheets required by the War Department for the manufacture of helmets. The production of the class of steel used for these helmets presented many difficult problems. It had previously been considered impossible to roll steel of the character required for helmets into sheets of as light gauge as this product necessitated. After much experimental work it was, however, successfully accomplished through revising materially the methods of rolling previously in use.

The American Bridge Company, at the request of the War Department, undertook to design and fabricate a special railway mount for naval guns. Three of the company's technical experts were sent to France by the War Department in this connection. Up to the time of signing of the armistice 17 gun mounts for this purpose had been completed and shipped by the company. A number of these mounts performed effective service at the front.

The Research Department of the National Tube Company, in co-operation with the Engineering Division, Army Ordnance Department, and the Chemical Warfare Service, conducted extended experimental work on designs for Livens gas shells and Stokes mortar shells made from welded pipe; also on Livens mortars with the object of decreasing their weight and increasing their strength. As a result the Company was directed on July 15, 1918, to proceed with the manufacture of shells of the design it had submitted. The first shipment of shells (designed to be used for phosgene gas) was made on July 26, 1918, and the entire order was completed by November 15, 1918. It is understood the shells furnished by National Tube Company were the only ones of this kind delivered in France in time to be used, and that they were satisfactory in every particular.

Large quantities of standard forms of material of the production of the subsidiary companies were furnished for war purposes. A great deal of this tonnage was of special analysis and shape, or produced under special conditions as to heat treatment, rolling, finish and assembling. All this called for much research work, the revising of methods of manufacture and procedure and close co-operation with the various departments and bureaus of the Government. In this way results were secured as to quantity production and according to the Government's schedule in a manner which met every expectation and desire.

Upwards of 200 officials and experienced employes of the Corporation and its subsidiary companies were granted leaves of absence during the war to connect themselves with various governmental departments, bureaus and commissions, including the Red Cross, Y. M. C. A. and kindred associations. These officials and employes included executives, experienced operating officers, engineers, scientific and technical men, as well as trained artisans and office employes. In addition many of the leading officials of the Corporation and the subsidiary companies took an active part from the beginning of the war in serving locally in their respective communities as members of Draft Boards, Red Cross, Y. M. C. A., Liberty Loan and Food Committees, and other governmental and quasi-governmental agencies. Employes to the number of 34,407, or about one-eighth of the total average number of employes, entered the active military and naval service of the United States.

There were turned over to the Government on requisition and for use in the Army and Navy service, seven of the ocean-going steamers owned by the Corporation; also five vessels of its fleet operating on the Great Lakes, together with one tug boat. The U. S. Steel Products Company (a subsidiary of the Corporation) also husbanded five vessels for account of the Naval Overseas Transport Service, i. e., furnished supplies for Deck, Engine and Steward's Departments in addition to supervising necessary repairs to the vessels.

The U. S. Shipping Board was permitted to utilize the Corporation's entire fleet on the Great Lakes in training Naval Reserves. There were placed on these vessels 590 Naval Reserves who received instruction and training under the direction of the fleet officers. In the Fall of 1917, at the request of the U. S. Shipping Board, the Corporation's fleet organization took charge of the work of manning and delivering at Montreal and Quebec vessels commandeered by the Shipping Board on the Great Lakes. This work involved furnishing the hulks (which had been cut in two to enable them to pass through the locks) with provisions and fuel and making all necessary arrangements for handling and towing them through the lakes, canals and rivers to the lower St. Lawrence River ports. An important effort of the Corporation's Great Lakes fleet organization was in taking an active and leading interest in the mobilization of its fleet and other vessels by co-operating with the United States Food Administration in the movement of grain and other commodities vital for the successful prosecution of the war. The President of the Pittsburgh Steamship Company (the Corporation's subsidiary) was Chairman of the Mobilization Committee which handled all ships on the Great Lakes in the Fall of 1917. This Committee furnished about one-half million dollars to keep the channels open with ice breakers to enable the fleet to bring down the lakes the scheduled quantity of grain.

In October, 1917, at the request of the Navy Department, there was turned over to it under a leasehold arrangement the entire warehouse property, including buildings, equipment and docks of the Corporation, located on San Francisco Bay, San Francisco, Cal. This necessitated the Corporation removing from the premises its warehouse stocks of products and establishing temporary warehouse facilities elsewhere in San Francisco and on the Pacific Coast. The Navy Department remodeled the property for use in the construction of torpedo boat destroyers, on which work the plant has been constantly and is now employed. The Navy Department has advised that the plant will be returned in the fall of 1919.

In May, 1918, the Corporation entered into a contract with the United States at the solicitation of the Secretary of War, to construct for the Government a large plant for the complete manufacture of heavy 12" to 18" guns, and of projectiles for such guns. The plant was designed to manufacture the guns and projectiles complete from the furnishing of pig iron and steel to the final finished products. The contract provided that the Corporation should take entire charge of the designing and construction of the plant, subject to approval of general plans by the Secretary of War, and that it should be reimbursed for only the exact cost of outlays made directly for the work which, in accordance with the offer of the Corporation, included no compensation for the services of its officials, experts, or its general organization in supervising the work; nor for interest upon considerable sums advanced for the payment of labor, material and other construction expenditures. The Corporation at once organized a special department to take charge of the work, appointed a general committee composed of ten of its officials, who, assisted by their respective staffs and under the direction of the Chairman and President of the Corporation, undertook the general supervision of the project, all without any charge for services. There were also detached from the service of the Corporation and its subsidiary companies 64 of their administrative officials, engineers, and other technical and trained employes experienced in construction work, whose time was exclusively devoted to the work. The site selected for the plant was on Neville Island, in the Ohio River, about six miles below Pittsburgh. Rapid progress was made in clearing the site, all general plans were prepared, approved, and to a very large extent worked out in detail; necessary construction buildings were erected and some work was done on permanent structures. Contracts were placed with machinery builders for a large quantity of equipment for the plant. A special committee of engineers was sent abroad to study the construction of large gun and projectile plants in England, France and Italy, all with the view of delivering the Government a plant of the most modern, efficient and economically operated type. Shortly after the armistice was signed, the War Department requested that the work be suspended and later that the contract be cancelled. This is now in process of accomplishment, only so much of the operating staff being retained at present as is necessary to consummate settlements with contractors for such work as they have performed under construction contracts. All physical property on the plant site has been surrendered to the War Department. The Corporation has been advised by the Secretary of War that its conduct of the work of organization and construction has been in every way entirely satisfactory.

From time to time, prior to the United States entering the war, the Corporation purchased an aggregate of $84,683,000 of various loans issued by the Allies, and since April, 1917, there have been purchased an additional $15,117,400, a total acquired of $99,800,400. A portion of the obligations included in these purchases have matured and been paid and some have been sold.

The Corporation and its subsidiary companies have subscribed for and purchased United States Liberty Loan Bonds of the First, Second, Third and Fourth issues, as follows:

Total amount purchased...	$127,950,900
Delivered to employes to February 1, 1919, on their fully paid subscriptions entered through the Corporation and subsidiary companies	6,645,000
Balance, held February 1, 1919...	$121,305,900
At February 1, 1919, of the above bonds there were held for account of employes partially paid subscriptions...	24,171,000
Leaving amount of bonds held by the Corporation and its subsidiaries....	$97,134,900

The Corporation's original subscriptions to the First and Second Liberty Loan Bonds were reduced materially on allotment by the United States Treasury Department.

The Corporation and its subsidiaries have in addition from time to time subscribed for and purchased U. S. Treasury Certificates of a net aggregate amount (not counting exchanges and reissues) of $352,340,500. Of this total, $196,063,500 have been used to pay Federal income taxes, leaving $156,277,000 on hand at February 1, 1919.

In connection with the Government's offerings of Third and Fourth Liberty Loan Bonds, the Corporation arranged to accept subscriptions from its employes payable in monthly installments. The plan permitted employes to cancel their subscriptions in case for good and sufficient reasons they elected to do so, or were unable to complete payment for the bonds in full. Subscriptions were received as follows:

	Employes Subscribing	*Amount Subscribed*
Third Liberty Loan....................................	179,374	$14,028,900
Fourth Liberty Loan.................................	202,140	22,871,600
Total		$36,900,500
To February 1, 1919, cancellation of subscriptions had been received to the number of 74,039 for a total of bonds of..............................		6,084,500
Balance		$30,816,000
Of this amount there had been paid in full bonds to the amount of..........		6,645,000

Leaving amount of subscriptions for bonds (at par) in force at February 1, 1919 $24,171,000

The employes also subscribed liberally to the First and Second Liberty Loan Bonds, but as these subscriptions were not made through the Corporation and the subsidiary companies, a statement of the exact amount cannot be given. This same condition prevails in respect of subscriptions to the Third and Fourth Liberty Loan Bonds not entered through the Corporation. From such data as it has been possible to obtain from local sources, Liberty Loan Committees and otherwise, it is known that subscriptions to these loans were made by employes other than through their employing companies of at least the sum of $16,250,000.

The Corporation and its subsidiary companies between April 1, 1917, and December 31, 1918, subscribed a total of $7,375,662 to various funds for war purposes raised by the Red Cross, United War Work Campaign, Young Men's Christian Association, Knights of Columbus and the Salvation Army. These subscriptions were made for the purpose of assisting in furthering the welfare of the large number of employes who had entered the military and naval establishments of the United States, and as a necessary means of protecting the properties of the Corporation and its subsidiaries. In addition an extra Red Cross dividend of 1 per cent. on the Common Stock, amounting to $5,083,025, was paid on July 28, 1917, for the purpose of aiding the stockholders in contributing to the American Red Cross Fund if they desired to do so. The use of the dividend by the stockholders for that purpose was expressly stated to be wholly optional with them in accordance with their interests and patriotic instincts. It is known that a very large part of the dividend was contributed to the Red Cross.

The subsidiary companies also assisted the Red Cross, United War Work Campaign and kindred associations in collecting subscriptions to war funds by employes, through accepting orders from the latter to be paid out of their salaries and wages. The amounts deducted accordingly from salaries and wages and paid over to the organizations named, together with certain subscriptions known to have been made by employes directly to these interests, equaled at least the sum of $2,825,000.

During the period of the European war eight general increases in wage rates were made. These increases, stated in percentages on basis of rates paid for common labor, were as follows:

Date of Increase	Percentage of Increase	Cumulative Percentage of Increase compared with rates paid in January, 1915
February 1, 1916	10	10
May 1, 1916	13.6	25
December 15, 1916	10	37.5
May 1, 1917	9	50
October 1, 1917	10	65
April 16, 1918	15	90
August 1, 1918	10.5	110
October 1, 1918 (See explanation below)	10	131

The percentage of increase stated for October 1, 1918, is that attaching to employes working 10 hours per day. For those working a longer number of hours the percentage of increase was greater. This arises from the adoption in nearly all departments of the basic 8-hour day, October 1, 1918, and the payment of increased rates for overtime service, the employes generally continuing after the adoption of this plan to work the same number of hours as theretofore.

The wage increases to common labor as above stated extended in substantially the same degree to other classes of employes, except to the higher paid wage earners and salaried employes. The general average increase in the earnings per employe per day in December, 1918, compared with the year 1914, was as follows:

Average for	December, 1918	Year 1914	Percentage of Increase
All employes except Administrative and Selling....	$6.23	$2.88	116%
Total employes including Administrative and Selling	6.26	2.97	111%

The average number of employes in each of the past five years and the total payroll of the organization were as follows:

	Average Number Employes	Total Pay Roll	Average Annual Earnings per Employe
1914	179,353	$162,379,907	$905
1915	191,126	176,800,864	925
1916	252,688	263,385,502	1,042
1917	268,058	347,370,400	1,296
1918	268,710	452,663,524	1,685
In month of December, 1918	......	....	1,950

The demands upon the entire personnel of the organization in every department during the period of the war were extraordinary and exacting. All were zealous and loyal in the discharge of their respective duties under conditions which at times were trying, but were assumed from a desire to assist in the effort to "win the war." The Board takes pleasure in acknowledging to the officers and employes of the Corporation and the several subsidiary companies the efficient and loyal services rendered by them to the Corporation and to the country.

BY ORDER OF THE BOARD OF DIRECTORS,

ELBERT H. GARY, *Chairman.*

UNITED STATES STEEL CORPORATION AND SUBSIDIARY COMPANIES

CONDENSED GENERAL PROFIT AND LOSS ACCOUNT

For year ending December 31, 1918

GROSS RECEIPTS—Gross Sales and Earnings (see page 24).. **$1,744,312,162.97**

OPERATING CHARGES, VIZ.:

Manufacturing and Producing Cost and Operating Expenses, including ordinary maintenance and repairs and provisional charges by subsidiary companies for depreciation.. $1,211,150,063.77

Administrative. Selling and General Expenses, employes' compensation under merit plan and pension payments (not including general expenses of transportation companies)...... 29,786,575.73

Taxes (except as included in following item)... 23,367,213.57

Allowance for estimated amount of Federal income, war-profits and excess-profits taxes.. 274,277,834.80

Commercial Discounts and Interest.. 9,646,361.49

$1,548,228,049.36

Less, Amount included in the above charges for provisional allowances for depreciation here deducted for purpose of showing the same in separate item of charge, as see below.. 33,117,398.16

1,515,110,651.20

Balance.. **$229,201,511.77**

Sundry Net Manufacturing and Operating Gains and Losses, including idle plant expenses, Royalties received, adjustments in inventory valuations, etc............................... $3,402,409.83

Rentals received 255,568.02

Compensation accrued for use of subsidiary railroads under Federal control (estimated)...... 15,510,511.34

19,168,489.19

Total Net Manufacturing. Producing and Operating Income before deducting provisional charges for depreciation... **$248,370,000.96**

OTHER INCOME

Net Profits of properties owned, but whose operations (gross revenue, cost of product, expenses, etc.) are not classified in this statement... $349,192.11

Income from sundry investments and interest on deposits, etc................................. 20,957,142.72

21,306,334.83

Total.. **$269,676,335.79**

Less the following adjustments and charges, viz.:

Reserved for amount of actual cost or market value in excess of normal prices of inventory stocks on hand at close of year... $20,297,000.00

Allowance for proportion of cost of facilities installed for production of articles contributing to prosecution of the present war (see also additional allowance for this purpose charged Balance of Net Income—page 37).................................... 40,000,000.00

Net Balance of Profits earned by subsidiary companies on sales made and service rendered account of materials on hand at close of year in purchasing companies' inventories, and which profits have not yet been realized in cash from the standpoint of a combined statement of the business of all companies............................... 1,098,231.56

61,395,231.56

Total Earnings in the year 1918 per Income Account, page 37........................... **$208,281,104.23**

Less, Interest Charges on Subsidiary Companies' Bonds, Mortgages and Purchase Money Obligations.......: 8,930,424.33

Balance of Earnings for the year before deducting provisional charges for depreciation................ **$199,350,679.90**

LESS, CHARGES AND ALLOWANCES FOR DEPRECIATION, VIZ.:

By Subsidiary Companies.. $33,117,398.16

By U. S. Steel Corporation.. 7,601,425.54

40,718,823.70

Net Income in the year 1918... **$158,631,856.20**

1919 ANNUAL REPORT

Inventory Reserve and Allowance for Extraordinary Cost Continues

UNITED STATES STEEL CORPORATION AND SUBSIDIARY COMPANIES

CONDENSED GENERAL PROFIT AND LOSS ACCOUNT

For year ending December 31, 1919

GROSS RECEIPTS—Gross Sales and Earnings (see page 24)..		$1,448,557,834.78
OPERATING CHARGES, VIZ.:		
Manufacturing and Producing Cost and Operating Expenses, including ordinary maintenance and repairs and provisional charges by subsidiary companies for depreciation..	$1,178,597,456.17	
Administrative, Selling and General Expenses, employes' compensation under merit plan and pension payments (not including general expenses of transportation companies).....	31,632,076.28	
Taxes (except as included in following item)...	29,594,336.89	
Allowance for estimated amount of Federal income and excess profits taxes..............	52,000,000.00	
Commercial Discounts and Interest..	9,062,142.40	
	$1,300,886,011.74	
Less, Amount included in the above charges for provisional allowances for depletion and depreciation here deducted for purpose of showing the same in separate item of charge, as see below...	37,608,819.42	
		1,263,277,192.32
Balance...		$185,280,642.46
Sundry Net Manufacturing and Operating Gains and Losses, including idle plant expenses, Royalties received, adjustments in inventory valuations, etc..............................	$2,840,639.27	
Rentals received	323,282.40	
Compensation accrued for use of subsidiary railroads under Federal control (estimated)......	15,582,723.76	
		18,746,645.43
Total Net Manufacturing, Producing and Operating Income before deducting provisional charges for depreciation..		$204,027,287.89
OTHER INCOME		
Net Profits of properties owned, but whose operations (gross revenue, cost of product, expenses, etc.) are not classified in this statement..	$381,794.64	
Income from sundry investments and interest on deposits, etc.................................	12,764,360.70	
		13,146,155.34
Total..		$217,173,443.23
Add, Net Balance of Profits earned by subsidiary companies on sales made and service rendered account of materials which were on hand at first of year in purchasing companies' inventories, and which profits have since been realized in cash from the standpoint of a combined statement of the business of all companies...................................		12,125,446.16
Total ....:		$229,298,889.39
Less the following adjustments and charges, viz.:		
Reserved for amount of actual cost or market value in excess of normal prices of inventory stocks on hand at close of year...	$38,710,396.41	
Allowance for proportion of extraordinary cost, resulting from war requirements and conditions, of facilities installed..	38,297,853.74	
		77,008,250.15
Total Earnings in the year 1919 per Income Account, page 33		$152,290,639.24
Less, Interest Charges on Subsidiary Companies' Bonds, Mortgages and Purchase Money Obligations..........		8,701,576.72
Balance of Earnings for the year before deducting provisional charges for depreciation................		$143,589,062.52
LESS, CHARGES AND ALLOWANCES FOR DEPLETION AND DEPRECIATION, VIZ.:		
By Subsidiary Companies...	$37,608,819.42	
By U. S. Steel Corporation...	7,937,107.01	
		45,545,926.43
Net Income in the year 1919...		$98,043,136.09

1920 ANNUAL REPORT

Inventory Reserve at its Zenith

The Guns are Silent but the Allowance for Extraordinary Cost Continues

INVENTORIES

OF

Manufacturing and Operating Materials and Supplies and Semi-Finished and Finished Products, Including Net Advances on Contract Work, Etc.

The net book valuation of the inventories of the above classes of assets for all the subsidiary companies equalled at December 31, 1920, after allowing credit for reserve of $95,000,000 for account of actual cost or market value of inventory stocks in excess of unit prices therefor at close of 1915, the sum of $258,363,497, an increase of $31,566,819 in comparison with the total at close of preceding year.

Inventory values, before allowing for credit for the reserve above mentioned, are on the basis of the actual purchase or production cost of the materials to the respective subsidiary companies holding the same (unless such cost was above the market value on December 31, 1920, in which case the market price was used) except that in respect of such commodities in stock at the close of the year as had been purchased by one subsidiary company from another there has been excluded the approximate amount of profits in such sales price which had accrued to the subsidiaries selling the same or furnishing service in connection therewith. These profits are not carried into the currently reported earnings of the entire organization until converted into cash or a cash asset to it. Accordingly, in the combined assets for all of the companies the inventories of those materials and products on hand which have been transferred and sold from one subsidiary company to another, are carried at net values which are substantially the production cost to the respective subsidiary companies furnishing the same.

The following is a general classification of the inventory valuations at December 31, 1920, in comparison with the valuations at the close of the preceding year:

	Dec. 31, 1920	Dec. 31, 1919
Ores—Iron, Manganese and Zinc	$79 430 633	$75 855 858
Limestone, Fluxes and Refractories	6 021 870	4 270 425
Coal, Coke and Other Fuel	10 587 353	7 517 024
Pig Iron, Scrap, Ferro and Spiegel	19 544 070	31 010 340
Pig Tin, Lead, Spelter, Copper, Nickel, Aluminum and Dross and Skimmings	11 980 704	11 541 018
Rolls, Molds, Stools, Annealing Boxes, etc.	15 788 150	15 431 459
Ingots—Steel	2 541 799	5 309 136
Blooms, Billets, Slabs, Sheet and Tinplate Bars, etc.	20 542 256	23 404 675
Wire Rods	1 880 580	1 728 715
Skelp	2 391 445	2 155 834
Finished Products	68 146 896	49 062 768
Manufacturing Supplies, Stores and Sundry Items not otherwise classified	57 807 450	51 600 101
Mining Supplies and Stores (for ore and coal properties)	9 914 547	9 145 370
Railroad Supplies and Stores	10 481 934*	2 600 301
Merchandise of Supply Companies	1 880 723	1 747 452
Material, labor and expense locked up in uncompleted Bridge and Structural Work and Ship Construction and Other Contract Work. $50 913 162		
Less Bills rendered on account. 41 412 104		
	9 501 058	3 981 504
Stocks abroad and on consignment	15 681 950	10 459 768
Material in transit	9 240 079	9 974 930
Total	$353 363 497	$316 796 678
Less, Reserve for account of actual cost or market value of stocks in excess of unit prices therefor at December 31, 1915	95 000 000	90 000 000
Balance	$258 363 497	$226 796 678

*Includes inventories of subsidiary railroads which were not included at December 31, 1919 account of roads being then under Federal control.

UNITED STATES STEEL CORPORATION AND SUBSIDIARY COMPANIES
CONDENSED GENERAL PROFIT AND LOSS ACCOUNT
For the year ending December 31, 1920

GROSS RECEIPTS—Gross Sales and Earnings (see page 24)		$1,755,477,025.13
OPERATING CHARGES, VIZ.:		
Manufacturing and Producing Cost and Operating Expenses, including ordinary maintenance and repairs and provisional charges by subsidiary companies for depreciation..	$1,440,734,562.52	
Administrative, Selling and General Expenses, employes' compensation under merit plan and pension payments (not including general expenses of transportation companies)	35,945,536.86	
Taxes (except as included in following item)...	38,724,289.12	
Allowance for estimated amount of Federal income and excess profits taxes..............	37,500,000.00	
Commercial Discounts and Interest..	10,849,880.54	
	$1,563,754,269.04	
Less, Amount included in above charges for allowances for depletion and depreciation here deducted for purpose of showing same in separate item of charge, as see below.........	38,245,601.92	
		1,525,508,667.12
Balance...		$229,968,358.01
Sundry Net Manufacturing and Operating Gains and Losses, including idle plant expenses, Royalties received, etc.	5,726,463.39	
Adjustments of Inventory Valuations (In addition, adjustments of $720,201 are charged in Manufacturing Costs and Operating Expenses)..Dr.	14,385,649.46	
Rentals received	991,569.72	
Compensation accrued in January and February for use of subsidiary railroads under Federal control (estimated)...	2,179,000.76	
		Dr. 5,488,615.59
Total Net Manufacturing, Producing and Operating Income before deducting provisional charges for depreciation..		$224,479,742.42
OTHER INCOME AND CHARGES		
Net Profits of properties owned, but whose operations (gross revenue, cost of product, expenses, etc.) are not classified in this statement..	$321,346.76	
Income from sundry investments and interest on deposits, etc...	16,199,187.57	
Allowance for depreciation in book value of U. S. Govt. bonds and other securities owned..Dr.	9,780,769.85	
		6,739,764.48
Total...		$231,219,506.90
Less, Charges as follows, viz.:		
Accrued estimated payment by subsidiary railroads to the United States under Transportation Act	$4,500,000.00	
Reserved for proportion of actual cost or market value of inventory stocks on hand in excess of pre-war unit values...	5,000,000.00	
Allowance for estimated proportion of extraordinary cost resulting from the world war conditions of new facilities and improvements installed............................	27,000,000.00	
		36,500,000.00
Balance		$194,719,506.90
Less, Net balance of Profits earned by subsidiary companies on sales made and service rendered account of materials on hand at close of year in purchasing companies' inventories and which profits have not yet been realized in cash from the standpoint of a combined statement of the business of all companies..........		9,624,147.62
Total Earnings in the Year 1920 per Income Account, page 35		$185,095,359.28
Less, Interest Charges on Subsidiary Companies' Bonds, Mortgages and Purchase Money Obligations..........		8,408,460.87
Balance of Earnings for the year before deducting provisional charges for depreciation.................		$176,686,898.41
LESS, CHARGES AND ALLOWANCES FOR DEPLETION AND DEPRECIATION, VIZ.:		
By Subsidiary Companies..	$38,245,601.92	
By U. S. Steel Corporation..	8,438,762.40	
		46,684,364.32
Net Income in the year 1920..		$130,002,534.09

1921 ANNUAL REPORT

$73 Million Drop in Net Earnings

Dividends Remain the Same

Negative Amount Transferred to Surplus

Deflation from War Period Prices Leads to Absorption of Reserve

Operations Fall to 29% of Capacity in July

Depreciation . . . Fair and Reasonable

Inventories . . . a Substantial Writedown to the Reserve

COMPARATIVE INCOME ACCOUNT

For the Fiscal Years ending December 31, 1921 and 1920

	1921	1920	+Increase —Decrease
EARNINGS—Before charging interest on Bonds and Mortgages of Subsidiary Companies:			
First Quarter	$34 342 006 44	$44 212 019 49	— $9 870 013 05
Second Quarter	23 911 921 99	45 268 551 34	— 21 356 629 35
Third Quarter	20 916 498 75	50 145 301 18	— 29 228 802 43
Fourth Quarter	21 620 852 32	45 469 487 27	— 23 848 634 95
Total for year	*$100 791 279 50	*$185 095 359 28	— $84 304 079 78
Less, Interest on outstanding Bonds and Mortgages of the Subsidiary Companies	8 065 221 58	8 408 460 87	— 343 239 29
Balance of Earnings	$92 726 057 92	$176 686 898 41	— $83 960 840 49
Less, Charges and Allowances for Depletion and Depreciation applied as follows, viz.:			
To Depreciation and Replacement Funds and Sinking Funds on Bonds of Subsidiary Companies.........	27 905 045 44	38 245 601 92	— 10 340 556 48
To Sinking Funds on U. S. Steel Corporation Bonds.....	8 863 180 35	8 438 762 40	+ 424 417 95
Net Income in the year.......................	$55 957 832 13	$130 002 534 09	— $74 044 701 96
Deduct:			
Interest on U. S. Steel Corporation Bonds outstanding.....	19 679 582 49	20 105 559 58	— 425 977 09
Premium paid on Bonds redeemed, viz.:			
On Subsidiary Companies' Bonds...................	27 835 57	118 104 19	— 90 268 62
On U. S. Steel Corporation Bonds.................	719 626 39	717 228 49	+ 2 397 90
Balance	$35 530 787 68	$109 061 641 83	— $73 530 854 15
Add: Net Balance of sundry charges and credits, including adjustments of various accounts	1 086 229 51	632 585 81	+ 453 643 70
	$36 617 017 19	$109 694 227 64	— $73 077 210 45
Dividends on U. S. Steel Corporation Stocks, viz.:			
Preferred, 7%	25 219 677 00	25 219 677 00	....
Common, 5%	25 415 125 00	25 415 125 00	....
Surplus Net Income	†$14 017 784 81	$59 059 425 64	— $73 077 210 45
Less, Appropriated from Surplus Net Income on account of expenditures made on authorized appropriations for additional property and construction........................	....	30 000 000 00	— 30 000 000 00
Balance	†$14 017 784 81	$29 059 425 64	— $43 077 210 45

*Balance of Earnings after making allowances for estimated amount of Federal income and excess profits taxes.
†Deficit provided from Undivided Surplus.

INVENTORIES

OF

MANUFACTURING AND OPERATING MATERIALS AND SUPPLIES AND SEMI-FINISHED AND FINISHED PRODUCTS, INCLUDING NET ADVANCES ON CONTRACT WORK, ETC.

The net book valuation of the inventories of the above classes of assets for all the subsidiary companies equalled at December 31, 1921, the sum of $241,504,369, a decrease of $16,859,128 in comparison with the total at close of preceding year. The valuation as stated is the net after allowing credit for a reserve of $60,710,255 set aside from earnings of previous years to absorb deflation in value from war period prices which may from time to time develop in respect of inventory items.

Inventory values, before allowing for credit for the reserve above mentioned, are on the basis of the actual purchase or production cost of the materials to the respective subsidiary companies holding the same (unless such cost was above the market value on December 31, 1921, in which case the market price was used) except that in respect of such commodities in stock at the close of the year as had been purchased by one subsidiary company from another there has been excluded the approximate amount of profits in such sales price which had accrued to the subsidiaries selling the same or furnishing service in connection therewith. These profits are not carried into the currently reported earnings of the consolidated organization until converted into cash or a cash asset to it. Accordingly, in the combined assets for all of the companies the inventories of those materials and products on hand which have been transferred and sold from one subsidiary company to another, are carried at net values which include no inter-company profits accruing to any subsidiary company in connection with the sale of materials to another subsidiary.

The following is a general classification of the inventory valuations at December 31, 1921, in comparison with the valuations at the close of the preceding year:

	Dec. 31, 1921	Dec. 31, 1920
Ores—Iron, Manganese and Zinc	$84 725 188	$79 430 633
Limestone, Fluxes and Refractories	4 440 739	6 021 870
Coal, Coke and Other Fuel	13 054 195	10 587 353
Pig Iron, Scrap, Ferro and Spiegel	18 869 057	19 544 070
Pig Tin, Lead, Spelter, Copper, Nickel, Aluminum and Dross and Skimmings	7 714 557	11 980 704
Rolls, Molds, Stools, Annealing Boxes, etc.	13 123 821	15 788 150
Ingots—Steel	1 573 879	2 541 799
Blooms, Billets, Slabs, Sheet and Tinplate Bars, etc.	22 782 293	20 542 256
Wire Rods	1 363 220	1 880 580
Skelp	1 785 049	2 391 445
Finished Products	56 599 667	68 146 896
Manufacturing Supplies, Stores and Sundry Items not otherwise classified	37 050 148	57 807 450
Mining Supplies and Stores (for ore and coal properties)	7 291 199	9 914 547
Railroad Supplies and Stores	7 953 241	10 481 934
Merchandise of Supply Companies	1 363 816	1 880 723
Material, labor and expense locked up in uncompleted Bridge, Structural and other contract work ... $1 850 115 / Less Bills rendered on account ... 825 583	1 024 532	9 501 058
Stocks abroad and on consignment	17 260 930	15 681 950
Material in transit	4 239 093	9 240 079
Total	$302 214 624	$353 363 497
Less, Inventory Reserve	60 710 255	95 000 000
Balance	$241 504 369	$258 363 497

84

16

GENERAL

The marked decrease in the demand for iron and steel products which developed in the midsummer of 1920, continued until the early fall of 1921, when there was some improvement. As stated in the annual report for last year the subsidiary companies carried forward into 1921 a substantial tonnage of orders for steel products. This enabled them to operate at an average of somewhat over 70 per cent. of capacity during the first quarter. The degree of operations dropped in succeeding months and reached the low point for the year in July when the output was only about 29 per cent. The average production for the entire year in rolled and other finished products for sale was 47.5 per cent. of capacity, the lowest ratio of production to capacity in any year since the organization of the Corporation. Concurrently with the decrease in demand for steel products there were marked declines in the prices obtained for nearly all classes of the same. These price reductions as a rule exceeded the decreases it was possible to effect in the cost of production through the reduction in unit prices of factors entering into cost of operations and the exercise of rigid economies. A number of elements in the cost of producing steel show little if any recession from war-time figures, notably that of railroad transportation, which on basis of existing rate conditions averages in the case of the subsidiary companies upwards of forty per cent. of the total cost of producing steel. At the close of the year the prices prevailing for some products were below the cost of production. Since the beginning of 1922, and to the date of writing this report, the new orders received have been equal to about one-half the total capacity of the plants of the subsidiary companies.

Production

The production of the several principal departments during the year in comparison with results for the preceding year was as follows:

	1921 Tons	1920 Tons	Decrease Tons	Decrease Per Cent.
Iron Ore Mined..................................	16,422,682	27,021,009	10,598,327	39.2
Coal Mined: For use in making coke.................	14,546,103	24,384,925	9,838,822	40.3
For steam, gas and other purposes.......	7,081,836	6,443,409	638,427	9.9 *Inc.*
	21,627,939	30,828,334	9,200,395	29.8
Coke Manufactured	9,825,264	16,208,111	6,382,847	39.4
Limestone Quarried	4,607,486	5,981,022	1,373,536	23.0
Pig Iron, Ferro and Spiegel......................	8,678,262	14,532,646	5,854,384	40.3
Steel Ingots (Bessemer and Open Hearth)............	10,966,347	19,277,960	8,311,613	43.1
Rolled and Other Finished Steel Products for Sale.... (For classification see page 15)	7,860,334	14,228,502	6,368,168	44.8
	Bbls.	Bbls.	Bbls.	
Universal Portland Cement.........................	12,499,000	11,960,000	539,000	4.5 *Inc.*
Vessels completed and delivered from shipyards:				
Ocean steamers.............................	16	18	....	....
Barges and Car Floats.......................	16	5	....	....
D. W. tonnage.............................	195,240	171,890	....	....

24

Shipments

The shipments of all classes of products in comparison with shipments during the preceding year were as follows:

Domestic Shipments	1921 Tons	1920 Tons	Decrease or Increase Tons	Per Cent.
Rolled Steel and Other Finished Products............	6,832,038	12,453,243	5,621,205	45.1 Dec.
Pig Iron, Ingots, Ferro and Scrap...................	142,715	341,563	198,848	58.2 "
Iron Ore, Coal and Coke..........................	618,729	1,212,811	594,082	49.0 "
Sundry Materials and By-Products.................	103,265	175,735	72,470	41.2 "
Total tons all kinds of materials, except Cement..	7,696,747	14,183,352	6,486,605	45.7 "
Universal Portland Cement (Bbls.).................	12,211,285	11,380,260	831,025	7.3 Inc.
Export Shipments				
Rolled Steel and Other Finished Products...........	1,126,795	1,645,464	518,669	31.5 Dec.
Pig Iron and Scrap..............................	978	6,979	6,001	86.0 "
Sundry Materials and By-Products.................	80,384	55,657	24,727	44.4 Inc.
Total tons all kinds of materials.................	1,208,157	1,708,100	499,943	29.3 Dec.
Aggregate tonnage of Rolled Steel and Other Finished Products shipped to both Domestic and Export Trade	7,958,833	14,098,707	6,139,874	43.5 Dec.

TOTAL VALUE OF BUSINESS (Covering all of above shipments, including cement and completed steamships delivered and other business not measured by the ton unit)	1921	1920	Decrease Amount	Per Cent.
Domestic (not including inter-company sales)......	$563,093,812	$1,071,739,500	$508,645,688	47.5
Export	92,313,756	147,905,404	55,591,648	37.6
Total	$655,407,568	$1,219,644,904	$564,237,336	46.3

The decrease in operations necessarily called for less outlays for maintenance and upkeep than were expended in previous year, as well as for smaller allowances for depletion and depreciation. The expenditures and appropriations for these purposes in comparison with similar charges in 1920, were as follows:

	1921	1920	Decrease Amount	Per Cent.
Ordinary repairs and maintenance...................	$92,480,126	$147,468,478	$54,988,352	37.3
Extraordinary replacements	2,361,582	5,757,480	3,395,898	59.0
Total expended	$94,841,708	$153,225,958	$58,384,250	38.1
Net allowances made from earnings (being the excess of same over amount expended and included in above) for exhaustion of minerals and depreciation of plants and properties	33,934,444	42,524,256	8,589,812	20.2
Total expended and appropriated for maintenance, depletion and depreciation	$128,776,152	$195,750,214	$66,974,062	34.2

The aggregate amount of inventories at the close of the year, valued at cost or market price (whichever was the lower) was $302,214,624, compared with a valuation of $353,363,497, at the close of 1920. During the year there was written off for shrinkage in inventory values the sum of $34,289,746. This amount of depreciation in values was charged to the Inventory Reserve Fund set aside from earnings of previous years to ab-

25

sorb any marked deflation of values from war period prices. Of the amount so charged to the Inventory Reserve, $20,005,548 were used in writing down to market prices at December 31, 1921, the values of various inventory materials and products then in stock, and the balance, $14,284,198, was similarly applied at various times during the year in respect of materials which were used in the manufacture of products shipped within the year. At December 31, 1921, the balance remaining in the Inventory Reserve Fund was $60,710,255. This balance of Inventory Reserve Fund is stated in the Condensed Balance Sheet as a reduction in the total value for Inventories on basis of cost or market (whichever was the lower) as carried in current assets.

88

CERTIFICATE OF INDEPENDENT AUDITORS

New York, March 10, 1922.

To the Stockholders of the United States Steel Corporation:

We have examined the books of the United States Steel Corporation and Subsidiary Companies for the year ending December 31, 1921, and certify that the balance sheet at that date and the relative income account are correctly prepared therefrom.

The charges to property account during the year cover only actual additions and extensions to the properties and plants. Having regard to the curtailment of operations during the year, the provision made for depletion and depreciation is, in our opinion, fair and reasonable. The item of deferred charges represents expenditures reasonably and properly carried forward to operations in subsequent years.

The valuations of the stocks of materials and supplies on hand, as shown by inventories certified by the responsible officials, have been carefully made at prices not in excess of cost or market, and, as stated in the directors' report, a substantial reserve has been deducted from the values so determined. Full provision has been made for bad and doubtful accounts receivable and for all ascertainable liabilities.

We have verified the cash and securities by actual inspection or by certificates from the depositaries, and are of opinion that the marketable bonds and stocks included in current assets are worth the value at which they are stated in the balance sheet, and

WE CERTIFY that, in our opinion, the balance sheet is properly drawn up so as to show the financial position of the Corporation and Subsidiary Companies on December 31, 1921, and the relative income account is a fair and correct statement of the net earnings for the fiscal year ending at that date.

PRICE. WATERHOUSE & CO.

1922 ANNUAL REPORT

The Inventory Reserve Shrinks Again

INVENTORIES

OF

MANUFACTURING AND OPERATING MATERIALS AND SUPPLIES AND SEMI-FINISHED AND FINISHED PRODUCTS, INCLUDING NET ADVANCES ON CONTRACT WORK, ETC.

The net book valuation of the inventories of the above classes of assets for all the subsidiary companies equalled at December 31, 1922, the sum of $220,707,251, a decrease of $20,797,118 in comparison with the total at close of preceding year. The valuation as stated is the net after allowing credit for a reserve of $49,460,082 set aside from earnings of previous years to absorb deflation in value from war period prices which may from time to time develop in respect of inventory items.

Inventory values, before allowing for credit for the reserve above mentioned, are on the basis of the actual purchase or production cost of the materials to the respective subsidiary companies holding the same (unless such cost was above the market value on December 31, 1922, in which case the market price was used) except that in respect of such commodities in stock at the close of the year as had been purchased by one subsidiary company from another there has been excluded the approximate amount of profits in such sales price which had accrued to the subsidiaries selling the same or furnishing service in connection therewith. These profits are not carried into the currently reported earnings of the consolidated organization until converted into cash or a cash asset to it. Accordingly, in the combined assets for all of the companies the inventories of those materials and products on hand which have been transferred and sold from one subsidiary company to another, are carried at net values which include no inter-company profits accruing to any subsidiary company in connection with the sale of materials to another subsidiary.

The following is a general classification of the inventory valuations at December 31, 1922, in comparison with the valuations at the close of the preceding year:

		Dec. 31, 1922	Dec. 31, 1921
Ores—Iron, Manganese and Zinc		$76 275 064	$84 725 188
Limestone, Fluxes and Refractories		5 091 428	4 440 739
Coal, Coke and Other Fuel		10 807 030	13 054 195
Pig Iron, Scrap, Ferro and Spiegel		12 374 219	18 869 057
Pig Tin, Lead, Spelter, Copper, Nickel, Aluminum and Dross and Skimmings		8 288 802	7 714 557
Rolls, Molds, Stools, Annealing Boxes, etc.		11 591 006	13 123 821
Ingots—Steel		2 533 616	1 573 879
Blooms, Billets, Slabs, Sheet and Tinplate Bars, etc.		16 283 993	22 782 293
Wire Rods		1 499 913	1 363 220
Skelp		1 588 148	1 785 049
Finished Products		47 619 421	56'599 667
Manufacturing Supplies, Stores and Sundry Items not otherwise classified		35 578 946	37 050 148
Mining Supplies and Stores (for ore and coal properties)		7 256 390	7 291 199
Railroad Supplies and Stores		6 210 753	7 953 241
Merchandise of Supply Companies		1 818 297	1 363 816
Material, labor and expense locked up in uncompleted Bridge, Structural and other contract work	$26 638 598		
Less Bills rendered on account	21 097 612		
		5 540 986	1 024 532
Stocks abroad and on consignment		12 940 727	17 260 930
Material in transit		6 868 594	4 239 093
Total		$270 167 333	$302 214 624
Less, Inventory Reserve		49 460 082	60 710 255
Balance		$220 707 251	$241 504 369

1923 ANNUAL REPORT

Return to "Normalcy"

COMPARATIVE INCOME ACCOUNT

For the Fiscal Years ending December 31, 1923 and 1922

	1923	1922	+Increase —Decrease
EARNINGS—Before charging interest on Bonds and Mortgages of Subsidiary Companies:			
First Quarter	$36 874 674 77	$21 303 631 59	+ $15 571 043 18
Second Quarter	49 940 029 97	29 330 255 01	+ 20 609 774 96
Third Quarter	49 112 517 68	29 596 455 29	+ 19 516 062 39
Fourth Quarter	52 026 445 43	29 558 574 43	+ 22 467 871 00
Total for year	*$187 953 667 85	*$109 788 916 32	+ $78 164 751 53
Less, Interest on outstanding Bonds and Mortgages of the Subsidiary Companies	8 306 993 48	8 259 605 93	+ 47 387 55
Balance of Earnings	$179 646 674 37	$101 529 310 39	+ $78 117 363 98
Less, Charges and Allowances for Depletion and Depreciation applied as follows, viz.:			
To Depreciation and Replacement Reserves and Sinking Funds on Bonds of Subsidiary Companies..........	41 745 434 23	33 382 624 09	+ 8 362 810 14
To Sinking Funds on U. S. Steel Corporation Bonds.....	9 724 720 38	9 305 884 70	+ 418 835 68
Net Income in the year.......................	$128 176 519 76	$58 840 801 60	+ $69 335 718 16
Deduct:			
Interest on U. S. Steel Corporation Bonds outstanding.....	18 764 567 62	19 232 304 87	— 467 737 25
Premium on Bonds redeemed and acquired for Sinking Fund, viz.:			
On Subsidiary Companies' Bonds..................	165 611 86	150 205 98	+ 15 405 88
On U. S. Steel Corporation Bonds..................	774 464 84	724 873 04	+ 49 591 80
Balance	$108 471 875 44	$38 733 417 71	+ $69 738 457 73
Add: Net Balance of sundry receipts and charges, including adjustments of various accounts	235 188 82	920 037 52	— 684 848 70
	$108 707 064 26	$39 653 455 23	+ $69 053 609 03
Dividends on U. S. Steel Corporation Stocks, viz.:			
Preferred, 7%	25 219 677 00	25 219 677 00	....
Common { 1923, Regular 5%, Extra ¾% } { 1922, Regular 5% }	29 227 393 75	25 415 125 00	+ 3 812 268 75
Surplus Net Income.........................	$54 259 993 51	†$10 981 346 77	+ $65 241 340 28
Less, Sums appropriated and expended or to be expended account of additions, improvements or betterments to plants and property..	40 000 000 00	....	+ 40 000 000 00
Balance carried forward to Undivided Surplus....	$14 259 993 51	†$10 981 346 77	+ $25 241 340 28

*Balance of Earnings after making allowances for estimated amount of Federal income taxes.
†Deficit provided from Undivided Surplus.

7

1929 ANNUAL REPORT

Surplus Built-Up and then Depleted

Housecleaning of Reserves

Redemption Loss to Surplus

Appreciated Cost (Water) to Surplus

Working Capital Contribution Wiped-Out

Recession Starts in October

Treasury Stock as Asset

Property Write-Offs Detailed

History of Amortization of Investment Cost

History of Net Profits and Undivided Surplus Since
Inception

Inventories Without Reserve

SURPLUS OF U. S. STEEL CORPORATION AND SUBSIDIARY COMPANIES

(Since April 1, 1901)

Balance of Undivided Surplus, December 31, 1928, exclusive of Profits earned by subsidiary companies on inter-company sales of products on hand in inventories, per Annual Report for 1928	$410,277,349.27
Add: Surplus Net Income earned in year 1929, per Income Account, page 1	108,523,342.99
Refunds received in 1929 of Federal Income and Excess Profits Taxes of earlier years.....	15,756,595.72
Balance of Inventory Reserve originally provided to absorb deflation in values because of post-war economic adjustment, now transferred to Surplus	47,076,404.12
Reserve set aside to provide against possible failure to realize Mining Royalties on unmined iron ore from specific properties, now transferred to Surplus, being no longer required for that purpose	7,000,000.00
	$588,633,692.10

Less, Charges to and Appropriations of Surplus:

Premium and unamortized discount on Bonds of United States Steel Corporation and subsidiary companies retired and called for redemption during the year	$40,626,554.25	
Surplus appropriated for amortization of appreciated cost to U. S. Steel Corporation of its investment in capital stocks of Subsidiary Companies in excess of their investment in tangible property.....	88,296,020.09	
Capital provided in organization (in 1901) and heretofore carried in "Surplus" account written off in reduction of Property Investment Account..	25,000,000.00	
		153,922,574.34
Balance of Earned Undivided Surplus, December 31, 1929, exclusive of Profits earned by subsidiary companies on inter-company sales of products on hand in inventories (see note below)		$434,711,117.76

NOTE.—Surplus of Subsidiary Companies amounting to $44,898,748.23, and representing Profits on sales of materials and products to other subsidiary companies which are on hand in latters' Inventories December 31, 1929, is deducted from the amount of Inventories included under Current Assets in Consolidated General Balance Sheet.

APPROPRIATED SURPLUS INVESTED IN CAPITAL EXPENDITURES

Amount at December 31, 1929......	$270,000,000.00

OPERATIONS FOR THE YEAR

The active demand for steel products which marked the closing months of 1928, continued in steadily broadening proportions into and through the summer of 1929; not until October was there any appreciable recession in deliveries. During the first nine months of the year operations equalled 94 per cent. of full capacity of finished products for sale, peak production of 100 per cent. having been reached in the month of May, while the average for the entire second quarter was 98.5 per cent. During the closing quarter of the year, however, the output dropped to 74.5 per cent. For the entire year the average was 89.2 per cent. of capacity compared with 83.4 per cent. in 1928.

These uniform and favorable conditions permitted the mills and plants to operate efficiently which, together with fairly stable prices received (virtually the same as the 1928 average in respect of domestic and a slight advance in case of export), produced satisfactory earnings results for the year.

Following the financial disturbances in the securities market in October and November there was up to January 1st a marked reduction in the tonnage of new business placed. But following that date there was an improvement which has continued to the date of writing this report. At December 31, 1929, the unfilled orders on the books of the subsidiary companies totalled 4,417,193 tons, compared with 3,976,712 tons at close of 1928. At March 1, 1930, the total was 4,479,748 tons. During the first two months of 1930, production of finished products for sale averaged 80 per cent. of capacity, while shipments were at a somewhat higher percentage account of considerable tonnage having been shipped from stock.

PRODUCTION

The production of the several principal departments for the year 1929 in comparison with results for the preceding year, was as follows:

	1929 Tons	1928 Tons	Increase Tons	Per Cent.
Iron and Manganese Ore............................	30,540,565	26,633,554	3,907,011	14.7
Limestone, Dolomite and Fluorspar...................	14,763,412	14,600,181	163,231	1.1
Coal	31,826,634	28,691,024	3,135,610	10.9
Coke	17,355,036	15,993,373	1,361,663	8.5
Pig Iron, Ferro and Spiegel.........................	16,484,985	15,237,717	1,247,268	8.2
Steel Ingots (Bessemer and Open Hearth)............	21,868,816	20,105,749	1,763,067	8.8
Rolled and Finished Steel Products for Sale...........	15,302,669	13,972,388	1,330,281	9.5
	Bbls.	Bbls.	Decrease	
Universal Portland Cement.........................	11,549,000	14,957,000	3,408,000	22.8

As will be observed from the foregoing the increases in output were general in all departments except Cement, the decrease in which latter reflects the diminution in demand for this product which evidenced itself in latter part of 1928 However, the demand this year to date is very largely in excess of same in similar period of last year, and it is confidently expected the lull in demand during 1929 was but a temporary recession. The relatively small increase in output of Limestone is wholly accounted for by the lesser quantity required for manufacture of Cement. On page 23 of this report will be found a table detailing by classes the production of finished steel products during 1929 in comparison with the results for preceding year.

CONSOLIDATED GENERAL BALANCE SHEET
December 31, 1929

ASSETS

PROPERTY INVESTMENT ACCOUNTS

PROPERTIES OWNED AND OPERATED BY THE SEVERAL COMPANIES
Balance of this account as of December 31, 1929, less Depletion, Depreciation
and Amortization Reserves per table on page 17... $ 1,541,492,587.42

MINING ROYALTIES

Mining Royalties on unmined ore, in respect of part of which notes of subsidiary
companies are outstanding in amount of $21,912,188.66, as see contra.................. 66,291,180.79

100

DEFERRED CHARGES (Applying to future operations of the properties)
Advanced Mining and other operating expenses and charges.....,.................. $ 1,306,160.37
Discount on subsidiary companies' bonds sold (net)............................... 368,669.17
1,674,829.54

INVESTMENTS
Outside Real Estate and Investments in sundry securities, including Real Estate
Mortgages .... $ 5,520,417.84
Land Sales Installment Contracts and Mortgages under Employes' Home-owning Plan 13,899,080.93
19,419,498.77

GENERAL AND RESERVE FUND ASSETS
Cash resources held by Trustees account Bond Sinking Funds...................... $ 570,998.10
(Trustees also hold $10,180,000 of redeemed bonds, not included as liabilities in this Balance Sheet.)

Cash deposits held by Trustees for payment of the $8,091,000 (par) of matured and
called bonds unpresented and the outstanding U. S. Steel 50 year non-callable
series, 5% Gold Bonds (see contra)... 8,915,166.73

Securities held as investment of Contingent Reserves and for account Employes'
Stock Subscriptions 27,704,946.54

Insurance and Depreciation Fund Assets:
Securities $57,807,301.79
Cash 74,638.09
57,881,939.88
95,073,051.25

CURRENT ASSETS
Inventories, less credit for amount of inventory values representing Profits earned
by subsidiary companies on Inter-Company sales of products on hand in Inven-
tories December 31, 1929. (See note opposite.) 288,572,969.54
Accounts Receivable.. 70,329,084.30
Bills Receivable... 6,401,586.47
Agents' Balances 1,431,634.87
Sundry Marketable Securities (including part of U. S. Gov't Securities owned)...... 60,544,918.56
Time and other special Bank Deposits.. 4,278,750.19
Cash (in hand and on deposit with Banks, Bankers and Trust Companies, subject
to cheque).. 130,673,563.21
562,232,507.14

We have audited the above Balance Sheet, and certify that in our opinion
it is properly drawn up so as to show the financial position of the United States
Steel Corporation and Subsidiary Companies on December 31, 1929.
PRICE, WATERHOUSE & CO.,

NEW YORK, MARCH 14, 1930.   Auditors.

$2,286,183,654.91

14

PROPERTY INVESTMENT ACCOUNTS

December 31, 1929

Gross Fixed Property Investment Account, December 31, 1928, exclusive of Stripping and Mine Development and Structural Erection Equipment..		$2,435,263,759.94
Add, Net Property Balances of Minority Companies not heretofore included and sundry property adjustments		265,426.05
		$2,435,529,185.99
Less: Specifically written off to cover amortization of cost to U. S. Steel of capital stocks of subsidiary companies in excess of latter's investment in tangible property, viz:		
From Bond Sinking Fund Reserves applicable for this purpose.............	$182,092,834.00	
From Profit and Loss Surplus...	88,296,020.09	
Working Capital provided in organization of U. S. Steel Corporation heretofore carried in "Surplus" formally applied in reduction of Property Investment Account	25,000,000.00	
		295,388,854.09
		$2,140,140,331.90
Capital Expenditures on Property Account in 1929 (ex. Stripping and Development)....	$ 61,043,036.06	
Less, Amounts written off in year 1929 to Depletion and Depreciation Reserves for investment cost of natural resources exhausted and of improvements, equipment and facilities abandoned and retired...	26,626,583.63	
		34,416,452.43
Gross Fixed Property Investment December 31, 1929		$2,174,556,784.33
Deduct: Balances in Depletion, Depreciation, Amortization and Current Maintenance Reserves, December 31, 1929:		
Depletion and Depreciation Reserves, exclusive of those specifically applied as per succeeding item	$538,785,901.80	
Specifically applied for redemption of bonds through Bond Sinking Funds of Subsidiary Companies	44,184,374.42	
Amortization Reserves account excess construction cost arising from war-time conditions	60,199,900.73	
Current Maintenance Reserves..	26,836,239.82	
		670,006,416.77
Net Fixed Property Investment Account, December 31, 1929		$1,504,550,367.56
Investment in Stripping and Development at Mines and Structural Erection Equipment:		
Balance at December 31, 1928..	$ 38,655,581.28	
Expended during the year 1929...	4,505,106.81	
	$ 43,160,688.09	
Less, Charged off in 1929 to operating expenses................................	6,218,468.23	
Balance December 31, 1929...		36,942,219.86
Total of Property Investment Account, December 31, 1929, per Consolidated General Balance Sheet.......		$1,541,492,587.42

INCOME AND SURPLUS RESERVED AND APPROPRIATED TO COVER AMORTIZATION OF INVESTMENT COST IN STOCKS OF SUBSIDIARY COMPANIES IN EXCESS OF THEIR OWN INVESTMENT IN TANGIBLE PROPERTY

Earnings heretofore reserved and applied in retirement of U. S. Steel Corporation Bonds through Sinking Funds specifically written off to Property Investment Account (see above)........................		$182,092,834.00
Earnings and Surplus appropriated to cover capital expenditures for additions, betterments and improvements, and which appropriations have been formally applied in reduction of the Property Investment Account, thus substituting tangible property values in lieu of this amount of above excess cost..............		207,708,569.68
Surplus specifically applied:		
Appropriated to close of 1928...	$30,205,076.23	
And in year 1929, as see table on page 2...................................	88,296,020.09	
		118,501,096.32
Total of Income and Surplus applied as above to December 31, 1929		$508,302,500.00

UNITED STATES STEEL CORPORATION AND SUBSIDIARY COMPANIES
SUMMARY OF NET PROFITS AND UNDIVIDED SURPLUS
April 1, 1901 to December 31, 1929.

NET INCOME after deducting all expenses incident to operations and allowances for depletion, depreciation, amortization and obsolescence, but exclusive of such allowances applied to U. S. Steel Corporation bond sinking funds **$3,876,161,774.98**

DEDUCT:

Interest on outstanding bonds, mortgages and securities of subsidiary companies	$227,350,857.92	
Interest on U. S. Steel Corporation bonds..	576,594,543.66	
Premium and unamortized discount on bonds redeemed:		
On Subsidiary Companies bonds	$5,101,756.52	
On U. S. Steel Corporation bonds	56,790,000.96	
	61,891,757.48	
		865,837,159.06

Balance of Net Income.. **$3,010,324,615.92**

From the foregoing balance there were set aside the following:

For expense (in year 1903) incurred in conversion of Preferred Stock and sale of Ten-Sixty Year 5% Bonds...	$6,800,000.00	
For permanent Pension Fund...	8,000,000.00	
		14,800,000.00

Balance **$2,995,524,615.92**

Dividends for the period on U. S. Steel Corporation stocks were paid as follows:

Preferred, 201¼%	$748,588,491.66	
Common, 153¼%	830,601,506.50	
Common, 40% Stock Dividend June 1, 1927...........................	203,321,000.00	
		1,782,510,998.16

Balance of Net Income.. **$1,213,013,617.76**

From this Surplus there have been appropriated the following amounts for allowances to amortize cost to U. S. Steel of stocks of subsidiary companies in excess of their investment in tangible property:

Amount reserved for retirement of U. S. Steel Corp'n Bonds through Sinking Funds	$182,092,834.00	
To cover capital expenditures for additions, betterments and improvements and formally applied in reduction of the Property Investment Account..........................	207,708,569.68	
Specifically appropriated in 1928 and 1929...	118,501,096.32	
		508,302,500.00

Total Surplus, December 31, 1929.. **$704,711,117.76**

Division of above Total Surplus

Appropriated Surplus to cover Capital Expenditures......................................	$270,000,000.00	
Undivided Surplus	434,711,117.76	
	$704,711,117.76	

NOTE.—Surplus of Subsidiary Companies at December 31, 1929, amounting to $44,898,748.23 and representing Profits accrued on sales of materials and products to other subsidiary companies and on hand in latters' inventories at that date, is not included in the Surplus of the consolidated organization, but is deducted from the amount of Inventories included under Current Assets in Consolidated General Balance Sheet.

INVENTORIES

OF

MANUFACTURING AND OPERATING MATERIALS AND SUPPLIES AND SEMI-FINISHED AND FINISHED PRODUCTS,
INCLUDING NET ADVANCES ON CONTRACT WORK, ETC.

Inventory values as stated herein are on the basis of the actual purchase or production cost of the materials to the respective subsidiary companies holding the same (unless such cost was above the market value on December 31, 1929, in which case the market price was used) except that in respect of such commodities in stock at the close of the year as had been purchased by one subsidiary company from another there has been excluded the approximate amount of profits embraced in the purchase prices accruing to the subsidiaries selling the same or furnishing service in connection therewith.

The reserve of $47,076,404 carried at December 31, 1928, to absorb possible further deflation in inventory values by reason of post war conditions and deducted from total valuation for Inventories as carried in general balance sheet, was in 1929 transferred to Undivided Surplus (see page 2).

The following is a general classification of the inventory valuations at December 31, 1929 in comparison with the valuations at the close of the preceding year:

	Dec. 31, 1929	Dec. 31, 1928
Ores—Iron, Manganese and Zinc	$ 67,765,584	$ 71,147,894
Limestone, Fluxes and Refractories	4,593,333	4,470,900
Coal, Coke and Other Fuel	10,848,016	9,981,972
Pig Iron, Scrap, Ferro and Spiegel	22,001,625	21,648,897
Pig Tin, Lead, Spelter, Copper, Nickel, Aluminum and Dross and Skimmings	9,752,433	9,280,860
Rolls, Molds, Stools, Annealing Boxes, etc.	11,748,160	12,713,279
Ingots—Steel	1,339,984	1,778,612
Blooms, Billets, Slabs, Sheet and Tinplate Bars, etc.	21,974,296	22,639,424
Wire Rods	1,529,229	1,502,533
Skelp	1,198,186	1,594,321
Finished Products	67,948,733	63,894,798
Manufacturing Supplies, Stores and Sundry Items not otherwise classified	29,800,598	29,875,045
Mining Supplies and Stores (for ore and coal properties)	3,522,262	3,853,582
Transportation Companies' Supplies and Stores	6,071,176	5,579,938
Merchandise of Supply Companies	1,816,756	1,677,301
Material, labor and expense locked up in uncompleted Bridge, Structural and other contract work ... $55,492,318		
Less Bills rendered on account ... 51,351,398		
	4,140,920	3,817,864
Stocks abroad and on consignment	17,459,088	25,092,122
Material in transit	5,062,591	6,291,858
Total	$288,572,970	$296,841,200
Less, Inventory Reserve	....	47,076,404
Balance	$288,572,970	$249,764,796

1930 ANNUAL REPORT

Earnings Per Share Disclosed
Operating Capacity to 47.9% in Last Quarter

TWENTY-NINTH ANNUAL REPORT

TO STOCKHOLDERS OF

United States Steel Corporation

OFFICE OF UNITED STATES STEEL CORPORATION,
51 Newark Street, Hoboken, New Jersey,
March 10, 1931.

To the Stockholders:

The Board of Directors submits herewith a combined report of the operations and affairs of the United States Steel Corporation and Subsidiary Companies for the fiscal year which ended December 31, 1930, together with a statement of the condition of the finances and property at the close of that year.

CONSOLIDATED INCOME ACCOUNT FOR YEAR 1930

The total earnings were, after deducting all expenses incident to operations, including ordinary repairs and maintenance (approximately $96,000,000), allowance for employes' profit sharing fund, and taxes (including reserve for Federal income taxes), per Consolidated Income Account, page 17... $157,710,231.72

Less, Charges and allowances for Depletion, Depreciation and Obsolescence............. 58,550,120.14

Net Income in the year 1930 .... $ 99,160,111.58

Deduct, Interest on outstanding bonds and mortgages:
Of Subsidiary Companies $5,593,367.37
Of U. S. Steel Corporation 46,729.05

5,640,096.42

Balance .... $ 93,520,015.16

Add: Special income receipts for the year, including net interest on Federal Tax
Refunds and net adjustments of various accounts 10,901,555.99

Total Net Income... $104,421,571.15

Dividends for the year 1930 on U. S. Steel Corporation stocks:

Preferred, 7 per cent...$25,219,677.00
Common, 7 per cent... 60,365,796.75*

85,585,473.75

Surplus Net Income in the year 1930 .... $ 18,836,097.40

Earnings per share on Common Stock (on average shares outstanding)...$9.18

---

* Includes $11,373.25 for March 30, 1931, dividend on Common Stock issued in January and February, 1931, under Employees' Stock Subscription Plan.

1

OPERATIONS FOR THE YEAR

The marked recession in demand for products of the subsidiary companies which developed in the Fall of 1929, continued during the first half of 1930, and in the last half of the year the decline became further pronounced, the output in the last quarter equalling only 47.9 per cent. of capacity. For the entire year the production of rolled and other finished products for sale averaged 65.6 per cent. of capacity compared with 89.2 per cent. in the previous year. The ratio of output to capacity in 1930 was next to the lowest for any year since the organization of the Corporation, the lowest having been in the year 1921, when the ratio was 47.5 per cent.

The continued lessening in demand during the year for products was accompanied with a substantial decline in prices secured. As a result the average selling price received for the total tonnage of rolled and other finished products shipped in 1930, compared with the prices received in 1929 for an equal tonnage of similar products, respectively, was $3.61 per ton less for domestic and $2.03 per ton less for export shipments. These decreases in prices account for a reduction of approximately $40,600,000 of the total reduction of $108,128,700 in the net earnings realized in 1930 compared with those for 1929. At the close of 1930 the prices then being secured were somewhat less than the average received, but appeared to be quite well stabilized with a slight advancing tendency due to an improved prospective demand.

109

PRODUCTION

Production of the several principal departments for the year 1930 in comparison with results for the preceding year, was as follows:

	1930 Tons	1929 Tons	Decrease Tons	Per Cent.
Iron and Manganese Ore	24,282,767	30,540,565	6,257,798	20.5
Limestone, Dolomite, Fluorspar and Cement Rock	14,611,927	18,035,082*	3,423,155	19.0
Coal	25,388,265	31,826,634	6,438,369	20.2
Coke	13,113,382	17,355,036	4,241,654	24.4
Pig Iron, Ferro and Spiegel	12,758,333	16,484,985	3,726,652	22.6
Steel Ingots (Bessemer and Open Hearth)	16,726,472	21,868,816	5,142,344	23.5
Rolled and Finished Steel Products for Sale	11,609,265	15,302,669	3,693,404	24.1
	Bbls.	Bbls.	Bbls.	
Portland Cement	24,294,154	24,843,057*	548,903	2.2

On page 22 of this report will be found a table detailing by classes the production of finished steel products during the year, together with that of miscellaneous products not included in above general classifications.

* Includes production in 1929 of Atlas Portland Cement Co. plants acquired January 1, 1930.

SHIPMENTS AND BUSINESS

The shipments of all classes of products in comparison with shipments during the preceding year were as follows:

Domestic Shipments	1930 Tons	1929 Tons	Increase or Decrease Tons	Per Cent.
Rolled and Finished Steel Products	10,800,638	14,027,128	3,226,490	23.00 Dec.
Pig Iron, Ingots, Ferro and Scrap	314,525	339,867	25,342	7.46 Dec.
Coal, Coke, Iron Ore and Limestone	4,469,396	6,217,942	1,748,546	28.12 Dec.
Sundry Materials and By-Products	276,341	169,557	106,784	62.98 Inc.
Total tons all kinds of materials, except Cement	15,860,900	20,754,494	4,893,594	23.58 Dec.
Portland Cement (Bbls.)	23,084,305	12,234,733*	10,849,572	88.68 Inc.

* Exclusive of shipments of Atlas Portland Cement Co.

3

1931 ANNUAL REPORT

Net Income Rescued by Sales of Fixed Assets

THIRTIETH ANNUAL REPORT

TO STOCKHOLDERS OF

United States Steel Corporation

OFFICE OF UNITED STATES STEEL CORPORATION,
51 Newark Street, Hoboken, New Jersey,
March 8, 1932.

To the Stockholders:

The Board of Directors submits herewith a combined report of the operations and affairs of the United States Steel Corporation and Subsidiary Companies for the fiscal year which ended December 31, 1931, together with a statement of the condition of the finances and property at the close of that year.

CONSOLIDATED INCOME ACCOUNT FOR YEAR 1931

The total earnings after deducting all expenses incident to operations, including ordinary repairs and maintenance (approximately $60,000,000), and taxes (including reserve for Federal Income taxes), but exclusive of inventory price adjustments at December 31st, amounting to $5,395,996.32, charged against previously established reserves, were .... $ 46,483,999.93

 Less, Charges and allowances for Depletion, Depreciation and Obsolescence 47,317,894.72

Deficit .... $ 833,894.79

Interest on outstanding bonds and mortgages:
  Of Subsidiary Companies $5,435,405.37
  Of U. S. Steel Corporation 34,218.48

5,469,623.85

Total Deficit .... $ 6,303,518.64

Special income receipts for the year arising from profits in sales of fixed property, and net adjustments of various accounts 19,341,659.51

Net Income for the year.. $ 13,038,140.87

Dividends for the year 1931 on U. S. Steel Corporation stocks:
  Preferred, 7 per cent...$25,219,677.00
  Common, 4¼ per cent.. 36,983,949.50

62,203,626.50

Net Deficit in year 1931 (provided from Undivided Surplus) .... $ 49,165,485.63

I

1932 ANNUAL REPORT

Overhead and Taxes Not a Part of Net Earnings

Dividends Still Paid but Cut

Operating Capacity to 18.3%

Administrators on Part-Time Service

Wage Cuts

THIRTY-FIRST ANNUAL REPORT

TO STOCKHOLDERS OF

United States Steel Corporation

OFFICE OF UNITED STATES STEEL CORPORATION,
51 NEWARK STREET, HOBOKEN, NEW JERSEY,
March 7, 1933.

TO THE STOCKHOLDERS:

The Board of Directors submits herewith a combined report of the operations and affairs of the United States Steel Corporation and Subsidiary Companies for the fiscal year which ended December 31, 1932, together with a statement of the condition of the finances and property at the close of that year.

CONSOLIDATED INCOME ACCOUNT FOR YEAR 1932

The deficit for the year resulting from operations after charging all expenses incident thereto including ordinary repairs and maintenance (approximately $29,000,000), and taxes (including reserve for Federal Income taxes), but exclusive of inventory price adjustments at December 31st, amounting to $3,135,148.85, charged against previously established reserves, was $12,729,566.44

Charges and allowances for Depletion, Depreciation and Obsolescence 39,321,603.42

Deficit $52,051,169.86

Interest charges on outstanding bonds and mortgages:

Of Subsidiary Companies..	$ 5,298,850.85	
Of U. S. Steel Corporation..	14,609.71	
		5,313,460.56

Total Deficit from Operations... $57,364,630.42

Proportion of overhead expenses and taxes of the Lake Superior Iron Ore properties and Great Lakes Transportation service normally included in the value of the season's production of ore carried in Inventories, but which because of extreme curtailment in tonnage of ore mined and shipped in 1932 is not so applied, to wit:

Taxes	$11,436,772.85	
Depreciation	998,190.73	
Other Overhead Expenses.......................................	1,500,126.66	
		13,935,090.24
		$71,299,720.66

Less, Net balance of sundry receipts and charges, including adjustments of various accounts (credit) 124,016.06

Net Deficit before charging Dividends.. $71,175,704.60

Dividends for the year 1932 on U. S. Steel Corporation Preferred Stock, 5¼ per cent........... 20,716,163.25

Total Deficit in year 1932 (provided from Undivided Surplus) $91,891,867.85

1

OPERATIONS FOR THE YEAR

The extreme depression which prevailed during the year 1932 in all lines of business activities severely affected the iron and steel industry. The output of finished steel products of the subsidiary companies of the Corporation was the lowest of any year since its organization in 1901. This output for the year equalled but 18.3 per cent. of the finished product capacity, reaching the extremely low ratio of 13.6 per cent. in August. The improvement which then followed was not maintained in the last two months of the year, and December averaged but 14.4 per cent. The shipments of rolled and finished steel products in the year totalled 3,974,062 tons, compared with 7,676,744 tons in 1931, a decrease of 48 per cent, and 11,260,293 tons compared with 1929, or 74 per cent. The export shipments aggregated 232,255 tons, a decrease of 282,130 tons, or 55 per cent. compared with 1931, and a decrease of 974,972 tons compared with 1929. Total tonnage shipped exceeded by 382,588 tons the tonnage produced, the stocks on hand in inventories at the beginning of the year having been reduced during 1932. The reduction in the demand for these products extended to all lines of consumption but was most marked in materials used by the railroads, in building construction and by the automobile industry.

The abnormally low volume of business necessarily produced unsatisfactory profit and loss results. The burden imposed upon the industry for overhead expenses including maintenance of organization, administrative expenses and taxes which a low volume of business enforces, and to which attention was called in preceding year's report, was materially greater during 1932 than in the preceding year.

Because of the closing down of many ore mines in the Lake Superior District, and the extremely low tonnage of ore mined and moved to furnaces, a large part of the overhead charges of the mining and lake transportation subsidiaries to the amount of $13,935,090 (of which $11,436,773 were for taxes) could not be absorbed in iron ore production costs without increasing such cost above its market price or value. Accordingly, the above amount of overhead expenses and taxes was charged direct to Profit and Loss.

Further drastic economies, following those instituted in 1931, were made in all controllable expenses. Many plants were closed entirely. At administrative headquarters forces were fixed at the minimum number required for care of the current business and as many of the administrative employes as practicable were placed on part-time service. In addition, on May 16, 1932, salaries and wages of all employes, other than such of the transportation companies' employes whose rates are subject to statutory control, were reduced 15 per cent. This reduction following those made in the fall of 1931 resulted in a cumulative decrease in salaries and wages of approximately 25 per cent. from the rates in effect prior to August, 1931.

The regular quarterly dividend of $1.75 per share on the Preferred stock of the Corporation was paid for the first three quarters of the year. In January, 1933, the Board of Directors declared a dividend of 50 cents per share on the Preferred stock for the fourth quarter, and announced in respect of same as follows:

"Including allowances for deterioration, exhaustion and retirement of fixed property, the year's reduction in net assets, working and fixed, has been $90,186,000. The year's reduction in net working assets, including cash, U. S. Government securities, receivables and inventories, has been $70,000,000.

"A large draft has accordingly been made upon the cash and working resources of the Corporation notwithstanding the introduction of drastic economies as well as reduction of wages and salaries.

"In view of current conditions as set forth, the Board of Directors has today declared upon the Preferred stock a dividend of 50 cents per share. The difference between this payment and the full rate of $1.75 for the quarter is deferred under the cumulative dividend provisions of the Preferred stock."

3

1933 ANNUAL REPORT

Refunds Taken to Surplus

Reversals of Reserves Taken to Surplus

New Reserves

Encouragement Reported

U. S. Steel and the NIRA

Working Capital Shown

SURPLUS OF UNITED STATES STEEL CORPORATION AND SUBSIDIARY COMPANIES

(*Since April 1, 1901*)

Balance of Undivided Surplus, December 31, 1932, exclusive of Profits earned by subsidiary companies on inter-company sales of products on hand in inventories, per Annual Report for 1932..			$329,100,247.55
Less: Net Deficit in year 1933, per Income Account..............................	$43,706,744.89		
Premium on bonds of United States Steel Corporation retired.........	2,550.00		
Reserve for possible loss on deposits in closed banks..................	541,050.35		
Federal Capital Stock Tax applied to last half of 1932................	499,183.90		
		44,749,529.14	
			$284,350,718.41
Add: Refunds under provisions of Emergency Railroad Transportation Act of 1933 of Railroad Recapture payments made in previous years........	$ 6,355,750.25		
Reversal of reserves set up in previous years for account Railroad Recapture...	18,624,038.04		
	$24,979,788.29		
Less, Appropriated from preceding, viz:			
For reserve for contingencies including losses which may arise through disposition of obsolete and slow moving inventory products and materials.........	$ 1,000,000.00		
For general reserve for plant and property amortization and obsolescence, to be allocated to particular properties as may be required..................	21,000,000.00		
		22,000,000.00	
			2,979,788.29
Balance of Earned Undivided Surplus, December 31, 1933, exclusive of Profits earned by subsidiary companies on inter-company sales of products on hand in inventories (see note below)....			$287,330,506.70

NOTE.—Surplus of Subsidiary Companies amounting to $23,083,263.56 and representing Profits on sales of materials and products to other subsidiary companies which are on hand in latters' inventories December 31, 1933, is deducted from the amount of Inventories included under Current Assets in Consolidated General Balance Sheet.

APPROPRIATED SURPLUS INVESTED IN CAPITAL EXPENDITURES

Amount at December 31, 1933.. $270,000,000.00

DIVIDEND DECLARATIONS FOR YEAR

PREFERRED

No. 128—½ per cent. paid May 29, 1933................	$1,801,405.50
No. 129—½ per cent. paid August 30, 1933..............	1,801,405.50
No. 130—½ per cent. paid November 29, 1933............	1,801,405.50
No. 131—½ per cent. payable February 27, 1934..........	1,801,405.50
Total Preferred.............................	$7,205,622.00

Cumulative dividend arrearages on Preferred Stock to the date of the latest payment amount to 6¼% or $22,517,568.75.

No dividend declarations have been made on Common Stock since that paid March 30, 1932, which was charged against Surplus at December 31, 1931, as reported.

OPERATIONS FOR THE YEAR

The business activities of the subsidiary companies of the Corporation for the year 1933, in spite of the adverse conditions which prevailed, show many encouraging features compared with the preceding year. Thus while in 1932 the earnings of the entire organization before dividends fell short of covering expenses and charges (exclusive of charges for depletion and depreciation) by the amount of $30,855,910, in the year 1933 the corresponding result was a profit of $7,083,376, a net betterment of $37,939,286.

This improvement resulted largely from a substantial increase in the volume of business. Steel manufacturing plant facilities were operated during 1933 to extent of approximately 29 per cent. of capacity, compared with an average of 18 per cent. in 1932. In 1933 the production of finished iron and steel products was 5,536,000 tons compared with 3,591,000 tons in the previous year. Plant operations reached the low point in the first quarter, averaging but 16 per cent. of capacity, rising to 27.5 per cent. in the second quarter, 41 per cent. in the third and 31 per cent. in the final quarter. The improvement in business was progressive during each of the first seven months. Beginning with August there was a gradual recession until December, which showed a considerable increase over the preceding month.

The iron mining properties and facilities in the Lake Superior district and the Great Lakes transportation service for moving ore to furnaces, were operated to only about 40 per cent. of their capacity in 1933, although on a much larger scale than in 1932. On account of the preceding a large amount of fixed expenses (principally taxes) could not be absorbed as production cost of the ore mined and moved. Accordingly, the proportion of these fixed expenses not allocable to cost of ore shipped has been charged direct to Profit and Loss, this amount being $7,468,237, of which $6,341,435 represented taxes on idle properties and plants.

The average prices received for steel products shipped during the year were less than in 1932. Based on the same relative tonnages of respective products shipped in both years, the net price received for domestic shipments was $2.00 per ton less than in 1932, for export shipments $5.01 less than in 1932, and for the two combined $2.21 less than in the preceding year. During the earlier months of the year there was a constant decrease in the average price received monthly, the average domestic price realized in July having been $4.06 per ton less than the average for 1932, which latter was $8.74 per ton less than the 1929 realized average price. Beginning with August prices became better stabilized and some products showed moderate increases.

The Corporation and subsidiaries have given hearty cooperation to plans of the Administration at Washington for bringing about a nation-wide economic recovery. The steel manufacturing subsidiary companies of the United States Steel Corporation are members of the Code of Fair Competition of the Iron and Steel Industry, formulated under the National Industrial Recovery Act. The Code was approved by the President on August 19, 1933, to continue in effect for ninety days, at expiration of which period it was extended on the President's approval until May 31, 1934. The purpose it was desired to accomplish through the National Industrial Recovery Act as stated in the text of the President's message to Congress, May 17, 1933, was to—

> " * * * provide for the machinery necessary for a great cooperative movement throughout all industry in order to obtain a wide reemployment, to shorten the working week, to pay a decent wage for the shorter week, and to prevent unfair competition and disastrous over-production."

The Code for the Iron and Steel Industry contains provisions for making effective the above purposes of the law. The Code fixes minimum wage rates in various districts and provides for an average maximum working week not to exceed 40 hours, thus permitting the employment of a larger number than would be possible with a greater number of hours per working week. The subsidiary companies of the Corporation had, however, to a very considerable extent anticipated and made effective this feature of the Code through application of the "Share the Work" movement inaugurated in the early Fall of 1930. Since the adoption of the Code the average hourly wage and salary

3

rates have been advanced approximately 25 per cent. over the rates paid in June, 1933. This has added materially to the costs of production and was only in part offset through increased prices realized for steel shipped in the last five months of 1933. The Corporation's subsidiaries have whole-heartedly cooperated in carrying out the spirit and intent of the Code and the law in respect of "collective bargaining" by and with employes. At practically all plants employes have organized under "Employes' Representation Plans," choosing their own representatives to deal with the employing company in all matters relating to wages and other conditions of employment. These plans have proven eminently satisfactory in promoting harmony in industrial relations and are conducive to the best interests of the employes, the employers and the general public. The Steel Code as approved by the Administration also contains provisions for effecting the additional purpose mentioned in the President's message above quoted, namely, to prevent unfair competition.

It is hoped the purposes sought to be accomplished through the National Industrial Recovery Act will be realized. A sufficient time has not yet elapsed to definitely determine to what extent these efforts will prove successful and whether the Steel Code in its present form should be continued beyond the date of its expiration, May 31, 1934.

124

FINANCIAL POSITION

The financial position of the organization has been maintained to a creditable degree, notwithstanding the payment of dividends on Preferred Stock of $7,205,622 not earned in the year. This has been accomplished through rigid economies both in costs of operations and outlays on capital account, and aided by special cash receipts as shown by the Surplus Account (page 2). The comparative status of net working assets at close of the year compared with December 31, 1932, was as follows:

	Dec. 31, 1933	Dec. 31, 1932	Increase or Decrease
Gross Working Assets	$414,969,392	$410,382,837	$4,586,555 Inc.
Current Liabilities	52,283,704	46,987,376	5,296,328 "
Net Working Assets	$362,685,688	$363,395,461	$ 709,773 Dec.

1934 ANNUAL REPORT

Reclassification of Overhead and Taxes Continued

UNITED STATES STEEL CORPORATION AND SUBSIDIARY COMPANIES

CONDENSED GENERAL PROFIT AND LOSS ACCOUNT

FOR THE YEAR ENDING DECEMBER 31, 1934

GROSS RECEIPTS—Gross Sales and Earnings (see page 5)		$591,609,497.39
Operating Charges:		
Manufacturing and Producing Cost and Operating Expenses, including inventory price adjustments, ordinary maintenance and repairs and provisional charges of $44,121,258.91 by subsidiary companies for depletion, depreciation and obsolescence	$532,235,150.92	
Administrative, Selling and General Expenses, including appropriations under pension plan, but exclusive of general expenses of transportation companies included in item above	37,986,702.75	
Taxes (including reserve for Federal income taxes)	28,844,419.41	
Commercial Discounts	2,938,247.25	
		602,004,520.33
Deficit		$ 10,395,022.94
Sundry Net Manufacturing and Operating gains and losses, etc..Dr.	$879,332.84	
Idle Plant Expenses ....Dr.	2,694,390.03	
Rentals and Royalties received	1,493,984.25	
		Dr. 2,079,738.62
Total Manufacturing, Producing and Operating Net Deficit after deducting charges for depletion, depreciation and obsolescence		$12,474,761.56

OTHER INCOME AND CHARGES

Net Profits of properties owned, but whose operations (gross revenue, cost of product, expenses, etc.) are not classified in this statement	$115,155.82	
Interest and discount and income from sundry investments	4,384,427.03	
		4,499,582.85
Balance		$ 7,975,178.71
Net Balance of Subsidiaries' Inter-Company Profits not yet realized as cash assets*		Dr. 927,721.14
Deficit		$ 8,902,899.85
Less, net balance of sundry receipts and charges account adjustments of various accounts (credit)		92,114.35
		$ 8,810,785.50
Proportion of overhead expenses and taxes of the Lake Superior Iron Ore properties and Great Lakes Transportation service normally included in the value of the season's production of ore carried in Inventories, but which because of curtailment in tonnage of ore mined and shipped in 1934, is not so applied		7,305,942.63
Total Net Operating Loss		$ 16,616,728.13
Interest charges on outstanding bonds and mortgages:		
Of Subsidiary Companies	$5,037,601.82	
Of U. S. Steel Corporation	13,450.00	
		5,051,051.82
Total Deficit before charging Dividends		$ 21,667,779.95

* These profits have been earned by individual subsidiary companies on inter-company sales made and service rendered to/for other subsidiaries but being locked up in the inventory value of materials held by the purchasing companies at close of 1934, are not to that date included as part of the reported earnings of the combined organisation. Such profits are so embraced only in the year in which they are converted into a cash asset.

17

1935 ANNUAL REPORT

Reduction of Net Book Values of Fixed Assets

Reduction of Expected Lives of Fixed Assets

Future Depreciation Charges Averted

$778 Million Appropriated to Cover Original Investment Valuation and Subsequent Capital Expenditures

BALANCE SHEET, STATEMENTS OF ACCOUNTS AND STATISTICS

The consolidated general balance sheet and the statements of accounts and statistics in this annual report present the combined results for the United States Steel Corporation and its subsidiary companies for the year ending December 31, 1935. In the balance sheet all inter-company accounts and inter-company profit in inventories of the subsidiary companies have been eliminated.

There was completed during the year a detailed analysis of the investment in depreciable property, which, as stated in the annual report for 1934, had been undertaken by the subsidiary companies. This analysis resulted in adjustments of the Property Investment account effecting a reduction of net book values. Broadly, these adjustments are attributable to the developments in the art and mechanics of steel making which have operated to reduce the normally expected life of such facilities, and to changes in plant location based upon shifting markets and transportation facilities. The factors involving present or prospective abandonments of obsolete units, from time to time, impose unusual depreciation charges which the property survey has attempted to record as reflecting present conditions. The above adjustment, amounting to a net of $88,720,028.04, has been effected by transferring that amount from the Surplus account termed "Appropriated for and Invested in Capital Expenditures," which heretofore was carried at $270,000,000. The remainder of the account, $181,279,971.96, has been transferred to and converted into a general reserve for amortization of property investment valuations.

In view of the fact that the surplus account "Appropriated For and Invested in Capital Expenditures" was invested in fixed property, it was considered advisable that the adjustment and transfer as described should be made as indicated. Capital investment expenditures to the amount of $181,279,971.96 having heretofore been financed specifically by such segregated surplus account, it follows that future depreciation allowances should not be made therefor in reporting consolidated net income. This reduction in annual depreciation allowances will, however, be offset, in part at least, by increased allowances in calculated future depreciation charges which will result from the revised depreciation rates indicated by the analysis above mentioned.

The gross Property Investment Account, inclusive of Intangibles, as shown in table on page 16 and as carried in the consolidated balance sheet, is based on the amount of capital stock and bonds of the Corporation issued for the acquirement of the subsidiary companies and cash, plus cash expenditures made for additional property acquired since the organization of the Corporation and less (a) the sum of $508,302,500, heretofore written off for Intangible values which was provided from Earned Surplus, and (b) credits for investment value of property sold, retired or otherwise disposed of. As shown also in table on page 16, the balance of the reserves provided from income and surplus for accrued depletion, depreciation, obsolescence and amortization of the present gross investment in plant and property amounts at December 31, 1935, to an aggregate of $1,124,107,707.52. These reserves include the adjustments of $88,720,028.04 and the transfer of the $181,279,971.96 mentioned in the preceding paragraphs.

The accounts of United States Steel Corporation and of the subsidiary companies for the year 1935 have been examined by Price, Waterhouse & Co., the independent auditors selected for this purpose by the stockholders at the annual meeting held April 1, 1935. The independent auditors report is printed below.

131

UNITED STATES STEEL CORPORATION AND SUBSIDIARY COMPANIES

PROPERTY INVESTMENT ACCOUNT

DECEMBER 31, 1935

Gross Fixed Property Investment Account, December 31, 1934, inclusive of balance of Intangibles but exclusive of Stripping and Mine Development and Structural Erection Equipment...		$2,422,493,040.70
Net of sundry adjustments to Property Account in 1935 (Credit).................		85,390.77
		$2,422,407,649.93
Capital Expenditures on Property Account in 1935 (ex. Stripping and Development).....................................	$35,313,455.23	
Less, Realizations from Sales and Dismantlement of property creditable Investment Account.......................	2,186,614.35	
Net Expenditures for new construction in the year..................		33,126,840.88
		$2,455,534,490.81
Less, Amounts written off in year 1935 to Depletion, Depreciation and Amortization Reserves for investment cost of natural resources exhausted and of improvements, equipment and facilities abandoned and retired (Net).........		28,365,155.37
Gross Fixed Property Investment December 31, 1935..............		$2,427,169,335.44
Less, Balances at December 31, 1935, per table on page 26, in Depletion, Depreciation, Obsolescence, Amortization and Current Maintenance Reserves, including balance previously carried as "Appropriated Surplus".....................		1,124,107,707.52
Net Fixed Property Investment December 31, 1935................		$1,303,061,627.92
Investment in Stripping and Development at Mines and Structural Erection Equipment:		
Balance at December 31, 1934............................	$36,882,836.87	
Expended during the year 1935...........................	1,276,444.37	
	$38,159,281.24	
Less, Charged off in 1935 in operating expenses..............	2,698,050.20	
Balance December 31, 1935.....................................		35,461,231.04
Total Property Investment Account, December 31, 1935, inclusive of balance of Intangibles, per Consolidated General Balance Sheet...............		$1,338,522,858.96

UNITED STATES STEEL CORPORATION AND SUBSIDIARY COMPANIES

SUMMARY OF NET PROFITS AND UNDIVIDED SURPLUS

APRIL 1, 1901 TO DECEMBER 31, 1935

NET INCOME, as currently reported, after deducting all expenses incident to operations and allowances for depletion, depreciation, amortization and obsolescence, but exclusive of such allowances applied to U. S. Steel Corporation bond sinking funds $3,915,842,616.02

DEDUCT:

Interest on outstanding bonds, mortgages and securities of subsidiary companies.....	$258,547,101.17		
Interest on U. S. Steel Corporation bonds.....................................	576,730,760.22		
Premium and unamortized discount on bonds redeemed:			
On Subsidiary Companies bonds............................. $5,367,761.82			
On U. S. Steel Corporation bonds............................. 56,944,650.96			
	62,312,412.78		
		897,590,274.17	
Balance of Net Income..		$3,018,252,341.85	

From the foregoing balance there were set aside the following:

For expense (in year 1903) incurred in conversion of Preferred Stock and sale of Ten-Sixty Year 5% Bonds..	$ 6,800,000.00	
For permanent Pension Fund..	8,000,000.00	
	14,800,000.00	
Balance	$3,003,452,341.85	

Dividends for the period on U. S. Steel Corporation stocks were paid as follows:

Preferred, 227%..	$841,360,874.91	
Common, 164½%..	927,951,252.75	
Common, 40% Stock Dividend, June 1, 1927..................................	203,321,000.00	
	1,972,633,127.66	
Balance of Net Income applied as below....................................	$1,030,819,214.19	

Appropriated to amortize cost to U. S. Steel Corporation of stocks of subsidiary companies in excess of their investment in tangible property $508,302,500.00

Appropriated to cover capital expenditures:

Transferred to Depreciation Reserves (See page 13)	$ 88,720,028.04	
Transferred and converted to an amortization reserve for investment in tangible property (See page 13)	181,279,971.96	
	270,000,000.00	778,302,500.00
Balance of Net Income carried in Earned Surplus Account, December 31, 1935................		$ 252,516,714.19

NOTE.—Surplus of subsidiary companies at December 31, 1935, amounting to $24,473,384.22 and representing profits accrued on sales of materials and products to other subsidiary companies and on hand in latters' inventories at that date, is not included in the Surplus of the consolidated organization, but is deducted from the amount of inventories included under current assets in consolidated general balance sheet.

1936 ANNUAL REPORT

Intangibles Finally Disclosed

Original Valuation in 1901 Mentioned as Part of Intangibles

UNITED STATES STEEL CORPORATION AND SUBSIDIARY COMPANIES

COMPARATIVE CONSOLIDATED GENERAL BALANCE SHEET

DECEMBER 31, 1936 AND DECEMBER 31, 1935

ASSETS	December 31, 1936	December 31, 1935
PROPERTY INVESTMENT ACCOUNT		
PROPERTIES OWNED AND OPERATED BY SUBSIDIARY COMPANIES, PER TABLE PAGE 18		
Tangible	$2,231,817,567.96	$2,202,051,089.78
Intangible	260,557,544.31	260,579,476.70
	2,492,375,112.27	2,462,630,566.48
Less, Depletion, Depreciation, Obsolescence, Amortization and Current Maintenance Reserve Balances	1,142,337,830.43	1,124,107,707.52
	1,350,037,281.84	1,338,522,858.96
MINING ROYALTIES (on unmined ore)	7,819,553.31	8,192,895.12
DEFERRED CHARGES (applying to future operations of the properties)		
Advanced Mining and other operating expenses and charges	1,400,222.07	2,052,386.72
Discount on subsidiary companies' bonds sold (net)	80,930.82	164,598.83
	1,481,152.89	2,216,985.55
INVESTMENTS		
Outside Real Estate, Real Estate Mortgages and Investments in Sundry Securities, including those deposited under statutory requirements—less reserves	8,410,938.45	8,874,728.85
House and Land Sales Installment Contracts and Mortgages under Employes' Home Owning and other Property Sales Plans—less reserves	6,048,474.60	6,731,966.42
	14,459,413.05	15,606,695.27
GENERAL AND RESERVE FUND ASSETS		
Cash resources held in Bond Sinking Funds and Other Trusteed Accounts	1,484,171.38	804,843.82
U. S. Steel Corporation Common Stock Owned (2,782 shares in 1936 and 6,170 shares in 1935) less reserves	111,589.84	204,466.84
Advances on Contracts and to Railroad Credit Corporation, also Cash and Receivables due from banks and others in process of reorganization or liquidation or payment of which may be delayed, less reserves	3,416,997.59	3,669,457.15
	5,012,758.81	4,678,767.81
CURRENT ASSETS		
Inventories, less reserves (see table on page 21)	286,003,964.52	258,804,995.94
Accounts Receivable—less reserves	67,098,849.96	47,464,046.37
Bills Receivable—less reserves	7,431,714.31	5,249,240.12
U. S. Government and Other Marketable Securities, less reserves. (Market value 1936, $41,842,672.43; 1935, $56,583,652.37)	39,904,566.88	55,989,490.03
Cash Working Funds	786,418.09	790,192.98
Time and other special Bank Deposits	2,547,834.56	1,247,841.64
Cash (in hand, and on deposit with banks subject to cheque)	81,393,010.44	83,637,731.74
	485,166,358.76	453,183,538.82
	$1,863,976,518.66	$1,822,401,741.53

Property Classifications	Gross Property Investment December 31, 1935	Capital Expenditures on Property Account in 1936 (Net)	Write-offs to Depletion, Depreciation and Amortization Reserves and Other Adjustments	Gross Property Investment December 31, 1936
Real Estate..............	$ 108,218,056.25	Cr. $ 463,397.27	$ 145,557.02	$ 107,609,101.96
Plant, Mineral and Manufacturing Properties and Equipment (a).................	1,720,453,500.19	60,801,637.12	32,684,703.38	1,748,570,433.93
Transportation Properties—Railroads, Lake and Ocean Steamships.....................	337,918,302.30	12,394,508.03	6,844,378.49	343,468,431.84
Intangibles (see note).........	260,579,476.70	Cr. 19,523.25	2,409.14	260,557,544.31
Total.......................	$2,427,169,335.44	$72,713,224.63	(b)$39,677,048.03	$2,460,205,512.04

Less, Balances at December 31, 1936, per table on page 19, in Depletion, Depreciation, Obsolescence, Amortization and Current Maintenance Reserves........................	1,142,337,830.43
Net Fixed Property Investment December 31, 1936..................	$1,317,867,681.61

Investment in Stripping and Development at Mines and Structural Erection Equipment:
Balance at December 31, 1935.............................. $35,461,231.04
Expended during the year 1936........................... 2,139,975.75

$37,601,206.79
Less, Charged off in 1936 to operating expenses............. 5,431,606.56

Balance December 31, 1936.......................	32,169,600.23
Property Investment Account, December 31, 1936 (inclusive of Intangibles) per Consolidated General Balance Sheet.............................	$1,350,037,281.84

(a) Includes Dock and River Transportation equipment auxiliary to and a part of manufacturing properties.
(b) Includes:

Write-offs to Depletion, Depreciation and Amortization Reserves...	$38,441,149.87
Write-offs charged to Profit and Loss and/or operating expense for facilities abandoned or retired and not replaced........	1,402,902.86
Net of Sundry Adjustments to Property Account...	Dr. 167,004.70
	$39,677,048.03

NOTE: Following the completion of the detailed analysis of the investment in depreciable property, which was referred to in the annual report for the year ended December 31, 1935, a calculation has been made of the amount which is comprehended in the combined assets of the Corporation and the subsidiary companies as represented in the Consolidated Balance Sheet, for the investment cost of the capital stocks of the subsidiary companies in excess of their own investments in tangible assets. This calculation is based in part on the valuations assigned to the tangible assets as estimated by the United States Bureau of Corporations in its survey and report on the formation of the Corporation in 1901, and in part upon net book values of the tangible assets of companies subsequently acquired. It is subject to possible adjustment as further continuing investigations under way indicate may be necessary.

137

1937 ANNUAL REPORT

U. S. Steel . . . The Good Employer

Change in Capital Structure Detailed

Intangibles to $1

Inherent Value Not Affected

ACCIDENT PREVENTION, RELIEF AND SANITATION

The Corporation continued during the year its long-standing policy of providing and maintaining safe, healthful and comfortable working conditions for employes engaged in the operations of its subsidiary companies. It is particularly gratifying to be able to report that as a result of these intensive endeavors and regardless of the fact that there was a material increase in operating activity and number of employes, it was possible to maintain the progress which has attended the Corporation's past efforts in the prevention of accidents.

In comparison with the year 1912, when a determination of the rate of disabling accidents was first established and the accident severity rating was re-classified, it has been calculated that the 1937 accident rate shows an improvement over that for 1912 of over 88 per cent.

A comparison of expenditures for accident prevention, accident relief and sanitation during the year 1937 with that for the previous year follows:

	1937	1936	Increase
For accident prevention work, including installation of safety devices and appliances.............................	$ 950,040	$ 713,861	$ 236,179
For accident relief, including obligations under State compensation laws...................................	4,302,894	3,362,199	940,695
For sanitary facilities, maintenance and improvement of healthful working conditions for employes in directions elaborated upon in previous annual reports...........	3,949,806	2,786,101	1,163,705

141

HOUSING, WELFARE AND UNEMPLOYMENT RELIEF

Contracts were entered into during the year 1937 with 404 employes desiring to avail themselves of the opportunity afforded by subsidiary companies to secure homes on reasonable terms through loans payable in installments and secured by liens on the property under established Home Owning Plans. The total activity since inception is summarized as follows:

	Year 1937	Year 1920 to Dec. 31, 1937
Number of contracts entered into.........................	404	6,925
Contracts liquidated in full.............................	305	3,358
Contracts in force December 31, 1937.....................	...	2,793

Principal amount invested by the subsidiary companies in contracts in force December 31, 1937, secured by mortgage liens on the properties and other protective features. $5,633,501.41
This latter amount compared with similar investment at close of 1936 shows an increase of... 104,665.45

On December 31, 1937, there were 2,296 employes carrying insurance amounting to $4,870,200 under the group life insurance plan adopted in 1928 in conjunction with the Home Owning Plan for the specific protection of their interests in the purchase of these homes. The general group life insurance plan is separately referred to under another caption.

The policy of giving close attention to the general welfare of employes has been continued by the Corporation and subsidiary companies. The necessity for the rendering of assistance decreased in a large measure in 1937, owing to generally improved operating conditions; but during the year direct relief and credits, principally the latter, were extended to employes in the amount of $103,527 to provide food, rent, fuel, medical aid and other necessities. Good Fellowship Clubs and other employe organizations have continued to render assistance to their fellow employes where necessity has required, and have provided relief to the extent of $105,847 during 1937.

As in previous years employes cultivated vegetable gardens during the summer of 1937, although interest in this work was somewhat curtailed owing to improved plant operations. A total of 40,250 garden plots was worked during the year, covering 6,247 acres, or the equivalent of nearly 10 square miles, which yielded to the employes so occupied raw produce of an estimated value of $540,000. These garden projects, in addition to providing fresh vegetables for the table, have afforded wholesome and instructive outdoor occupation with its physical and other incidental benefits to employes and their families. The subsidiary companies, as usual, rendered assistance to the employes in plowing, plotting and fertilizing the land and in securing vegetable seeds.

9

CHANGES PROPOSED IN CAPITAL STRUCTURE

At the annual meeting on April 4th, 1938, the stockholders of the Corporation will be asked to authorize certain changes in the Corporation's capital structure. In a letter dated February 21, 1938, addressed to the stockholders, the object and scope of the proposed changes were set forth. The changes are in the form of two amendments to the certificate of incorporation, and may be summarized as follows:

1. To change each share of authorized common stock of the Corporation with par value ($100) into one share of common stock without par value; to decrease the capital of the Corporation by reducing to $75 the capital represented by each share of the issued and outstanding common stock as so changed; and to increase the authorized common stock as so changed from 12,500,000 shares to 15,000,000 shares.

2. Without impairing any of the charter restrictions as to the issuance of secured obligations, to confer on the Board of Directors authority to issue, at such times and for such consideration as the Board of Directors may determine, bonds, debentures and other obligations of the Corporation convertible into common stock of the Corporation.

The Board of Directors believes it is important and in the best interests of the stockholders that the capital structure of the Corporation be made more flexible so as to give the Board a wider choice in selecting from time to time the method of financing most suitable to the particular occasion. The Board cannot now authorize the issue and sale of the common stock for less than $100 per share or the issue and sale of any bonds, debentures or other obligations convertible into common stock. When the proposed amendments shall have become effective, the issue and sale of common stock without par value or of bonds, debentures or other obligations convertible into common stock will be legally possible at such price as the Board may, from time to time, deem advisable. However, the common stockholders will have pro rata subscription rights as to any common stock or any obligations convertible into common stock hereafter issued and sold for cash.

Although it is proposed that the now outstanding 8,703,252 shares of common stock with a par value of $100 per share be changed into common stock without par value, share for share, it is necessary to name some amount as the stated capital for each such share of common stock without par value. The Board of Directors have accordingly proposed that such stated capital for the outstanding common stock without par value shall be $75 per share. This will effect a decrease of the capital of the Corporation to the extent of $217,581,300, this sum being the difference between the capital represented by the 8,703,252 shares at the stated value of $75 per share and the aggregate par value of the now outstanding 8,703,252 shares of common stock of the par value of $100 each. This decrease of $217,581,300 in capital will add an equal amount to the capital surplus of the Corporation (which now amounts to $81,250,021.42, representing the premium above par heretofore received by the Corporation upon the issuance of certain shares of its par value common stock), thereby increasing the capital surplus to $298,831,321.42.

It is contemplated that as soon as the amendment with respect to common stock without par value has become effective, the item of intangible assets which appears as $260,368,521.53 in the consolidated balance sheet at December 31, 1937, will be reduced to $1.00, the difference of $260,368,520.53 to be charged against the abovementioned capital surplus of $298,831,321.42. The value of these intangible assets will not be affected by the

14

change of the amount at which they are carried on the consolidated balance sheet; nevertheless it seems advisable in view of their intangible character, to carry them on the consolidated balance sheet, at the nominal value of $1.00. When such readjustment shall have been made, the balance sheet will show a capital surplus of $38,462,800.89, in addition to earned surplus, which at December 31, 1937, amounted to $280,356,143.55.

The proposed amendments will effect no change in the intrinsic value of the Corporation's assets or in the number of shares or intrinsic value of the common stock now outstanding. No change is made in the preferred stock. However, additional common stock without par value or obligations convertible into common stock, to which the common stockholders will have the right to subscribe if sold for cash, may thereafter be issued and sold as above stated.

The adoption of each of these amendments requires the approval of holders of record at the close of business March 5, 1938, of two-thirds of each class of the then outstanding shares of preferred and common stock. These amendments have been declared advisable by the Board of Directors, who recommend that they be approved and adopted by the stockholders at the annual meeting.

143

1938 ANNUAL REPORT

Substantial Amount of Intangibles Occurred at Formation
Writedown to $1
Real Value of Intangibles Impossible to Determine
Recapitalization from $100 Par Value to $75 Par Value
Writedown to Capital Surplus

DISPOSITION OF INTANGIBLE ASSETS

At various times through the early years following the formation of the Corporation in 1901, the extent of the probable intangible values inherent in and created through its formation and comprehended in the consolidated balance sheet, was frequently a matter of review. It was recognized that a substantial amount of value for intangibles existed, although to what degree such values were present could not be conclusively determined on any basis of tangible property valuations available.

As far back as 1917 when the war-time Excess Profits Tax laws were in force, the Internal Revenue Department in its calculations to determine and verify Invested Capital for tangibles accepted a plan designed to fix such investment values at the date of the formation of the Corporation on April 1, 1901. This plan was based upon values appraised some years prior to 1917 by the United States Department of Commerce and Labor, Bureau of Corporations. With the enactment of the Federal Securities Exchange Act of 1934 and the regulations promulgated thereunder, the necessity developed for a segregation in the accounts of the intangible values. Accordingly, the plan accepted by the Internal Revenue Department, as above outlined, was utilized as the initial basis from which to obtain this separation of intangible values.

In pursuance of this plan, the amount of the intangible assets present in the accounts of the Corporation and its consolidated subsidiaries at December 31, 1937, after deducting the aggregate sum of $508,302,500 which up to that date had been written off during the preceding thirty-six years (the Corporation having from its inception in 1901 commenced currently to write down the intangible values through bond sinking and other appropriations from income and surplus), was determined to be $260,368,521.53.

Following the changes in the Corporation's capital structure adopted in 1938, the Board of Directors authorized a further allowance for amortization of intangibles through the application of capital surplus, arising largely through reduction in the stated capital of common stock from $100 per share to $75 per share, in the amount of $260,368,520.53, to the end that the intangible investment appearing in the consolidated balance sheet of the Corporation and its subsidiary companies at December 31, 1937, be reduced to the nominal sum of $1.00, at which figure it is carried on the books at December 31, 1938.

It is, of course, not possible to evaluate convincingly what real value the intangible assets possess, but whatever that value may be, it is still in existence and is not affected in any manner by the book reduction mentioned above.

UNITED STATES STEEL CORPORATION AND SUBSIDIARY COMPANIES

COMPARATIVE CONSOLIDATED GENERAL BALANCE SHEET

DECEMBER 31, 1938 AND DECEMBER 31, 1937

148

ASSETS	December 31, 1938	December 31, 1937
PROPERTY INVESTMENT ACCOUNT		
PROPERTIES OWNED AND OPERATED BY SUBSIDIARY COMPANIES		
Tangible.	$2,344,316,957.25	$2,298,303,932.40
Intangible.	1.00	260,368,521.53
GROSS PROPERTY INVESTMENT (PER TABLE PAGE 20)	2,344,316,958.25	2,558,672,453.93
Less, Depletion, Depreciation, Obsolescence, Amortization and Current Maintenance Reserve Balances.	1,177,797,445.32	1,148,239,539.46
	1,166,519,512.93	1,410,432,914.47
MINING ROYALTIES (Paid in advance on unmined ore)	8,581,954.10	7,729,627.28
DEFERRED CHARGES (applying to future operations of the properties)		
Advanced mining and other operating expenses and charges	923,336.96	391,127.49
Discount and expense on long term debt (net)	3,130,722.13	86,668.66
	4,054,059.09	477,796.15
INVESTMENTS		
Outside Real Estate, Real Estate Mortgages and Investments in Sundry Securities, including those deposited under statutory requirements, less reserves	12,357,555.19	9,427,788.52
House and Land Sales Installment Contracts and Mortgages under Employes' Home Owning and other Property Sales Plans, less reserves	6,537,957.21	6,507,634.40
	18,895,512.40	15,935,422.92
OTHER ASSETS		
Cash resources held in Bond Sinking Funds and Other Trusteed Accounts	683,831.55	627,688.42
U. S. Steel Corporation Common Stock Owned (2,766 shares in 1938 and 1937)	111,157.84	111,157.84
Accounts and Notes Receivable not collectible within one year and other delayed items, less reserves	2,094,467.69	2,677,561.71
	2,889,457.08	3,416,407.97
CURRENT ASSETS		
Inventories, less reserves (see table on page 23)	307,479,017.73	331,479,126.00
Accounts Receivable, less reserves	56,998,861.44	53,917,022.63
Bills Receivable, less reserves	7,714,966.72	9,379,984.44
U. S. Government and Other Marketable Securities, less reserves. (Market Value 1938, $20,439,282.91; 1937, $40,621,801.10)	19,660,075.72	39,600,687.01
Cash Working Funds	949,143.59	908,735.84
Time and other special Bank Deposits	2,225,349.06	802,830.41
Cash (in hand, and on deposit with banks subject to cheque)	115,311,096.04	44,648,733.54
	510,338,510.30	480,737,119.87
	$1,711,279,005.90	$1,918,729,288.66

18

UNITED STATES STEEL CORPORATION AND SUBSIDIARY COMPANIES

COMPARATIVE CONSOLIDATED GENERAL BALANCE SHEET

DECEMBER 31, 1938 AND DECEMBER 31, 1937

LIABILITIES	December 31, 1938	December 31, 1937
BONDED, MORTGAGE AND DEBENTURE DEBT OUTSTANDING (See page 25 for detailed statement) (Payments due in 1939 aggregate $9,456,226.61)		
UNITED STATES STEEL CORPORATION		
Ten Year 3¼% Debentures...	$ 100,000,000.00	....
SUBSIDIARY COMPANIES ISSUES		
Guaranteed by U. S. Steel Corporation...................................	50,230,000.00	$ 53,315,000.00
Not Guaranteed by U. S. Steel Corporation...............................	79,839,000.00	52,851,000.00
Real Estate Mortgages and Purchase Money Obligations—Guaranteed $195,249.90	1,200,257.17	1,005,623.78
BONDS FOR PAYMENT OF WHICH CASH IS SPECIALLY HELD BY TRUSTEES...........	305,000.00	318,000.00
	231,574,257.17	107,489,623.78
SUBSIDIARY COMPANIES PURCHASE MONEY OBLIGATIONS—Issued at various dates from 1913 to 1925, inclusive, in connection with acquirement of the fee title to certain ore properties previously held under mining leases........................	12,138,082.37	13,082,583.22
(The December 31, 1938, obligations mature over a period of 20 years, of which there are guaranteed by U. S. Steel Corporation $11,508,082.37; not guaranteed $630,000.00; non-interest bearing $11,987,959.72; interest bearing $150,122.65. Maturities in 1939 aggregate $941,850.16).		
CURRENT LIABILITIES		
Current Accounts Payable and Pay Rolls (at end of 1938 includes $1,491,448.48 accrued for Personal Injury Claims payable after 1939).............................	39,583,181.72	46,074,599.86
Accrued Taxes including reserves for Federal Income, Capital Stock, Excess Profits, and Social Security Taxes...	31,369,881.73	63,469,971.65
Accrued Interest, Unpresented Coupons and Unclaimed Dividends...................	2,003,346.24	1,481,580.08
Preferred Stock Dividends (No. 154 payable February 20, 1939 and No. 150 payable February 19, 1938)..	6,304,919.25	6,304,919.25
	79,261,328.94	117,331,070.84
RESERVES		
CONTINGENT, MISCELLANEOUS OPERATING AND OTHER RESERVES.................	38,567,298.12	37,511,269.77
INSURANCE RESERVES...	45,694,174.69	45,966,321.60
SUBSIDIARY COMPANIES STOCKS NOT HELD BY U. S. STEEL CORPORATION (book value)...	5,137,050.86	5,135,754.48
CAPITAL STOCK AND SURPLUS		
UNITED STATES STEEL CORPORATION		
Preferred 7% Cumulative Stock—Par Value $100...................... (Authorised 4,000,000 shares; issued 3,602,811 shares)	360,281,100.00	360,281,100.00
Common Stock		
Common—Par Value $100 (a)................................... (Authorised 12,500,000 shares; issued 8,703,252 shares)	....	870,325,200.00
Common—No Par—Stated Capital $75 per share.................... (Authorised 15,000,000 shares; issued 8,703,252 shares)	652,743,900.00	....
Capital Surplus..	38,462,800.89	81,250,021.42
Earned Surplus of U. S. Steel Corporation and Subsidiary Companies...........	247,419,012.86	280,356,143.55
TOTAL CAPITAL STOCK AND SURPLUS....................	1,298,906,813.75	1,592,212,464.97
	$1,711,279,005.90	$1,918,729,288.66

(a) Changed on April 4, 1938 to Common Stock without par value.

UNITED STATES STEEL CORPORATION AND SUBSIDIARY COMPANIES
GROSS PROPERTY INVESTMENT ACCOUNT
DECEMBER 31, 1938

PROPERTY CLASSIFICATIONS	Gross Property Investment December 31, 1937	Additions During Year at Cost	Retirements and Property Sales During Year	Changes in Classification and Adjustments	Gross Property Investment December 31, 1938
Real estate.........................	$ 100,259,308.76	$ 169,376.70	$ 1,382,979.87	$481,455.43	$ 98,564,250.16
Plant, mineral and manufacturing properties and equipment (a).......	1,804,259,049.63	67,788,066.44	20,466,597.89	620,847.27	1,852,201,365.45
Transportation properties—railroads, lake and ocean steamships.........	366,906,240.46	2,825,101.64	2,442,582.28	139,391.84	367,149,367.98
	$2,271,424,598.85	$70,782,544.78	$ 24,292,160.04(b)	....	$2,317,914,983.59
Investment in stripping and development at mines and structural erection equipment..................	26,879,333.55	2,195,895.21	2,622,525.15(c)	50,729.95	26,401,973.66
Total tangible property........	$2,298,303,932.40	$72,978,439.99	$ 26,914,685.19	$ 50,729.95(d)	$2,344,316,957.25
Intangibles.........................	260,368,521.53	....	260,368,520.53(e)	....	1.00
Gross property investment account per balance sheet......	$2,558,672,453.93	$72,978,439.99	$287,283,205.72	$ 50,729.95	$2,344,316,958.25

(a) Includes dock and river transportation equipment auxiliary to and forming a part of manufacturing properties.

(b) Includes:

Write-offs to depletion, depreciation, amortization and current maintenance reserves.....................................	$20,313,980.46
Write-offs to profit and loss or operating expense to cover abandonments or investment amortization not provided for otherwise...	622,507.25
Proceeds creditable to investment account from dismantlement and sales of property.................................	3,355,672.33
	$24,292,160.04

(c) Expense absorbed in current year's operations.

(d) Net of transfers to other accounts.

(e) Write-off to capital surplus.

CAPITAL SURPLUS

Balance at December 31, 1937, representing premium above par value heretofore received by the Corporation upon the issuance of par value common stock...................	$ 81,250,021.42
Add, amount of capital surplus arising in 1938 through changing the par value common stock of $100 per share to shares without par value, being the difference between the aggregate capital represented by the 8,703,252 shares outstanding at the present stated capital of $75 per share, and the total of the par value of the shares prior to such change...	217,581,300.00
Total..	$298,831,321.42
Deduct, amount applied in 1938 in reduction of the value of intangible assets as heretofore carried in the consolidated balance sheet to the nominal sum of $1.00........	260,368,520.53
Balance of Capital Surplus at December 31, 1938, per consolidated balance sheet..........	$ 38,462,800.89

1939 ANNUAL REPORT

Depreciation . . . Wage for the Use of Facilities

Savings of Nearly 250,000 People Stressed

Public Interest Governs

Supplies Reclassified from Current Assets

Balance Sheet Format Changed

HOW THE CORPORATION EARNED
ITS LIVING IN 1939

	Total Amount (Millions of Dollars)	Per Cent of Total	Total Amt. Per Employe
U. S. STEEL SOLD TO THE PUBLIC GOODS & SERVICES . .	$857	100.0	$3,829
This revenue was disposed of as follows:			
GOODS & SERVICES PURCHASED FROM OTHERS	$310	36.2	$1,384
WEAR & USAGE OF FACILITIES (Depletion & Depreciation) .	61	7.1	274
TAXES	67	7.8	299
INTEREST PAID (for the use of savings, the ownership of which is evidenced by outstanding bonds and other obligations) . .	9	1.1	42
LEAVING FOR WAGES FOR THE SERVICES OF MEN AND FACILITIES	410	47.8	1,830
This was disposed of as follows:			
WAGES AND SALARIES FOR MEN (being 90%)	369		
WAGES FOR THE USE OF FACILITIES	41		

This was equal to a *wage of 3.0% for the use of tools* in the form of plants, facilities, equipment and other assets essential to the production and sale of goods and services and the payment of wages and salaries. These tools or assets represented savings, the ownership of which is evidenced by outstanding preferred and common stock.

This wage was disposed of as follows:			
TO THE HOLDERS OF PREFERRED STOCK	25		
SET ASIDE FOR FUTURE NEEDS	16		

(This is a rearranged approximate statement of the Corporation's financial activities—for formal statements see pages 16, 17 & 18)

152

ABOUT OUR FINANCIAL AFFAIRS

The United States Steel Corporation is not itself an operating organization. Operations are carried on by subsidiary companies, which are in the nature of a great cooperative enterprise in which the savings from nearly a quarter of a million people have been pooled to provide the tools for the creation of wealth in the form of iron, steel and other products. The tools range from tiny and infinitely delicate laboratory devices through plants, mines, railways, steamships, warehouses and hospitals to the common implements which are usually classed as tools. These pooled savings provided the tools for the use of each of the 224,000 employes of the United States Steel Corporation and its operating subsidiaries.

I. HOW THE CORPORATION EARNED ITS LIVING

To operate the Corporation's facilities in 1939 required the services of about a quarter of a million men and women of varied skills and authorities. The tools were operated and the men and women had jobs because the public bought from the Corporation's subsidiaries some 11.7 million tons of rolled and finished steel in many forms and of many kinds, more than 12.6 million barrels of cement and a variety of steamships, bridges and other products.

In order to supply the wants of the public as expressed in its orders, the subsidiaries had to go outside their own facilities and resources and purchase great quantities of goods and services from those enterprises which were engaged in producing and selling such goods and services. Thus were set in motion a large number of transactions

which in turn set in motion further series of transactions. We know that these processes, flowing out of the purchases made by the subsidiaries, extend throughout the United States and reach in some fashion or other almost to the ends of the earth, and that all require at some point the services of tools and of men.

The operations, if they could be viewed in detail, would be too complex for comprehension, but, grouped according to their elements, they become simple and understandable.

The owners in considerable measure depend and the employes of the Corporation altogether depend for their livelihoods upon the manner in which the Corporation serves the public, and those who are in the chain of events related to the Corporation's operations depend, in part, for

HOW THE CORPORATION HAS EARNED ITS LIVING SINCE 1902
(IN MILLIONS OF DOLLARS)

YEAR	SALES OF GOODS & SERVICES	Goods & Services Purchased from Others	Depletion, Deprec. & Amortization	Taxes	Interest Paid	LEAVING FOR WAGES FOR THE SERVICES OF MEN AND FACILITIES	Wages and Salaries for Men	Wages for the Use of Facilities	Pfd. Dividends	Com. Dividends	Balance
1902	422.2	159.9	27.8	2.4	21.3	210.8	120.5	90.3	35.7	20.3	34.3
1903	395.3	161.2	29.3	3.0	25.6	176.2	120.8	55.4	30.4	12.7	12.3
1904	324.7	143.3	18.2	3.1	30.1	130.0	99.8	30.2	25.2	..	5.0
1905	409.4	151.3	28.0	3.6	29.8	196.7	128.1	68.6	25.2	..	43.4
1906	484.5	169.2	35.6	4.4	29.4	245.9	147.8	98.1	25.2	10.2	62.7
1907	504.7	171.6	32.9	5.4	29.4	265.4	160.8	104.6	25.2	10.2	69.2
1908	331.8	106.5	22.4	5.4	31.3	166.2	120.5	45.7	25.2	10.2	10.3
1909	442.5	142.3	29.3	8.7	31.5	230.7	151.7	79.0	25.2	20.3	33.5
1910	492.6	160.2	30.2	9.2	30.6	262.4	175.0	87.4	25.2	25.4	36.8
1911	433.0	149.6	26.0	9.6	31.1	216.7	161.4	55.3	25.2	25.4	4.7
1912	535.5	218.4	31.1	9.8	32.6	243.6	189.4	54.2	25.2	25.4	3.6
1913	561.7	194.9	31.9	13.2	33.3	288.4	207.2	81.2	25.2	25.4	30.6
1914	413.2	156.5	25.1	12.6	33.2	185.8	162.4	23.4	25.2	15.2	17.0
1915	524.9	193.4	32.4	13.6	32.8	252.7	176.8	75.9	25.2	6.4	44.3
1916	903.0	270.0	26.6	32.0	534.9	263.4	271.5	25.2	44.5	201.8
1917	1276.4	370.9	50.6	252.3	31.0	571.6	347.4	224.2	25.2	91.5	107.5
1918	1328.2	381.2	40.7	297.6	30.7	578.0	452.7	125.3	25.2	71.2	28.9
1919	1109.9	396.4	45.5	81.6	30.1	556.3	479.5	76.8	25.2	25.4	26.2
1920	1295.8	452.3	46.7	76.2	29.3	691.3	581.6	109.7	25.2	25.4	59.1
1921	725.9	253.4	36.8	37.7	28.5	369.5	332.9	36.6	25.2	25.4	14.0
1922	809.3	340.1	42.7	35.8	28.4	362.3	322.7	39.6	25.2	25.4	11.0
1923	1093.6	380.8	51.5	55.1	28.0	578.2	469.5	108.7	25.2	29.2	54.3
1924	920.7	271.6	48.9	45.3	27.3	527.6	442.5	85.1	25.2	35.6	24.3
1925	1023.8	342.4	56.1	50.9	27.1	547.3	456.7	90.6	25.2	35.6	29.8
1926	1087.2	359.7	64.2	52.4	26.8	584.1	467.4	116.7	25.2	35.6	55.9
1927	962.0	312.1	58.9	46.3	26.1	518.6	430.7	87.9	25.2	49.8	12.9
1928	1011.0	339.3	67.2	51.0	25.7	527.8	413.7	114.1	25.2	49.8	39.1
1929	1094.1	343.3	63.3	55.0	14.9	617.6	420.1	197.5	25.2	63.8	108.5
1930	840.2	232.2	58.6	48.1	5.6	495.7	391.3	104.4	25.2	60.4	18.8
1931	551.1	184.2	47.3	34.2	5.5	279.9	266.9	13.0	25.2	37.0	42.2
1932	288.7	148.6	40.3	31.7	5.3	62.8	134.0	71.2	20.7	..	91.9
1933	377.2	170.0	43.6	31.7	5.2	126.7	163.2	36.5	7.2	..	43.7
1934	423.2	148.9	44.6	35.8	5.1	188.8	210.5	21.7	7.2	..	28.9
1935	544.2	200.5	47.6	38.4	5.0	252.7	251.6	1.1	7.2	..	6.1
1936	791.7	287.7	56.8	52.9	4.9	389.4	338.9	50.5	50.4	..	.1
1937	1028.8	337.0	60.9	88.0	5.1	537.8	442.9	94.9	58.5	8.7	27.7
1938	611.4	230.6	49.2	48.8	8.3	274.5	282.2	7.7	25.2	..	32.9
1939	857.1	309.9	61.2	67.0	9.3	409.7	368.6	41.1	25.2	..	15.9

The above figures are based on the earnings reported to stockholders each year and have not been adjusted to reflect surplus charges and credits. The data are in some respects necessarily approximate rather than exact figures. For example, wages represented in inventory expansion in one year are more properly a subdivision of the succeeding year's sales than of the given year's. Sales of goods and services include small amounts of "other income." Payroll includes wages paid for new construction. Taxes are as accrued before adjustments. "Sales" above are after approximating inter-company transportation revenues. (Deficit in *Italics*.)

[10]

154

their livelihoods upon the manner in which they serve the Corporation.

The policies of the Corporation, therefore, must always be consonant with the interests of the public which it serves, with the interests of the men and women who have entrusted their savings to it and with the interests of the employes who depend upon it for a living. Since the owners and employes are also members of the public and since some of the employes are also owners, no interest can conflict with another interest without also conflicting with itself—and in the end ruining itself.

The dollars paid by the public are controlling. How did the dollars paid by that part of the public which at the moment was buying move through the circulatory system of the Corporation?

The accounts of the Corporation for 1939, as duly audited by the auditors elected by the stockholders, give the complete financial picture of the Corporation, and these accounts appear on pages 16, 17 and 18 of this report. They tell the financial history of the Corporation in the required fashion. A different grouping of financial data is made under the heading "How the Corporation Earned Its Living in 1939" which appears on page 8. Similar groupings for each of the years of the Corporation's existence are shown on page 10. The figures do not exactly correspond with those in the statements certified by the auditors and in some respects the aggregate items specified are approximated as to the totals reported. These divergencies, however, are not substantial and, consequently, in a broad manner the tabulation shows in simplified form the results of the major economic classifications of "How the Corporation Earned Its Living in 1939."

The subsidiaries sold to the public either in the form of goods or services a total of $857 million. That was the amount the Corporation had from which to pay the cost of producing the goods and services purchased by the public.

The Corporation is to a high degree self-contained or, as it is called, integrated. Nevertheless, in the course of doing business it had to go outside its own organization to purchase a considerable amount of goods and services—freight being a substantial item. As freight rates are in all instances fixed by law, the producing subsidiaries are without discretion as to what they will pay for transportation. Of course, there is a choice of modes of transport, but the area of selection is restricted. As to the other goods and services which it bought, the Corporation had a certain selectivity and a certain bargaining power, but again the discretion was within narrow bounds and to all intents and purposes the Corporation had little control over the amounts which it laid out for goods and services purchased from others. The purchases amounted to $310 million.

As a condition of doing business, the Corporation had to pay taxes levied upon it by federal, state and local authorities. These taxes were of various sorts. In the year 1939 the Corporation paid many kinds of taxes levied by hundreds of taxing authorities. Some of the taxes were assessed upon valuations of the Corporation's property regardless of the amount of business done, while others were regulated by the results of operations. These taxes amounted to $67 million

155

and as to their payment the Corporation had neither control nor any kind of discretion.

The tools and machinery owned by the subsidiaries are subject to wear and tear in the course of production, and each pound of mineral removed from the mines of the Corporation makes the property that much less valuable. This depreciation and depletion of property is an inescapable cost element in production and, unless an adequate sum be currently set aside to cover these unseen costs, the Corporation might at some future time find that its facilities had been worn out or depleted and that provision for their replacement had not been made.

156

Thus depreciation and depletion are the currently incurred portion of the expenditures which have been made in the past to create the facilities, and which will have to be re-expended in the future in order to replace them with new facilities as need arises. Over these costs the Corporation had only a limited, engineering discretion. The sum set aside was $61 million.

The Corporation has borrowed money, issuing bonds and other obligations as evidences of the debt. The interest charges on this money borrowed may or may not be costs of production, but the Corporation has no discretion as to the payments if it desires to continue in business. The interest payments came to $9 million.

The total cost of these four general items for the production of the goods and services required by the customers was $447 million and the management had relatively little control over the payments for these items of expense.

There remained in the hands of the management the sum of $410 million, being 48% of the sales to the public of goods and services. The Corporation paid $369 million, or 90% of this sum remaining for the wages and salaries of the men and women employed in various capacities to operate the various facilities. As to these payments, the Corporation nominally had a considerable discretion, for nominally it may bargain as to the rates it will pay. But actually, the bargaining power has been much limited by law.

After paying wages and salaries, there was left over the sum of $41 million which was the only sum available to the Corporation for payment to the owners for the use of their savings or for retention as a reserve fund for future contingencies.

The taxes accrued in the year were $67 million. That is, the many units of government, which had put no savings into the property and had taken no risk, received $26 million more than the owners (from earnings), who had ventured their savings and thereby created $369 million in wages for our employes.

The figures as exhibited are of very great moment in considering the system under which we work and how it may be improved, for, while the account is of United States Steel, all industrial business has about the same components. In the item "Goods and Services Purchased from Others" are represented the products of thousands of corporations, firms and individuals whose affairs, in turn, contain essentially the same elements as the affairs of United States Steel.

The important item is the "Leaving for Wages for the Services of Men and Facilities," for out of that item must come the returns to the owners and to the workers. No matter what form of industrial or social organization may be adopted, the three items "Goods and Services Purchased from Others," "Taxes" and "Depreciation and Depletion" will exist in some form, for no enterprise can be wholly self-contained, every government must, in some fashion, be supported, and no one can prevent tools and machinery from wearing out. These facts are inexorable and can not be changed.

II. WHAT THE CORPORATION HAD TO WORK WITH

The preceding comments describe the flow of money through the organization and the uses of those funds in order to produce goods for the public, wages for the employes and remunerations to those whose savings have been entrusted to the Corporation. As indicated, the accomplishment of these purposes has been made possible only by providing tools which may be utilized for the creation of wealth in the form of iron, steel and other products.

The diagram below provides an informal and condensed statement of the cost of the tools owned and the debts against them.

The formal balance sheet which presents the accounts in more detailed fashion appears on pages 16 and 17. In the diagram, the amounts of the several major accounts of properties and *assets* are shown on the *left*. The representation of the *liabilities* shown on the *right* has two fundamental divisions, the first of which shows the obligations of the Corporation to others than the owners of the business and the second division of which represents the equity of the nearly a quarter of a million stockholders who have pooled their capital and savings to provide the tools necessary for carrying on the enterprise.

157

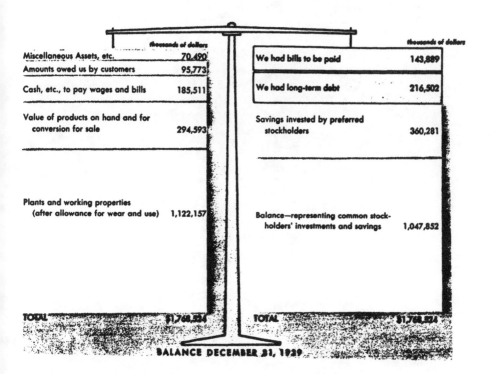

	thousands of dollars		*thousands of dollars*
Miscellaneous Assets, etc.	70,490	We had bills to be paid	143,889
Amounts owed us by customers	95,773		
Cash, etc., to pay wages and bills	185,511	We had long-term debt	216,502
Value of products on hand and for conversion for sale	294,593	Savings invested by preferred stockholders	360,281
Plants and working properties (after allowance for wear and use)	1,122,157	Balance—representing common stockholders' investments and savings	1,047,852
TOTAL	$1,768,524	TOTAL	$1,768,524

BALANCE DECEMBER 31, 1939

INVENTORIES

The total of inventories of materials and products on hand at December 31, 1939, amounted to $294,593,046, compared with $279,518,604 at the end of the preceding year, an increase of $15,074,442 or about 5.4 per cent.

There was a satisfactory absorption of materials in 1939. In the latter part of the year inventories expanded, but to a much smaller extent than the expansion in the volume of business.

Inventories on hand are not deemed excessive. The problem of balanced inventories receives constant review to the end that the investment therein be consistent with efficient operations and market conditions. It has been deemed advisable, as a refinement in balance sheet presentation, to transfer from the current asset classification at December 31, 1939, the investment in certain production materials and manufacturing supplies heretofore carried in the inventory classification. The amount so transferred was $25,674,829 compared with $27,960,413 at December 31, 1938. Both amounts appear in the balance sheet under the heading of Other Assets as *Inventory of Sundry Operating Parts, Supplies, etc.*

Inventories are valued at production and purchase costs or market — whichever is lower. The contract prices for materials for future deliveries are less than December 31 prices.

Where one subsidiary purchased from another, there has been excluded from the inventory values the approximate amount of profits of selling subsidiaries embraced in the purchase prices.

The following is a general inventory summary:

	Dec. 31, 1939	Dec. 31, 1938
Ores — iron, mang. & zinc	$ 73,012,408	$ 75,708,116
Limestone, fluxes & refractories	3,464,870	3,527,893
Coal, coke and other fuel	8,620,905	9,281,046
Pig iron, scrap, ferro & spiegel	20,995,312	25,503,731
Non-ferrous metals & other mfg. materials . . .	17,076,055	10,590,167
Semi-finished products — ingots, billets, etc. . .	29,248,679	29,245,888
Finished products . . .	88,577,673	89,016,319
Transportation co's' supplies & stores	4,194,621	4,295,168
Merchandise of supply co's	1,858,081	2,002,462
Cost (less billings) of uncompleted contracts . .	10,610,013	4,642,804
Material in transit . . .	7,929,648	2,614,718
Sundry items	29,004,781	23,090,292
TOTAL	$294,593,046	$279,518,604

159

A S S E T S

	Dec. 31, 1939	Dec. 31, 1938
CURRENT ASSETS		
Cash in banks and on hand	$ 165,190,478	$ 118,485,589
U. S. Government and other marketable securities, less reserves . . .	20,320,237	19,680,076
(Market value 1939, $21,376,464; 1938, $20,439,283)		
Accounts receivable, less reserves	88,632,482	56,998,861
Bills receivable, less reserves	7,140,894	7,714,967
Inventories, less reserves *(See page 15 for details)*	294,593,046	279,518,604
	575,877,137	482,378,097
INVESTMENTS		
Outside real estate & mortgs. & invest. in sundry securities, less reserves	9,594,980	12,357,555
U. S. Steel Corp. common stock owned (2,766 shares in 1939 and 1938)	111,158	111,158
Balances under employes' home-owning plans, less reserves	6,359,442	6,537,957
	16,065,580	19,006,670
FIXED ASSETS *(See page 20 for details)*		
Property, plant and equipment	2,339,203,909	2,344,316,957
Less reserves for depletion, depreciation, amortization & obsolescence . .	1,217,046,795	1,177,797,445
	1,122,157,114	1,166,519,512
INTANGIBLE ASSETS	1	1
OTHER ASSETS		
Inventory of sundry operating parts, supplies, etc.	25,674,829	27,960,413
Cash resources held in bond sinking funds & other trusteed accounts . .	14,058,079	683,832
Receivables not collectible within one year, less reserves	2,914,924	2,094,468
	42,647,832	30,738,713
DEFERRED CHARGES		
Prepaid royalties	8,383,014	8,581,954
Discount and expense on long term debt (net)	2,322,208	3,130,722
Other deferred charges	1,070,777	923,337
	11,775,999	12,636,013
	$1,768,523,663	$1,711,279,006

160

PRINCIPLES APPLIED IN CONSOLIDATION AND NOTES

The consolidated balance sheet and the statements of accounts present the combined results for the United States Steel Corporation and its subsidiaries for the year ending December 31, 1939. In the balance sheet inter-company accounts and inter-company profit in inventories of the subsidiary companies have been eliminated.

The statement of income and surplus presents the results from operations of the Corporation and its subsidiaries for 1939 resolved to a consolidated organization basis. In the case of subsidiary transportation companies the gross revenue reported includes revenues from services rendered to other subsidiary companies as well as revenues from outside sources, since under the system of accounting prescribed for transportation companies a segregation is not made.

Profits from these respective inter-company transactions are eliminated from consolidated profits to the extent that the materials to which the same attach remain on hand in inventory at the close of the year. This elimination of inter-company profits is comprehended in the cost of goods sold in the consolidated income statement.

The effect on the Consolidated Balance Sheet and related Income Account of the exchange situation with respect to investment in foreign assets and the earnings from foreign transactions is not material.

[16]

LIABILITIES

	Dec. 31, 1939	Dec. 31, 1938
CURRENT LIABILITIES		
Current accounts payable including payrolls	$ 59,350,845	$ 39,583,182
Accrued taxes	46,719,183	31,369,882
Accrued interest, unpresented coupons and unclaimed dividends . .	1,954,365	2,003,346
Preferred stock dividends (#154 payable Feb. 20, 1939, #158 Feb. 20, 1940) . .	6,304,919	6,304,919
Bonds, mortgages & debentures maturing within one year	29,559,379	10,244,967
	143,888,691	89,506,296
LONG-TERM DEBT *(See page 21 for detail)*		
United States Steel Corporation 10-Year 3¼% debentures	90,286,500	95,146,000
Subsidiary companies' issues	112,234,000	125,855,000
Bonds for payment of which cash is specially held by trustees	3,175,000	305,000
Real estate mortgages and purchase money obligations	10,806,709	12,161,373
	216,502,209	233,467,373
DEFERRED CREDITS	3,241,244	. . . .
RESERVES		
Contingent, miscellaneous operating and other reserves *(See page 20 for detail)*	38,638,389	38,567,298
Insurance reserves	46,301,124	45,694,174
MINORITY INTEREST IN COMPANIES NOT WHOLLY OWNED *(Book Value)*	5,144,935	5,137,051
CAPITAL STOCK AND SURPLUS:		
Preferred 7% cumulative stock—par value $100	360,281,100	360,281,100
(Authorized 4,000,000 shares; issued 3,602,811 shares)		
Common stock—no par—stated capital $75 per share	652,743,900	652,743,900
(Authorized 15,000,000 shares; issued 8,703,252 shares)		
Capital surplus	38,462,801	38,462,801
Earned surplus	263,319,270	247,419,013
TOTAL CAPITAL STOCK AND SURPLUS	$1,314,807,071	$1,298,906,814
	$1,768,523,663	$1,711,279,006

INDEPENDENT AUDITORS' REPORT TO STOCKHOLDERS

New York, March 12, 1940

To the Stockholders of United States Steel Corporation:

As auditors elected at the annual meeting of stockholders of the United States Steel Corporation held on April 3, 1939, we have examined the consolidated balance sheet of United States Steel Corporation and its subsidiary companies as at December 31, 1939 and the consolidated statement of income and surplus for the year 1939. We have reviewed the system of internal control and the accounting procedures of the companies and, without making a detailed audit of the transactions, have examined or tested accounting records of the companies and other supporting evidence by methods and to the extent we deemed appropriate.

In our opinion the accompanying consolidated balance sheet and related statement of income and surplus present fairly the position of United States Steel Corporation and its subsidiary companies at December 31, 1939 and the results of their operations for the year in conformity with generally accepted accounting principles applied on a basis consistent with that of the preceding year.

PRICE, WATERHOUSE & CO.

[17]

1941 ANNUAL REPORT

LIFO Adopted

Inventories $15 Million Lower

$25 Million for Contingencies

$10 Million for Amortization of Emergency Facilities

Excess Profits Taxes Noted

LIFO Inventory Adjustment

INDEPENDENT AUDITORS' REPORT TO STOCKHOLDERS

To the Stockholders of United States Steel Corporation: NEW YORK, MARCH 11, 1942.

As auditors elected at the annual meeting of stockholders of United States Steel Corporation held on May 5, 1941, we have examined the consolidated balance sheet of United States Steel Corporation and subsidiaries as at December 31, 1941, and the consolidated statement of income and surplus for the year 1941. We have reviewed the system of internal control and the accounting procedures of the companies and, without making a detailed audit of the transactions, have examined or tested accounting records of the companies and other supporting evidence by methods and to the extent we deemed appropriate. Our examination was made in accordance with generally accepted auditing standards applicable in the circumstances and included all procedures which we considered necessary.

In ascertaining net income for the year 1941 with respect to inventories of certain materials, work in process and finished goods of certain subsidiaries, the last-in, first-out inventory method was applied instead of the average cost method used heretofore. As a result of this change in method, which we approve, inventories at December 31, 1941, and income before Federal taxes for the year 1941 are approximately $15,000,000 less than they would have been under the method heretofore followed. Otherwise, the principles of accounting maintained by the companies during the current year were, in our opinion, consistent with those of the preceding year.

In our opinion, the accompanying consolidated balance sheet and related statement of income and surplus present fairly the position of United States Steel Corporation and subsidiaries at December 31, 1941, and the results of their operations for the year in conformity with generally accepted accounting principles.

PRICE, WATERHOUSE & CO.

U. S. STEEL CORPORATION & SUBSIDIARIES

CONSOLIDATED STATEMENT OF INCOME & EARNED SURPLUS

FOR THE YEARS ENDED DECEMBER 31, 1941 & 1940

	Year 1941	Year 1940
GROSS SALES, REVENUES OF TRANSPORTATION COMMON CARRIERS & MISCELLANEOUS OPERATIONS, *less discounts, returns & allowances*	$1,620,515,110	$1,076,471,158
COST OF GOODS SOLD & OPERATING EXPENSES OF TRANSPORTATION COMMON CARRIERS & MISCELLANEOUS OPERATIONS	1,112,143,410	736,523,709
BALANCE	508,371,700	339,947,449
OTHER OPERATING EXPENSES		
General administrative & selling expenses	58,499,935	54,547,051
Payments for current & future pensions	15,184,433	15,626,917
Provision for bad debts	3,105,107	1,798,235
Special provision for contingencies	25,000,000	—
Social security taxes	22,856,726	17,288,507
State, local & miscellaneous taxes	49,945,848	41,832,038
Depletion, depreciation, obsolescence & amortization allowances	83,472,483	69,085,116
Amortization of emergency facilities	9,948,140	—
Expenses of dismantling & rearranging facilities	2,394,466	2,013,380
	270,407,138	202,191,244
OPERATING INCOME	237,964,562	137,756,205
OTHER INCOME & *Deductions*		
Interest & dividend income, less miscellaneous interest paid	1,162,780	2,067,937
Discount on purchases	2,257,936	1,551,523
Rents & royalties	757,813	1,683,508
Patent settlement expense in excess of reserves provided	*120,300*	2,011,120
Profit and loss on sale of securities & valuation adjustments	508,203	866,688
Loss or gain on sale of capital assets	*1,885,708*	1,799
Minority portion of profits of companies not wholly owned	*35,580*	*42,499*
Miscellaneous income	294,767	275,391
TOTAL OTHER INCOME	2,939,911	4,393,227
INCOME BEFORE INTEREST & FEDERAL INCOME TAXES	240,904,473	142,149,432
INTEREST ON BONDS AND MORTGAGES (*including in 1940 $6,413,186 of premium & balance of unamortized discount on refinancings*)	6,033,398	13,638,150
INCOME BEFORE FEDERAL INCOME TAXES	234,871,075	128,511,282
PROVISION FOR ESTIMATED FEDERAL INCOME & EXCESS PROFITS TAXES		
Normal income taxes	73,147,800	26,300,000
Excess profits taxes & additional income taxes	45,552,200	—
	118,700,000	26,300,000
NET INCOME	116,171,075	102,211,282
DIVIDENDS—U. S. Steel Corporation Preferred Stock ($7.00 *per share*)	25,219,677	25,219,677
U. S. Steel Corporation Common Stock ($4.00 *per share*)	34,813,008	34,813,008
SURPLUS FOR THE YEAR	56,138,390	42,178,597
EARNED SURPLUS AT CLOSE OF PREVIOUS YEAR	305,497,867	263,319,270
Restoration of 1940 inventory write-downs preparatory to adoption of last-in, first-out inventory method in 1941	415,183	—
EARNED SURPLUS AT DECEMBER 31 (*per balance sheet*)	$362,051,440	$305,497,867

166

[18]

DETAILS OF BALANCE SHEET ITEMS

INVENTORIES

	Dec. 31, 1941	Dec. 31, 1940
Ores—Iron, Manganese & Zinc	$ 53,766,592	$ 63,510,158
Limestone, Fluxes & Refractories	4,694,176	4,095,668
Coal, Coke and Other Fuel	9,029,031	12,204,972
Pig Iron, Scrap, Ferro-Manganese & Spiegel	16,409,781	20,586,153
Non-Ferrous Metals & Misc. Manufacturing Materials	20,974,021	21,780,358
Semi-finished Products—Ingots, Billets, etc.	29,444,434	32,707,272
Finished Products	83,272,157	97,865,523
Transportation Companies' Supplies & Stores	6,558,403	4,934,954
Merchandise of Supply Companies	3,171,158	2,078,692
Cost (Less Billings) of Contracts in Progress	8,858,739	12,754,513
Material in Transit	8,460,914	7,408,883
Sundry Items	45,011,231	29,058,178
Total	**$291,650,637**	**$308,985,324**

Inventories at December 31, 1940, were carried at cost, or at market value, whichever was lower. At December 31, 1941, certain inventories are carried at cost, or at market value, whichever is lower; and certain others are carried at cost as determined under the provisions of the last-in, first-out (LIFO) inventory method, which was adopted, and made applicable to such inventories, by certain subsidiaries as of January 1, 1941. This means that costs of sales, calculated under the LIFO method, are on the basis of current costs of inventories, instead of the average cost method used heretofore. Inventory values exclude inter-company profits.

FIXED ASSETS

	Gr. Investment Dec. 31, 1940	Additions In Year	Retirements & Sales in Year	Reclassifications & Adjustments	Gr. Investment Dec. 31, 1941
Real Estate	$ 95,400,258	$ 494,919	$ 5,227,809	$ 79,573	$ 90,746,941
Plant, Mineral & Manufacturing*	1,849,228,082	84,251,090	46,074,150	13,100,895	1,900,505,917
Transport'n—R.R., Lake & Ocean S.S.	382,534,742	26,212,403	4,528,245	142,305	404,076,595
	2,327,163,082	110,958,412	55,830,204†	13,038,163	2,395,329,453
Investment in Mine Stripping, etc.	18,752,699	3,218,034	6,646,251	21,482	15,345,964
Total	**$2,345,915,781**	**$114,176,446**	**$62,476,455**	**$13,059,645**	**$2,410,675,417**

Values are based upon determinations by the U. S. Bureau of Corporations as at the date of organization of the Corporation, adjusted for additions and disposals since that date. * Includes transportation equipment auxiliary to and a part of manufacturing properties. † Comprises $6,676,356 credited to investment account for sales and salvage and $49,153,848 written off for value of natural resources exhausted and for investment in facilities retired or sold of which $7,329,180 was charged to current income or operations.

RESERVES

	Balances Dec. 31, 1940	Income Set Aside 1941	1941 Expends. & Charges	1941 Transfs. & Adjusts.	Balances Dec. 31, 1941
Depletion	$ 9,949,074	$ 3,890,108	$ 3,890,108	—	$ 9,949,074
Depreciation & Amortization	1,203,922,115	89,530,515	36,180,448	$15,155,960	1,272,428,142
Blast Furnace Relining	21,872,701	3,283,856	1,792,689	2,058,321	21,305,547
Total Property Reserves	**$1,235,743,890**	**$96,704,479**	**$41,863,245§**	**$13,097,639**	**$1,303,682,763**
General Contingent	33,607,918	29,937,558	1,858,065	3,717,508	65,404,919
Accident & Hospital	5,188,081	6,279,170	4,944,857	31,594	6,490,800
For Other Operating Expenses	451,062	1,161,190	988,239	20,395	603,618
Total	**$ 39,247,061**	**$37,377,918**	**$ 7,791,161**	**$ 3,665,519**	**$ 72,499,337**

§ Comprises expenditures of $38,577, and depletion and depreciation of $41,824,668 written off to credit of property investment account for value of natural resources exhausted and for investment in facilities retired or sold.

168

1942 ANNUAL REPORT

Pension Plan Changes Discussed

Further Pension Payments Made

Footnotes Given More Formal Presentation

Transition to Peacetime Provided by Reserve

Income Much Lower

Insurance and Pensions

Under the Employes' Group Life Insurance Plan, beneficiaries of 1,816 employes received death benefits of $4,227,750 in 1942. At the end of the year, 289,314 employes were insured for $685,740,000.

During the year 1942, pensions were granted under the U. S. Steel Pension Plan to 1,434 retiring employes and 1,085 pensions were terminated by the death of pensioned employes, or for other reasons. At the end of the year, there were 14,603 pensions in force. The average length of service of employes pensioned in 1942 was 35.65 years; the average monthly pension granted under the Plan in 1942 was $42.42. These pensions are in addition to any public pensions received by retired employes.

The rules, adopted under the U. S. Steel Pension Plan, consist of two parts — the contributory part and the non-contributory part of the Plan.

Contributory Part of Plan. Effective January 1, 1940, provisions for contributory pensions were put in force with respect to employes' earnings in excess of the maximum taxable limits under the Federal old age benefit laws. Under these provisions, employes who elect to participate contribute three per cent of their compensation in excess of these limits and the employing companies contribute such additional amount as may be sufficient, according to the determination of an actuary, to cover present and prospective benefits and expenses under the contributory part of the Pension Plan. The contributions of the employing companies are restricted, however, to five per cent of the compensation in excess of these limits paid to all employes eligible to participate. These contributions are held by a trustee upon the terms and conditions stated in this part of the Plan.

Non-Contributory Part of Plan. Changes in the Pension Rules made in 1940 continued the eligibility of employes for pensions with respect to service prior to January 1, 1940, subject to adjustments for public pensions. Employes do not contribute to the cost of this part of the Plan. These changes further provided that, for certain pension purposes, no credit would be granted under this part of the Plan for service rendered subsequent to December 31, 1939. However, provisions permitting pensions under special retirement conditions, including total and permanent incapacity, were continued.

Commencing in 1940, the non-contributory part of the Plan has provided for payment by the employing companies to a trustee of the present value, as determined by an actuary, of the expected future payments in respect of pensions granted to employes retiring each year under the non-contributory part of the Plan. Payments of this nature were made to a trustee in 1940, 1941 and 1942.

In 1942, further payments were made by the employing companies to a trustee toward the cost of pensions for employes retiring under the non-contributory part of the Plan after December 31, 1939.

No provision for the payment of pensions granted prior to January 1, 1940, under the non-contributory part of the Plan has been made, with the exception of the trust funds established by Andrew Carnegie and United States Steel Corporation, the income from which is applicable to the payment of pensions. As the income from these trust funds falls far below the amount required to pay these pensions, the payment of the larger part of these pensions still constitutes a current expense.

171

ASSETS

	Dec. 31, 1942	Dec. 31, 1941
CURRENT ASSETS		
Cash in banks and on hand	$ 198,666,196	$ 282,062,548
United States Government securities including Treasury tax notes, at cost . .	230,640,837	69,079,943
Other marketable securities, less reserves	63,429	67,971
Notes and accounts receivable (including approximately $69,000,000 in 1942 from U. S. Government), less reserves	157,784,200	140,599,758
Inventories, less reserves	319,615,944	291,650,637
	906,770,606	783,460,857
OTHER ASSETS		
Inventory of sundry operating parts and supplies	26,982,276	28,420,073
Cash resources held in bond sinking funds and other trusteed accounts . . .	5,761,219	3,173,718
Receivables not collectible within one year, less reserves	7,473,888	3,404,081
	40,217,383	34,997,872
INVESTMENTS		
Mortgages and sundry investments and advances, less reserves	12,343,711	10,771,084
U. S. Steel Corporation common stock owned (2,766 shares)	111,158	111,158
Balances under employes' home-owning plans, less reserves	5,053,130	6,682,620
	17,507,999	17,564,862
CASH DEPOSITS HELD ON DEFENSE CONTRACTS (per contra)	11,448,264	28,817,857
CASH SEGREGATED FOR CAPITAL EXPENDITURES	60,000,000	60,000,000
FIXED ASSETS (details on p. 31)		
Property, plant and equipment	2,411,857,582	2,397,374,900
Less — Reserves for depletion, depreciation and amortization	1,349,297,523	1,303,682,763
	1,062,560,059	1,093,692,137
INTANGIBLES	1	1
DEFERRED CHARGES		
Stripping and development	9,116,603	13,300,517
Prepaid royalties	8,852,506	8,851,020
Discount and expense on long-term debt (net)	1,265,923	1,689,045
Other deferred charges	5,695,920	2,646,920
	24,930,952	26,487,502
	$2,123,435,264	$2,045,021,088

NOTES TO ACCOUNTS

Renegotiation of Government Contracts. War profits control legislation gives the Government the right under certain conditions to renegotiate and adjust profits realized on contracts and subcontracts with resulting reduction in and refunding of profits realized on such contracts. Because of the uncertainties involved, it is impossible to estimate at this time the effect, if any, of such renegotiation upon the financial statements of the Corporation and its subsidiaries.

Basis for Federal Tax Provisions. The final liability for Federal income taxes for the years 1930, and 1935 through 1941, has not yet been determined. The Revenue Act of 1942 contains many provisions, including relief provisions, upon which various interpretations can be placed and it will be some time before its ultimate effect can be determined. Although additional taxes may be levied for these years, it is believed that reasonable reserves have been provided.

Depreciation and Amortization. Special amortization allowances for emergency facilities are computed over a period not in excess of five years and are subject to adjustment if the emergency terminates before the end of that period. Provision for depreciation of other facilities is being made to meet the added burden on plant and equipment resulting from pressure to secure maximum production.

Estimated Additional Costs Arising Out of War. For the year 1942, as in the year 1941, a reserve of $25,000,000 was provided for those costs applicable to this period arising out of war and which because of the high rate of operations must be deferred until a future time, as well as for transition to a peace-time basis at the end of the war.

Inventories. At December 31, 1942, certain inventories are carried at cost or market, whichever is lower, and certain others are carried at cost as determined under the last-in, first-out inventory method. As outlined in the annual report for 1941, the last-in, first-out inventory method was adopted as at January 1, 1941, and was made applicable

172

26

Consolidated General Balance Sheet

LIABILITIES

	Dec. 31, 1942	Dec. 31, 1941
CURRENT LIABILITIES		
Current accounts payable including payrolls	$ 119,009,170	$ 97,892,936
Accrued taxes	235,765,907	161,029,920
Accrued interest and unpresented coupons	1,494,188	1,678,761
Preferred dividend (declared in January, payable in February)	6,304,919	6,304,919
Common dividend (declared in January, payable in March)	8,703,252	8,703,252
Bonds, mortgages and debentures maturing within one year	12,214,543	12,056,773
	383,491,979	287,666,561
LONG-TERM DEBT (details on p. 30)	151,909,384	193,295,215
Less — Amount maturing within one year shown above	12,214,543	12,056,773
	139,694,841	181,238,442
LIABILITY FOR DEFENSE CONTRACT DEPOSITS (per contra)	11,448,264	28,817,857
DEFERRED CREDITS	4,886,920	7,724,430
RESERVES		
For estimated additional costs arising out of war	50,000,000	25,000,000
For insurance and loss replacement (details on p. 31)	54,174,131	48,395,104
For contingencies and miscellaneous expenses (details on p. 31)	50,180,654	47,499,337
MINORITY INTEREST IN COMPANIES NOT WHOLLY OWNED (book value)	4,233,350	5,140,116
CAPITAL STOCK AND SURPLUS		
Preferred stock, 7% cumulative, par value $100 (Authorized 4,000,000 shares; issued 3,602,811 shares)	360,281,100	360,281,100
Common stock, without par value, stated capital $75 per share (Authorized 15,000,000 shares; issued 8,703,252 shares)	652,743,900	652,743,900
Capital surplus	38,462,801	38,462,801
Earned surplus		
At beginning of year	362,051,440	305,497,867
Income after dividends	11,785,884	56,138,390
Restoration of write-downs upon adoption of last-in, first-out inventory method	—	415,183
At end of year	373,837,324	362,051,440
TOTAL CAPITAL STOCK AND SURPLUS	1,425,325,125	1,413,539,241
	$2,123,435,264	$2,045,021,088

NOTES TO ACCOUNTS

to certain materials. This method was extended to certain other materials in 1942, resulting in a reduction in inventories at December 31, 1942, and in income before calculating Federal taxes for the year 1942, of approximately $1,500,000 as compared with the method followed in 1941. Inventories at December 31, 1942, included cost, less billings, of contracts in progress of $28,475,595 as compared with $8,858,739 at December 31, 1941.

Fixed Asset Valuation. The gross values at which the tangible property, plant and equipment are carried in the consolidated balance sheet have been determined from and based upon the findings of the United States Bureau of Corporations, and accepted by the Bureau of Internal Revenue of the Treasury Department, as at the initial date of organization of the Corporation, plus actual cost of additions since, and less credits for the cost of properties sold, retired or otherwise disposed of.

Insurance Reserves. Although, in view of the present emergency, outside insurance against fire, windstorm, marine, war damage and related losses has been placed on a substantial part of the subsidiary companies' insurable assets, the balance in the reserve for insurance at December 31, 1942, is held available for absorbing possible losses of this character in connection with properties not so insured and for other emergencies.

Basis of Consolidation. The consolidated balance sheet and the statements of accounts present the combined results for United States Steel Corporation and subsidiaries for the year ended December 31, 1942. In these statements, intercompany accounts and intercompany profit in inventories of the subsidiary companies have been eliminated. The effect on the consolidated balance sheet and related income account of the exchange situation with respect to investment in foreign assets and the earnings from foreign transactions is not material.

Consolidated Statement of Income

	Year 1942	Year 1941
SALES AND REVENUES		
Sales and revenues, *less discounts, returns, allowances and bad debts*	$1,861,940,280	$1,617,410,003
Interest, dividends and other	4,011,412	4,945,919
TOTAL	1,865,951,692	1,622,355,922
COSTS		
Employment costs:		
Wages and salaries	725,750,899	590,233,976
Social security taxes	24,245,901	22,856,726
Payments for pensions *(details on page 16)*	32,664,901	15,184,433
	782,661,701	628,275,135
Purchased products and services	648,401,343	579,640,279
Depletion and depreciation	91,765,371	86,756,339
Amortization of emergency facilities	31,962,146	9,948,140
Loss on sale of fixed assets	4,434,013	1,885,708
Estimated additional costs applicable to this period arising out of war . . .	25,000,000	25,000,000
Interest and other costs on long-term debt	6,153,392	6,033,398
State, local and miscellaneous taxes	48,255,157	49,945,848
Estimated Federal taxes on income *(details on page 18)*	155,500,000	118,700,000
TOTAL	1,794,133,123	1,506,184,847
INCOME	71,818,569	116,171,075
DIVIDENDS–On cumulative preferred stock *($7.00 per share)*	25,219,677	25,219,677
On common stock *($4.00 per share)*	34,813,008	34,813,008
CARRIED FORWARD FOR FUTURE NEEDS	$ 11,785,884	$ 56,138,390

174

1943 ANNUAL REPORT

Wartime Reserve Grows Again
Treasury Stock Now in Equity Section

Consolidated Balance Sheet

U. S. Steel Corporation and Subsidiaries

ASSETS

	Dec. 31, 1943	Dec. 31, 1942
CURRENT ASSETS		
Cash in banks and on hand	$ 198,441,107	$ 198,666,196
United States Government securities at cost	176,988,072	230,640,837
Notes and accounts receivable (including approx. $79,000,000 in 1943 and $69,000,000 in 1942 from United States Government), less reserves	157,413,830	157,784,200
Inventories (*details on p. 32*)	334,446,623	312,039,243
	867,289,632	899,130,476
INVENTORY OF OPERATING PARTS AND SUPPLIES	28,618,018	34,558,977
MISCELLANEOUS INVESTMENTS AND OTHER ASSETS INCLUDING RECEIVABLES NOT COLLECTIBLE WITHIN ONE YEAR, less reserves	33,548,380	30,695,377
CASH DEPOSITS HELD ON EMERGENCY CONTRACTS (*per contra*)	9,932,465	11,448,264
CASH AND UNITED STATES GOVERNMENT SECURITIES SET ASIDE FOR PROPERTY ADDITIONS AND FOR EXPENDITURES ARISING OUT OF WAR	135,000,000	60,000,000
PLANT AND EQUIPMENT, less reserves (*details on p. 31*)	1,010,916,795	1,062,560,059
INTANGIBLES	1	1
MINE STRIPPING AND OTHER COSTS APPLICABLE TO FUTURE PERIODS	20,757,168	24,930,952
	$2,106,062,459	$2,123,324,106

176

LIABILITIES, CAPITAL AND SURPLUS

	Dec. 31, 1943	Dec. 31, 1942
CURRENT LIABILITIES		
Accounts payable	$ 141,962,674	$ 123,503,358†
Accrued taxes	183,310,064	233,335,907†
Preferred dividend (declared in January, payable in February)	6,304,919	6,304,919
Common dividend (declared in January, payable in March)	8,703,252	8,703,252
Bonds, mortgages and debentures maturing within one year	7,666,623	12,214,543
	347,947,532	384,061,979
LONG-TERM DEBT, less amount maturing within one year (*details on p. 30*)	128,993,645	139,694,841
LIABILITY FOR EMERGENCY CONTRACT DEPOSITS (*per contra*)	9,932,465	11,448,264
INCOME APPLICABLE TO FUTURE PERIODS	4,892,698	4,886,920
RESERVES (*details on p. 32*)		
For estimated additional costs arising out of war	73,876,739	50,000,000
For insurance and loss replacement	56,262,671	54,174,131
For contingencies and miscellaneous expenses	52,690,119	50,180,654
MINORITY INTEREST IN COMPANIES NOT WHOLLY OWNED	3,406,762	4,233,350
CAPITAL AND SURPLUS		
Preferred stock, 7% cumulative, par value $100 (Authorized 4,000,000 shares; issued 3,602,811 shares)	360,281,100	360,281,100
Common stock, no par value, stated capital $75 per share (Authorized 15,000,000 shares; issued 8,703,252 shares)	652,743,900	652,743,900
Capital surplus	38,462,801	38,462,801
Less – Cost of 2,766 shares common stock held in treasury	*111,158*	*111,158*
	1,051,376,643	1,051,376,643
Earned surplus		
At beginning of year	373,267,324	362,051,440
Income after dividends	3,415,861	11,215,884†
At end of year	376,683,185	373,267,324†
TOTAL CAPITAL AND SURPLUS	1,428,059,828	1,424,643,967†
	$2,106,062,459	$2,123,324,106

† After adjustment for renegotiation of contracts.

28

1945 ANNUAL REPORT

Additional Wartime Amortization Offset by Reserve
Was Income Smoothed

Consolidated Statement of Income

UNITED STATES STEEL CORPORATION AND SUBSIDIARIES

	1945	1944	Five Years 1941-1945
PRODUCTS AND SERVICES SOLD	$1,747,338,661	$2,082,186,895	$9,287,177,921
COSTS			
EMPLOYMENT COSTS			
Wages and salaries	778,391,800	902,162,021	3,849,805,592
Social Security taxes	18,081,595	21,995,708	113,192,507
Payments for pensions *(details on p. 19)* .	28,975,958	33,074,986	143,550,768
	825,449,353	957,232,715	4,106,548,867
PRODUCTS AND SERVICES BOUGHT	672,728,198	792,901,582	3,400,434,757
WEAR AND EXHAUSTION OF FACILITIES			
Depletion and depreciation	77,140,359	81,083,380	421,908,749
Amortization of emergency facilities . . .	44,215,710	56,765,012	300,232,623
Loss on sales of plant and equipment . .	2,064,848	1,149,183	14,725,877
	123,420,917	138,997,575	736,867,249
ADDITIONAL AMORTIZATION DUE TO ENDING OF EMERGENCY PERIOD, less associated Federal income tax adjustments	35,584,069	—	—
WAR COSTS INCLUDED HEREIN PROVIDED FOR IN PRIOR YEARS			
Additional amortization above . . .	*35,584,069*	—	—
Other	*2,600,883*	*3,517,648*	—
ESTIMATED ADDITIONAL COSTS APPLICABLE TO THIS PERIOD ARISING OUT OF WAR	—	25,000,000	57,174,139
INTEREST AND OTHER COSTS ON LONG-TERM DEBT .	3,500,653	4,979,675	26,918,580
STATE, LOCAL AND MISCELLANEOUS TAXES	36,825,367	40,801,715	217,394,466
ESTIMATED FEDERAL TAXES ON INCOME *(details on p. 25)*	30,000,000	65,000,000	372,982,140
TOTAL	1,689,323,605	2,021,395,614	8,918,320,198
INCOME	58,015,056	60,791,281	368,857,723
DIVIDENDS – On cumulative preferred stock *($7 per share)*	25,219,677	25,219,677	126,098,385
On common stock *($4 per share)*	34,813,008	34,813,008	174,065,040
INCOME REINVESTED IN BUSINESS			
ADDITION IN PERIOD	—	$ 758,596	$ 68,694,298
REDUCTION IN PERIOD	$ 2,017,629	—	—

179

Consolidated Statement of Financial Position

UNITED STATES STEEL CORPORATION AND SUBSIDIARIES

	Dec. 31, 1945	Dec. 31, 1944
CURRENT ASSETS		
Cash	$ 231,820,174	$ 215,649,601
United States Government securities, at cost	197,537,000	206,004,111
Receivables (including approximately $35,000,000 in 1945 and $75,000,000 in 1944 from United States Government), less estimated bad debts	117,803,916	158,170,097
Inventories *(details on p. 33)*	270,599,494	307,399,945
TOTAL	817,760,584	887,223,754
Less		
CURRENT LIABILITIES		
Accounts payable	147,526,167	167,175,414
Accrued taxes	40,388,532	149,491,151
Dividends payable	15,008,171	15,008,171
Long-term debt due within one year	14,077,462	6,195,835
TOTAL	217,000,332	337,870,571
WORKING CAPITAL	600,760,252	549,353,183
MISCELLANEOUS INVESTMENTS, less estimated losses	27,446,932	31,894,223
UNITED STATES GOVERNMENT SECURITIES SET ASIDE, at cost		
For property additions	250,000,000	100,000,000
For expenditures arising out of war	58,000,000	96,000,000
PLANT AND EQUIPMENT, less depreciation *(details on p. 33)*	702,504,137	913,222,736
OPERATING PARTS AND SUPPLIES	23,751,863	25,489,175
COSTS APPLICABLE TO FUTURE PERIODS	11,305,258	11,877,439
INTANGIBLES	1	1
TOTAL ASSETS LESS CURRENT LIABILITIES	1,673,768,443	1,727,836,757
Deduct		
LONG-TERM DEBT *(details on p. 34)*	78,638,831	92,919,209
RESERVES *(details on p. 33)*		
For estimated additional costs arising out of war	57,174,139	95,359,091
For insurance, contingencies and miscellaneous expenses	111,971,482	111,556,837
EXCESS OF ASSETS OVER LIABILITIES AND RESERVES	$1,425,983,991	$1,428,001,620

		Dec. 31, 1945	Dec. 31, 1944
OWNERSHIP EVIDENCED BY			
Preferred stock, 7% cumulative, par value $100 (3,602,811 shares)		$ 360,281,100	$ 360,281,100
Common stock (8,703,252 shares)		1,065,702,891	1,067,720,520
Stated capital, $75 per share	$652,743,900		
Capital in excess of stated amount, less cost of treasury stock	38,351,643		
Income reinvested in business *(see p. 29 for reduction of $2,017,629 in 1945)*	374,607,348		
TOTAL		$1,425,983,991	$1,428,001,620

180

30

UNITED STATES STEEL CORPORATION AND SUBSIDIARIES

* *

Renegotiation of Government Contracts. The subsidiary companies whose war contracts are subject to renegotiation under the Federal Renegotiation Act were notified by the Navy Price Adjustment Board, acting for all governmental agencies, that no excessive profits under these contracts were realized by any of these companies for the year 1944. It is believed by management that no excessive income was realized on similar contracts performed during 1945.

Amortization of Emergency Facilities. Amortization of emergency facilities was computed for the first nine months of 1945, as in prior years, in accordance with Section 124 (a) of the Internal Revenue Code, and the Federal taxes on income were calculated on this basis for the year 1945. As a result of the proclamation of the President of the United States on September 29, 1945, ending the period for amortization of emergency facilities, there was additional amortization for the period January 1, 1941, to September 30, 1945. As this additional amortization, together with the associated Federal income tax adjustment, applies to the war years as a whole, the effect thereof is reflected in the statement of income for the five years 1941 to 1945. The remaining cost of the facilities at September 30, 1945, was $113,688,733, and this amount has been added to the reserve for amortization. The associated Federal income tax adjustment is $78,104,664, which amount has been deducted from the accrued tax liability. The loss of $35,584,069 had been provided for in prior years and so has been charged to the Reserve for Estimated Additional Costs Arising out of War. In the statement of income the charge and an offsetting credit are both included.

Federal Taxes on Income. Audit of Federal income and excess profits tax returns for 1941 and subsequent years has not yet been completed by the Bureau of Internal Revenue, and certain relatively small items for the years 1935 through 1940 have not yet been finally agreed upon with the taxing authorities. It is believed that reasonable provision has been made for any additional taxes which may be levied.

Estimated Additional Costs Arising Out of War. During each of the previous four years, $25 million was set aside for estimated additional costs arising out of war. Of this $100 million total, $4,640,909 was used to December 31, 1944. As the balance remaining was considered adequate, no further amount was set aside for this purpose during 1945. In 1945, however, the additional amortization loss of $35,584,069, and other war costs representing inventory losses, deferred repair and maintenance and other expenditures, in the amount of $2,600,883, were charged to this reserve. These charges and offsetting credits are included in the statement of income.

Plant and Equipment Valuation. The gross values at which plant and equipment are carried in the consolidated accounts have been determined from and based upon the findings of the United States Bureau of Corporations, and accepted by the Bureau of Internal Revenue of the Treasury Department, as at the initial date of organization of the Corporation, plus actual cost of additions since, and less credits for the cost of properties sold, retired or disposed of otherwise.

Insurance Reserve. The subsidiary companies are, for the most part, self-insurers of their assets against fire, windstorm, marine and related losses. The balance of the insurance reserve is held available for absorbing possible losses of this character.

Wages and Salaries. Wages and salaries for the year 1945 totaled $786,721,918. Of this amount $778,391,800 was included in costs of products and services sold and the balance was charged to construction and other accounts.

181

1946 ANNUAL REPORT

6 Million Tons of Coal Lost in Strike

U. S. Steel Hit by Strike

New Labor Demands

60 Million Man Hours Lost Because of Strikes

Earnings Too Low

OPA Blamed for Keeping Prices Down

Volume Necessary

Reinvestment Lagging

Strike Costs Offset by Reserve

$500 Million Potential Liability for Portal-to-Portal Pay Suits

The Coal Strikes of 1946

During 1946, two strikes in the bituminous coal mines of the country shut off the supply of coal for steel making operations and threatened paralysis for all of American industry. These strikes caused an estimated loss in coal production by U. S. Steel of six million tons.

The first strike continued from April 1 to May 29, 1946. It ended after the Government took possession of practically all of the bituminous coal mines in the nation, including those of U. S. Steel, and entered into a new labor agreement with the United Mine Workers of America. The agreement, so made by the Government, provided for wage increases and for a "welfare fund" under which five cents a ton must be paid into a fund to be administered by a representative of the Union, a representative of the mine owners and a representative to be appointed by the Government. The agreement also granted many other demands of the Union.

In October, 1946, while the coal mines were still in the possession of the Government, a dispute arose between the United Mine Workers of America and the Government as to the right of the Union to reopen the agreement in an attempt to secure additional wage increases. This resulted in a second national coal strike lasting from November 21 to December 7, 1946, and in litigation between the Government and the Union, which is still pending. This second strike was terminated suddenly by the United Mine Workers of America with instructions to the miners to go back to work until March 31, 1947, without any change being made in the contract with the Government. The Government's control of the coal mines of the nation will terminate not later than June 30, 1947.

Steel Labor Situation

A country-wide steel strike lasting four weeks became effective on January 21, 1946. Full operations could not be resumed by U. S. Steel until several weeks after the strike was terminated on February 18, 1946. The circumstances surrounding the calling of this strike by the United Steelworkers of America (CIO) and U. S. Steel's efforts to avert such a serious blow to the economy of the nation need not be repeated in this report, as the story previously has been told fully in public statements, in a letter to the stockholders, and in the Annual Report of U. S. Steel for 1945.

At the conclusion of this strike, in an effort to secure a period of industrial peace, U. S. Steel's labor contracts with the Union were extended to February 15, 1947, with a renewed provision that there would be no strikes, work stoppages or lockouts during the life of the extended contracts, and a further provision designed to achieve "the highest level of employe performance and efficiency consistent with safety, good health and sustained effort. . . ."

In accordance with the terms of such extended contracts, negotiations with the United Steelworkers of America (CIO) for new labor contracts to replace those expiring on February 15, 1947, began in January, 1947. The demands then presented by the Union included a "substantial wage increase," portal-to-portal pay, a union shop, a guaranteed annual wage, and premium pay for all work on Saturdays and Sundays, regardless of whether these days fell within the span of a forty-hour week.

At the outset of these negotiations, U. S. Steel proposed that the existing contracts be extended to April 30, 1947, for the purpose of providing additional time for effective collective bargaining and to permit time to elapse for clarification by the Congress or the courts of the portal-to-portal pay problem resulting from the decision of the U. S. Supreme Court in the Mt. Clemens Pottery Company case. This proposal was accepted by the Union and these labor contracts have been extended to April 30, 1947.

The management of U. S. Steel earnestly desires to do everything in its power to obtain full and sustained collaboration of its employes in a cooperative effort to attain the greatest degree of productivity, consonant with good labor practices, and to utilize to best advantage the full resources of U. S. Steel for the mutual benefit of all persons concerned.

The major steel and coal strikes, together with other strikes and work stoppages, combined to make 1946 perhaps the worst year in U. S. Steel's recent history in terms of manhours lost. The estimated loss of manhours during the year as a result of strikes and work stoppages is about 60 million contrasted with 6 million manhours so lost in 1945.

Profit and Loss Facts and Factors

In the first full year of business following the end of hostilities U. S. Steel's results were distorted by war influences. The dislocation of relationships arising from war will continue to be felt for some time. In 1946, during the periods of the year when its operations were free from strike interruptions, U. S. Steel produced at a level not exceeded in any other year of peace in its forty-six year history and the rate of its receipts from customers during this time was an all-time record for peacetime years. The factors behind the figures are more significant than the dollar results themselves. But, even taken without regard to the factors behind them, the figures reveal that the 1946 earnings were the lowest per dollar of sales of any peacetime year of comparable volume of shipments.

187

There are specific reasons why U. S. Steel's 1946 earnings were too low under existing conditions, and why in the future it should earn at better rates.

Cost and Price Changes — Subnormal earnings at high levels of operations were partly the result of the wartime dislocations of wages and prices that persisted into 1946. In the war period, increases in steel prices were severely limited by OPA restrictions while wage costs were greatly increased. As costs increased in one industry they spread to many other industries, largely by government dictation, and soon the prices of goods and services, such as scrap, tin and freight, which U. S. Steel must purchase to continue operations, increased. Meanwhile, steel prices advanced relatively less than the prices of these and other goods and services purchased. The finished steel composite price at the end of January, 1947, would have had to be 43 per cent higher than it actually was to have kept pace with the average advance since 1940 in the wholesale prices of all commodities as computed by the U. S. Bureau of Labor Statistics.

Volume — U. S. Steel cannot expect operations to continue indefinitely at present peak levels. It is characteristic of the steel business that the volume of steel shipments and receipts from customers are subject to wide fluctuations. In years of peace, U. S. Steel has used from as little as two-tenths to as much as nine-tenths of its capacity to produce steel. Owing to substantial fixed costs, which have to be incurred irrespective of the rate of operations, it is equally characteristic of the steel business, as shown in the accompanying charts, that its income is subject to even more violent fluctuation than is the volume of its

23

business. For example, income has ranged from a loss of more than twenty cents for every dollar of sales to a profit of nearly twenty cents for every dollar of sales.

The table on the opposite page compares U. S. Steel's results in 1946 — the first full year of peace — with the average results of earlier peacetime periods, and also with the average results of the five years of World War II.

This table clearly establishes that U. S. Steel's wartime profits in no way were excessive, or out of the ordinary — in fact, quite the contrary. During the five years of World War II, when U. S. Steel had record shipments of steel averaging more than 20 million tons a year, the profit per dollar of sales was only 4 cents. This was about one-fifth less per dollar of sales than earned on the average from 1919-1940 inclusive, although average shipments during the war were two-thirds more than the 1919-1940 average. The wartime profit of 4 cents per dollar of sales was 60 per cent less than the average profit per dollar of sales in five good peacetime years, although average shipments during the war were one-third more than the average of these five good peacetime years.

For the twenty-two years of peace between World Wars I and II, as well as for all of the forty-six years of U. S. Steel's history, its shipments of steel products averaged about 12 million tons a year. In 1946, U. S. Steel's shipments of steel products were more than 15 million tons — or one-fourth more than such long-term average. In spite of these increased shipments, U. S. Steel's profit per dollar of sales in 1946 was only 6 cents, or 40 per cent less than the average of 10 cents for the five peacetime years of approximately the same volume of shipments.

Good management seems to require that all reasonable action be taken in an attempt to improve U. S. Steel's earnings in times of high operations so that it may have the financial means to maintain itself during periods when customers' demand for steel is small, and thus best serve the nation at all times.

Reinvestment in the Business — Price suppression, increased costs and heavy taxation during the high volume wartime years prevented U. S. Steel from setting aside those amounts for reinvestment in the business which its experience indicates as desirable. If the record of the past is any measure of the future, U. S. Steel has entered a period of peace in which the long-term outlook is for the average use of about two-thirds of its capacity with relatively inadequate provision for future needs having been made during recent periods of maximum production.

Need for New Tools — Construction costs have generally increased by at least two-thirds over their prewar levels. The replacement of U. S. Steel's tools of production as they wear out, become outmoded and are used up will cost much more than did the existing tools of production unless wages and prices in general move downward substantially toward the prewar levels. The purchase of such tools at advanced prices cannot be financed, without borrowing, unless profits attain a better relationship to the volume of business than has been previously experienced.

Neither wartime strength nor progress toward better peacetime living standards can be assured unless profits over the years are sufficient to maintain the incentives to supply tools, employ workers and provide goods and services. This means that profits in years of large volume must compensate for lesser profit or loss in years of reduced volume.

PERIOD	SHIPMENTS (Million Tons)	OPERATING RATE (% of Capacity)	PROFIT (Per $ of Sales)
First Full Postwar Year . . . . . (1946)	15.2	73	$ .06
5 War Years . . . . (1941-1945)	20.1	94	.04
5 Good Years . . . . (1920, 1923, 1926, 1928, 1940)	15.5	86	.10
5 Poor Years . . . . (1921, 1931, 1932, 1933, 1934)	6.9	33	— .06 (Loss)
22 Peace Years . . . . (1919-1940)	12.0	64	.05

(Data compared with those of 1946 are averages of similar annual measurements.)

Consolidated Statement of Income

	1946	1945
PRODUCTS AND SERVICES SOLD	$1,496,064,326	$1,747,338,661
COSTS		
EMPLOYMENT COSTS		
Wages and salaries	679,353,429	778,391,800
Social Security taxes	15,986,855	18,081,595
Payments for pensions (details on p. 18)	9,120,897	28,975,958
	704,461,181	825,449,353
PRODUCTS AND SERVICES BOUGHT	589,606,301	672,728,198
WEAR AND EXHAUSTION OF FACILITIES		
Depletion and depreciation	71,400,608	77,140,359
Amortization of emergency facilities	—	44,215,710
Loss (profit) on sales of plant and equipment	2,661,434	2,064,848
	68,739,174	123,420,917
ADDITIONAL AMORTIZATION DUE TO ENDING OF EMERGENCY PERIOD, less associated Federal income tax adjustments	—	35,584,069
WAR COSTS INCLUDED HEREIN PROVIDED FOR IN PRIOR YEARS, less associated Federal income tax adjustments		
Additional amortization above	—	35,584,069
Strike costs	27,626,351	—
Other war costs	1,586,363	2,600,883
INTEREST AND OTHER COSTS ON LONG-TERM DEBT	4,777,135	3,500,653
STATE, LOCAL AND MISCELLANEOUS TAXES	37,070,774	36,825,367
ESTIMATED FEDERAL TAXES ON INCOME	32,000,000	30,000,000
TOTAL	1,407,441,851	1,689,323,605
INCOME	88,622,475	58,015,056
DIVIDENDS — On cumulative preferred stock ($7 per share)	25,219,677	25,219,677
On common stock ($4 per share)	34,813,008	34,813,008
INCOME REINVESTED IN BUSINESS		
ADDITION IN PERIOD	$ 28,589,790	—
REDUCTION IN PERIOD	—	$ 2,017,629

191

29

Federal Taxes on Income. Audit of Federal income and excess profits tax returns for 1941 and subsequent years has not been completed by the Bureau of Internal Revenue, and certain relatively small items for the years 1935 through 1940 have not been finally agreed upon with the taxing authorities. It is believed that reasonable provision has been made for any additional taxes which may be levied.

Securities Set Aside for Property Additions. Of the $250 million of segregated funds invested in government securities at December 31, 1945, for property additions, $110 million was used in 1946 in the purchase of facilities from the Government. Of this amount, $75 million was paid out, and $35 million was deposited under an escrow agreement against payment to be made on or before June 19, 1948. The balance of invested funds segregated for property additions, after deducting the cost of these facilities, is $140 million. On December 31, 1946, additional expenditures planned for property additions and replacements amounted to $277.5 million.

Estimated Additional Costs Arising Out of War. The cost of the steel and coal strikes which occurred during the first half of the year was $46,035,917. After deduction of associated Federal income taxes, the amount of these strike costs charged to the reserve for estimated additional costs arising out of war, which had been set aside during the war years, was $27,626,351. Other war costs representing inventory losses, deferred repairs and maintenance, and other expenditures, totaling $1,586,363, also were charged to this reserve. These charges and offsetting credits are included in the consolidated statement of income.

Plant and Equipment Valuation. The gross values at which plant and equipment are carried in the consolidated accounts have been de-termined from and based upon the findings of the United States Bureau of Corporations, and accepted by the Bureau of Internal Revenue of the Treasury Department, as at the initial date of organization of the Corporation in 1901, plus actual cost of additions since, and less credits for the cost of properties sold, retired or disposed of otherwise. The depreciated amount shown in the consolidated statement of financial position for plant and equipment represents that portion of the gross values which is a cost applicable to operations of future periods, and does not purport to be either a realizable or replacement value.

Insurance Reserve. The subsidiary companies are, for the most part, self-insurers of their assets against fire, windstorm, marine and related losses. The balance of the insurance reserve is held available for absorbing possible losses of this character, and is considered adequate for this purpose.

Portal-to-Portal Pay Suits. Late in 1946 and early in 1947 certain subsidiary companies were sued by unions and individuals for alleged past "portal-to-portal" pay liability. The amounts claimed in such suits are in excess of $500 million. No provision has been made for any possible liability under these claims.

Wages and Salaries. Wages and salaries for the year 1946 totaled $694,258,238. Of this amount, $679,353,429 was included in costs of products and services sold and the balance was charged to construction and other accounts.

Products and Services Bought. Included in the amount of products and services bought are the changes during the year in inventories and deferred costs. Such changes are not considered to be significant in relation to sales or total costs.

193

1947 ANNUAL REPORT

Only 2.7% of Sales Reinvested in Business

Purchasing Power of Dollar Much Lower than in 1940

An Additional $26.3 Million of Replacement Cost Depreciation Deducted

Original Cost Depreciation Inadequate

Replacement Cost Depreciation Compared to LIFO

Long-term Inventories Analogy Used

30% Factor Applied to Original Cost Depreciation

Price Waterhouse Says Replacement Cost Depreciation Not in Accordance with Generally Accepted Accounting

How U. S. Steel's 1947 Sales Dollar was Divided

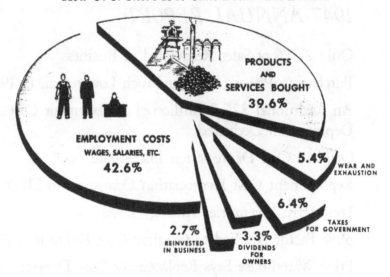

PRODUCTS AND SERVICES BOUGHT 39.6%

EMPLOYMENT COSTS
WAGES, SALARIES, ETC.
42.6%

5.4% WEAR AND EXHAUSTION

6.4% TAXES FOR GOVERNMENT

2.7% REINVESTED IN BUSINESS

3.3% DIVIDENDS FOR OWNERS

Income of United States Steel Corporation and subsidiaries for 1947 was $127.1 million after taxes, an increase of $38.5 million over the prior year when the income of the Corporation was affected adversely by serious steel and coal strikes. It will be recalled that these strikes in 1946 caused an estimated loss of 6.3 million tons of steel production to U. S. Steel and pulled down its average rate of steel making operations for the year to 72.9 per cent of rated capacity.

The income for the year 1947 is equivalent to a profit of six cents per dollar of sales, approximately the same return on the basis of sales as in 1946. This return of six per cent is the lowest for any peacetime year in the history of U. S. Steel when operations were near capacity. Such a return on sales is, for example, only slightly more than half of the average return on sales in 1920, 1923, 1926, 1928 and 1940.

U. S. Steel's profit in 1947 from all operations was $70 million less than in 1929, although in 1947 its sales were twice those of 1929. U. S. Steel's profit in 1947 of $127 million was $25 million more than it earned in 1940. However, in terms of the purchasing power of the 1940 dollar, the 1947 profit of $127 million was only $80 million, or one-fifth less than in 1940, and this despite much greater production in 1947.

U. S. Steel's relatively low earnings of six cents per dollar of sales in 1947 evidence the cumulative effect of rising costs in all fields of operation. As in the case of industry in general, U. S. Steel was faced during 1947 with this problem of rising costs. Wages, salaries and other employment costs continued to mount, as did the cost of the thousands of products and services bought by U. S. Steel.

In 1947, U. S. Steel derived a return of 7.4 per cent on its investment — total assets less liabilities other than long-term debt. The investment on which this return is computed is based on book values far below present replacement costs.

The above-mentioned income for 1947 reflects a cost of $26.3 million for the year covering wear and exhaustion of facilities in addition to a cost of $87.7 million for such wear and exhaustion based upon the original cost of facilities. This additional cost, although not presently deductible for income tax purposes, represents the judgment of the management of U. S. Steel as to what is advisable in view of the greatly increased present cost of facilities over the original cost of the facilities which are to be replaced.

During 1947, U. S. Steel paid four regular dividends of $1.75 a share on the cumulative preferred stock — aggregating $25.2 million — and total dividends of $5.00 a share on the common stock, aggregating $43.5 million. Dividends paid to the owners in 1947 represented about one-thirteenth of the year's payroll for U. S. Steel's employes.

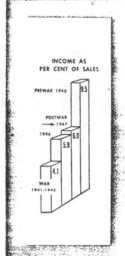

INCOME AS
PER CENT OF SALES

PREWAR 1940   9.5

POSTWAR
⟶ 1947
1946   6.0
               5.9

WAR
1941-1945   4.1

After declaration of dividends on the preferred and common stocks for the' year 1947, including those declared on January 27, 1948, there remained for reinvestment in the business $56.2 million, as compared with $28.6 million in 1946 when operations were on a substantially lower level.

Working capital of United States Steel Corporation and subsidiaries at December 31, 1947, after deducting dividends declared on January 27, 1948, and excluding the balance of funds segregated for property additions and war costs, was $548.7 million, compared with $629.1 million at December 31, 1946. The several factors causing this decrease of $80.4 million are fully set forth in the statement on page 30 of this report.

Long-term debt of U. S. Steel at December 31, 1947, was $77.2 million, excluding $5.7 million of bonds covered by deposits with trustees. Long-term indebtedness has been reduced to one-third of the amount in 1939 and is now the lowest in U. S. Steel's history.

5

Real Costs

The extent of real costs may be seriously obscured in periods of rapidly rising or falling wages and prices. Failure to establish and record the real costs in such periods weakens and may ultimately destroy the ability of a business to continue its job of profitably producing products and services for exchange. The period of 1940-1947 has been one of such marked increases in wages and prices.

Increased Wage Costs — In 1947, wages, salaries and other employment expenses accounted for 45 per cent of U. S. Steel's total costs. Since 1940, there has been a continual increase in the average hourly earnings of U. S. Steel's employes until — in December 1947 — the increase over 1940 was 80 per cent, as shown in the following table:

| | Increases Over 1940 | | | |
	5 War Years	1946	1947	December 1947
Average Hourly Earnings	29%	59%	73%	80%

Increased Cost of Products and Services Bought — In 1947, products and services bought accounted for 42 per cent of U. S. Steel's total costs. Since by far the major part of the total cost of all products and services in the nation is for wages and salaries, the advance from 1940 to the end of 1947 in general wage rates has been translated into higher prices for the things U. S. Steel must buy. Since 1940, it has been U. S. Steel's experience that every increase in hourly earnings has been followed shortly by a nearly equal percentage increase in the cost of products and services it must buy for its operations.

Increases in the costs of a few of the important items purchased by U. S. Steel are indicated by the following table:

| | Per Cent Increases Over 1940 | | | |
	5 War Years	1946	1947	December 1947
Zinc Ore	24	31	54	62
Copper	− 2	30	69	77
Tin	8	27	71	96
Fuel Oil	22	36	89	130
Scrap	7	32	75	93
Coke	28	58	91	111

Increased Cost of Replacing and Adding Facilities — Current construction costs likewise reflect the wage-price spiral. Merely to replace the tools of production (machinery, plants and mines) as they wear out requires, at present prices, an annual expenditure very much greater than the depreciation recovered on the basis of their original cost. The following table, based on virtually identical facilities acquired by U. S. Steel in 1940 and 1947, gives specific indication of how such costs have increased:

	Per Cent Increase 1947 Over 1940
Wire Drawing Machine	91
Standard Electric Crane	105
Reheating Furnace	108
Blast Furnace	105
By-Product Coke Ovens	150
Mine Locomotive	44
Large Electric Motor	50
Continuous Rolling Mill	84
Concrete Construction	124
Brick Construction	250

The cost of replacing existing tools and adding to plants and facilities continues to increase. For example, a new cold reduced sheet mill, authorized late in 1945 at an expenditure of $25,250,000 to expand capacity, is currently estimated to have a final cost of $43,220,000, or 71 per cent more than planned. Again, additional tin plate capacity, authorized late in 1945 at an expenditure of $13,250,000, is currently estimated to have a final cost of $19,542,000, or 47 per cent more than planned. The increase since 1940 in construction costs, as measured by the *Engineering News—Record* index shown in the accompanying chart, has been as follows:

	Increases Over 1940			
	5 War Years	1946	1947	December 1947
Cost of Construction	18%	43%	68%	79%

Construction costs continue to advance. Because of the upward trend of such costs, it is necessary continuously to revise upward the amounts initially estimated to complete projects under way. Thus merely to meet the increase in construction costs since original authorizations of facilities under way at December 31, 1947, U. S. Steel had to add $77 million to the amounts estimated initially. The amount necessary to complete all authorizations for additions to and replacements of facilities, including the $77 million, was $350 million at December 31, 1947.

Recording These Increases — These rising wages and prices mean that sums greater than originally expended must be spent currently to replace short-term inventories (stocks of goods) and long-term inventories (machinery, plants and mines) used up in production. Such additional amounts for replacement, required to be spent if production is to be sustained, must be recorded as a cost of doing business if overstatement of profits and dissipation of capital are to be avoided.

Short-Term Inventories — An accepted procedure for determining the cost of short-term inventories is the last-in, first-out method. This method recognizes fluctuations in the purchasing power of the dollar by reflecting current costs of employment and purchases — whatever the price change — in the cost of products currently sold. It is the most acceptable method yet developed of recording in costs purchasing power equivalent to that originally expended. It became a generally accepted accounting practice, legislatively recognized for tax purposes, many years after the heavy inventory losses experienced following World War I — a previous period of marked price changes.

U. S. Steel in 1941 substituted the last-in, first-out method of determining the cost of its major classifications of inventories for the average cost method previously used when prices were relatively stable. In 1942 and 1947, as it became practicable to do so,

Tools for Workers Cost More

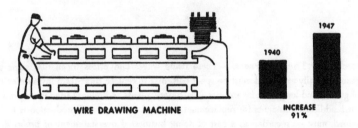

WIRE DRAWING MACHINE

1940

1947

INCREASE
91%

202

this method was extended to certain other inventories. Thus U. S. Steel's inventories, for the most part, are priced in 1940 dollars. By this change in method, rising wages and prices currently incurred by U. S. Steel to reproduce what is sold are recorded as cost and not as increased inventory valuation and seeming profit.

Long-Term Inventories – Believing that the same principle of recording the cost of short-term inventories consumed is applicable to recording the cost of long-term inventories consumed (wear and exhaustion of machinery, plants and mines), U. S. Steel in 1947 increased its provision for wear and exhaustion from $87.7 million based on original cost to $114.0 million, or by 30 per cent. This was a step toward stating wear and exhaustion in an amount which will recover in current dollars of diminished buying power the same purchasing power as the original expenditure.

If a business is to continue, it is necessary to recover the purchasing power of sums originally invested in tools so that they may be replaced as they wear out. Therefore, this added amount is carried as a reserve for replacement of properties. It is a simple truth that to buy similar tools of production takes many more dollars today than formerly; to count as profits, rather than as cost, the added sums required merely to sustain production is to retreat from reality into self-deception.

The 30 per cent increase in the provision for wear and exhaustion was determined partly through experienced cost increases and partly through study of construction cost index numbers. Although it is materially less than the experienced cost increase in replacing worn-out facilities, it was deemed appropriate in view of the newness of the application of this principle to the costing of wear and exhaustion. The use of index numbers for cost purposes gained recognition early in 1947 in a Tax Court decision in Hutzler Brothers Company, Petitioner v. Commissioner of Internal Revenue, Respondent. Although this case deals only with costing short-term inventories, the principles set forth are just as applicable to costing the wear and exhaustion of long-term inventories.

While awaiting accounting and tax acceptance, U. S. Steel believed that it was prudent for it to give some recognition to these increased replacement costs rather than to sit idly by and witness the unwitting liquidation of its business should inadequate recording of costs result in insufficient resources to supply the tools required for sustained production.

203

Cost-Price Balance — The discovery and measurement of real costs are not the end of the story. Knowing costs and covering costs are not the same thing. It is the balancing of real costs with competitive prices that determines whether the production and exchange of products and services in the end are to walk in step with the depreciation of the dollar.

How Steel Prices Have Lagged Behind Steel Wages

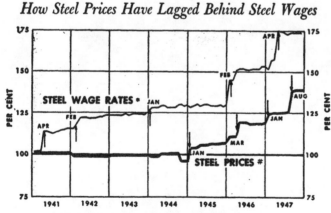

* Straight Time Hourly Earnings — Steel Manufacturing Operations (U S. Steel).
\# Composite Base Price of Finished Steel (Iron Age).

	1947	1946
PRODUCTS AND SERVICES SOLD	$2,122,786,243	$1,496,064,326
COSTS		
EMPLOYMENT COSTS		
Wages and salaries	872,496,549	679,353,429
Social Security taxes	20,663,936	15,986,855
Payments for pensions *(details on p. 18)*	10,402,279	9,120,897
	903,562,764	704,461,181
PRODUCTS AND SERVICES BOUGHT	841,915,356	589,606,301
WEAR AND EXHAUSTION OF FACILITIES		
Based on original cost	87,745,483	68,739,174
Added to cover replacement cost	26,300,000	—
	114,045,483	68,739,174
WAR COSTS INCLUDED HEREIN PROVIDED FOR IN PRIOR YEARS, less associated Federal income tax adjustments		
Strike costs	—	27,626,351
Other war costs	2,540,618	1,586,363
INTEREST AND OTHER COSTS ON LONG-TERM DEBT	2,507,729	4,777,135
STATE, LOCAL AND MISCELLANEOUS TAXES	45,197,381	37,070,774
ESTIMATED FEDERAL TAXES ON INCOME	91,000,000	32,000,000
TOTAL	1,995,688,095	1,407,441,851
INCOME	127,098,148	88,622,475
DIVIDENDS DECLARED		
On cumulative preferred stock *($7 per share)*	25,219,677	25,219,677
On common stock *($5.25 per share 1947, $4 per share 1946)*	• 45,692,073	34,813,008
INCOME REINVESTED IN BUSINESS	$ 56,186,398	$ 28,589,790

205

206

Inventories. Beginning in 1941 and 1942, the last-in, first-out method of determining costs was applied to major classifications of inventories of steel producing subsidiaries. This method was extended to certain other subsidiaries and to other inventory items as at January 1, 1947. As a result of this extension of such principle, inventories as at December 31, 1947, affected thereby are approximately $10 million less, and income for the year 1947 is $6 million less, than they would have been under the average cost method previously followed with respect to these particular inventories.

Federal Taxes on Income. Audit of Federal income and excess profits tax returns for 1941 and subsequent years has not been completed by the Bureau of Internal Revenue, and certain relatively small items for the years 1935 through 1940 have not been finally agreed upon with the taxing authorities. It is believed that reasonable provision has been made for any additional taxes which may be levied.

Securities Set Aside for Property Additions and Replacements. In 1947, $15 million of United States Government securities was segregated from current assets and was added to the balance of $140 million previously set aside for property additions and replacements. On December 31, 1947, additional expenditures planned for property additions and replacements amounted to approximately $350 million.

Plant and Equipment Valuation. The gross values at which plant and equipment are carried in the consolidated accounts have been determined from and based upon the findings of the United States Bureau of Corporations, and accepted by the Bureau of Internal Revenue of the Treasury Department, as at the initial date of organization of the Corporation in 1901, plus actual cost of additions since, and less credits for the cost of properties sold, retired or disposed of otherwise. The depreciated amount shown in the consolidated statement of financial position for plant and equipment represents that portion of the gross values which is a cost applicable to operations of future periods, and does not purport to be either a realizable or replacement value.

Reserve for Estimated Additional Costs Arising Out of War. Of the reserve for estimated additional costs arising out of war, provided during the war years, $2,540,618 was used in 1947 to cover the higher costs of replacing inventories depleted during the war. This charge and offsetting credit are included in the consolidated statement of income.

Insurance Reserve. The subsidiary companies are, for the most part, self-insurers of their assets against fire, windstorm, marine and related losses. The balance of the insurance reserve is held available for absorbing possible losses of this character, and is considered adequate for this purpose.

Wages and Salaries. Wages and salaries for 1947 totaled $890,112,230. Of this amount, $872,496,549 was included in costs of products and services sold and the balance was charged to construction and other accounts.

Products and Services Bought. Included in products and services bought are the changes during the year in inventories and deferred costs. Such changes are not considered to be significant in relation to sales or total costs.

Wear and Exhaustion of Facilities. Wear and exhaustion of facilities of $114,045,483 includes $87,745,483 based on original cost of such facilities and $26,300,000 added to cover replacement cost. The added amount is 30 per cent of provisions based on original cost, and is a step toward stating wear and exhaustion in an amount which will recover in current dollars of diminished buying power the same purchasing power as the original expenditure. Because it is necessary to recover the purchasing power of sums originally invested in tools so that they may be replaced as they wear out, this added amount is carried as a reserve for replacement of properties. The 30 per cent was determined partly through experienced cost increases and partly through study of construction cost index numbers. Although it is materially less than the experienced cost increase in replacing worn out facilities, it was deemed appropriate in view of the newness of the application of this principle to the costing of wear and exhaustion.

Independent
Auditors' Report

PRICE, WATERHOUSE & CO.

56 PINE STREET

NEW YORK 5

To the Stockholders of
United States Steel Corporation:

As independent auditors elected at the annual meeting of stockholders of United States Steel Corporation held on May 5, 1947, we have examined the consolidated statement of financial position of United States Steel Corporation and subsidiaries as at December 31, 1947, and the consolidated statement of income for the year 1947. Our examination was made in accordance with generally accepted auditing standards and included such tests of the accounting records and other supporting evidence and such other procedures as we considered necessary in the circumstances.

The corporation extended the application of the last-in, first-out method of inventory valuation which it adopted in 1941-42 to certain other subsidiaries and to other inventory items as at January 1, 1947. As a result of this extension of such principle, inventories as at December 31, 1947, affected thereby are approximately $10,000,000 less, and income for the year 1947 is $6,000,000 less, than they would have been under the average cost method previously followed with respect to these particular inventories.

During the year 1947, in partial recognition of the increased replacement cost of long-term facilities which are being worn out or exhausted in production, the corporation has included in costs additional depreciation of $26,300,000 (as indicated in the notes to the accounts) in excess of the amount determined in accordance with the generally accepted accounting principle heretofore followed of making provision for depreciation on the original cost of facilities.

In our opinion, except as set forth in the preceding paragraph, the accompanying consolidated statement of financial position and related statement of income, together with the notes thereto, present fairly the position of United States Steel Corporation and its subsidiaries at December 31, 1947, and the results of the year's operations in conformity with generally accepted accounting principles. Except as indicated in the two preceding paragraphs, the accounting principles were applied during the year on a basis consistent with that of the preceding year.

Price, Waterhouse & Co.

New York, March 2, 1948.

1948 ANNUAL REPORT

Pressure Exerted by SEC on U. S. Steel

AIA's Position Supported by SEC

U. S. Steel Adopts Accelerated Depreciation

Price Waterhouse Approves of Accelerated Depreciation

Wear and Exhaustion — In its accounts for 1947, U. S. Steel reflected in the total wear and exhaustion for the year an amount of $26.3 million in addition to the normal depreciation based on original cost of its facilities. This added amount, which represented 30 per cent of the normal depreciation, was determined partly through experienced cost increases and partly through study of construction cost index numbers. Although it was materially less than the experienced cost increase in replacing worn-out facilities. it was a step toward stating total wear and exhaustion in an amount which would recover in current dollars of diminished buying power the same purchasing power as the original expenditure.

This principle was continued during the first three quarters of 1948. In view of the continued increase in the cost of goods and facilities during 1948, the additional charge for wear and exhaustion was advanced, effective as of January 1, 1948, to 60 per cent of the depreciation based upon original cost, because the 30 per cent initially adopted was not sufficient to cover the true cost of property currently consumed.

In the release of the accounts for the third quarter of 1948, it was stated that, in view of the position taken by the American Institute of Accountants and the discussions between the Corporation and the Securities and Exchange Commission, further study was being made in an effort to agree upon principles satisfactory to the Commission for determining and reflecting additional wear and exhaustion cost.

U. S. Steel believes that the principle which it adopted in 1947 and continued in 1948 is a proper recording of the wear and exhaustion of its facilities in terms of current dollars as distinguished from the dollars which it originally expended for those facilities. However, in view of the disagreement existing among accountants, both public and private, and the stated position of the American Institute of Accountants, which is supported by the Securities and Exchange Commission, that the only accepted accounting principle for determining depreciation is that which is related to the actual number of dollars spent for facilities, regardless of when or of what buying power, U. S. Steel has adopted a method of accelerated depreciation on cost instead of one based on purchasing power recovery. This method is made retroactive to January 1, 1947. The amount of the accelerated depreciation for the year 1948 is $55,335,444, including a deficiency of $2,675,094 in the amount reported in 1947 as depreciation added to cover replacement cost. Such accelerated depreciation is not presently deductible for Federal income tax purposes.

211

INDEPENDENT AUDITORS' REPORT

PRICE, WATERHOUSE & CO.

56 PINE STREET

NEW YORK 5

To the Stockholders of
United States Steel Corporation:

As independent auditors elected at the annual meeting of stock-holders of United States Steel Corporation held on May 3, 1948, we have examined the consolidated statement of financial position of United States Steel Corporation and subsidiaries as at December 31, 1948, and the consolidated statement of income for the year 1948. Our examination was made in accordance with generally accepted auditing standards and accordingly included such tests of the accounting records and such other auditing procedures as we considered necessary in the circumstances.

During the year 1948 (as stated in the notes to the accounts) the Corporation adopted a policy, which we approve, of accelerating depreciation on the cost of new facilities retroactive to January 1, 1947. Under this policy the accelerated depreciation for the year 1947 is $28,975,094 or $2,675,094 more than the amount reported for the year as depreciation added to cover replacement cost. The amount of $55,335,444 provided for accelerated depreciation in 1948 includes this adjustment of $2,675,094. In all other respects the accounting principles were applied during the year on a basis consistent with that of the preceding year.

In our opinion, the accompanying consolidated statement of financial position and related statement of income, together with the notes thereto, present fairly the position of United States Steel Corporation and its subsidiaries at December 31, 1948, and the results of the year's operations in conformity with generally accepted accounting principles.

Price, Waterhouse & Co.

New York, February 23, 1949.

1949 ANNUAL REPORT

"Pot of Gold" Fallacy Attacked
Normal Depreciation Dollars Stressed
Tax Laws Cause Increased Borrowings
Income % Well Under U. S. Steel History

Financial Summary

The "Pot of Gold" Fallacy

THERE is a basic misconception of the meaning of accounting terms that is serious and widespread. Thus many people have been led to believe that the amount by which corporate income exceeds dividends — so-called undistributed profit — represents a stagnant pool of cash purchasing power, a "pot of gold," that has been "siphoned off" from the public. This is not true. It is a myth. The myth, nevertheless, becomes the basis for supposing that there is some sort of social responsibility to get the supposed "pot of gold" restored to the country's purchasing power flows. The supposed social responsibility is conveniently aligned with the self-interest of those who pretend that purchasing power flows would be increased by profit-sacrificing price reductions. That is why they confuse profit amounts with "pots of gold" and pretend the profit is bigger than it is.

Circulation of Cash

The fact is, of course, that so-called undistributed profit does not constitute a stagnant pool of cash buying power; on the contrary, undistributed profit is one of the names or tags that accountants put on buying power that has probably already been distributed.

In the case of U. S. Steel, undistributed profit, more properly designated "income re-invested," represents dollars that have been spent just as much as the dollars labeled wages have been spent. It is a grave mistake to assume that undistributed profit as recorded at the end of the year — or at any other time — constitutes a convenient pool of cash on which to lay hands for any purpose.

The continuous circulation of cash into, through and out of U. S. Steel during 1949 can be better understood by reference to the statement appearing below. This state-

Cash Flow — In and Out — Year 1949   (In Millions)

	Sales, Costs and Income	Adjustment to Cash Basis		Total Cash Receipts and Disbursement
		Explanation	Amount	
Receipts From Customers—The Public	$2,301.7	Add – Proceeds from sales of properties . . . Decrease in uncollected receivables . .	$ 4.2 23.4	$2,329.3
Disposed of as Follows EMPLOYMENT COSTS U. S. Steel's direct employment . .	931.7	Add – Decrease in unpaid employment costs .	4.8	936.5

PRODUCTS AND SERVICES BOUGHT
  Provides employment by suppliers
    and by their suppliers in turn . .
	899.9	Add – Payment of war costs and other items
		  charged reserves . . . .
		Increase in inventories and deferred
		  costs . . . .
		Decrease in amounts owed to suppliers .
			7.9
			
			33.7
			39.7
				981.2

WEAR AND EXHAUSTION
  Provides employment by suppliers of
    new plants and equipment
    and by their suppliers in turn . .
	119.7	Add – Use of proceeds from sales of properties .
		Other amounts expended . . . .
		Total expenditures for property additions
		  and replacements . . . .
			4.2
			55.2
				179.1

TAXES
  Provides employment by governments
    and by their suppliers in turn
    State, local and miscellaneous }
    Federal income . . . . . }
	182.2	Add – Decrease in unpaid taxes	2.6	184.8

INTEREST
  Compensation for savings loaned . }
DIVIDENDS
  Compensation for savings invested }
	83.6	Add – Decrease in unpaid dividends . . . .
		Repayment of borrowed money . . . . . .
			2.6
			5.6
				86.2
				5.6

TOTALS	2,217.1		$156.3	2,373.4
INCOME REINVESTED	$ 84.6	*Deficit* in cash		$ 44.1

		Met from
		  Sale of Government securities . . . . .
		Decrease in cash funds
		  Balance January 1, 1949 . . $225.4
		  Balance December 31, 1949 . 210.4
			$ 29.1
			
			15.0
				$ 44.1

Spent for Facilities vs. Wear and Exhaustion and Income Reinvested

POSTWAR PERIOD
September 30, 1945 — December 31, 1949

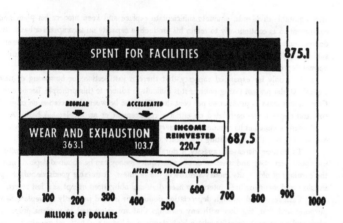

SPENT FOR FACILITIES 875.1

REGULAR   ACCELERATED

WEAR AND EXHAUSTION 363.1   103.7   INCOME REINVESTED 220.7   687.5

AFTER 40% FEDERAL INCOME TAX

0   100   200   300   400   500   600   700   800   900   1000

MILLIONS OF DOLLARS

ment shows, in the first column of figures, U. S. Steel's regular income statement and then shows its recasting to give an accounting, in the last column, of all the cash that came into and went out of U. S. Steel in the year.

The statement shows that despite an income reinvested of $84.6 million, U. S. Steel's cash disbursements in 1949 exceeded, by $44.1 million, its receipts from customers.

The $93.1 million of cash required for the increase in inventories and for property additions and replacements in excess of amounts covered by wear and exhaustion alone exceeded the $84.6 million of income reinvested.

Modernizing and Replacing Facilities

U. S. Steel's expenditures for properties have been far more for modernizing and replacing its facilities than for expanding its basic capacity.

U. S. Steel believes that a manufacturer should be able to recover out of receipts from customers, through depreciation and through income remaining for reinvestment after equitable dividends, amounts sufficient to replace and keep modern his plant and equipment so as continuously to retain his productive capacity on a competitive basis. By depreciation is meant depreciation on either a replacement or an accelerated basis whereby sufficient dollars are recovered currently to provide the same purchasing power as so-called normal depreciation dollars commanded when they were initially expended.

It is only for expanded capacity that there is justification for borrowing or new capital. Under present taxing policies it is difficult to adhere to this principle, because the Government taxes as profit at 40 per cent the difference between depreciation on original cost and depreciation calculated on either a replacement or an accelerated basis. As a result many companies have found it necessary to borrow merely to replace facilities which are wearing out, thereby diluting the equity of present investors.

To finance increased capacity a durable goods manufacturer should, if possible, use equity securities; and whether or not new equity money can be obtained depends upon the earnings of old equity money already in the business. A durable goods manufacturer should avoid incurring fixed interest or fixed dividend obligations except as a last resort.

Cash recovered through depreciation deductions is used primarily for replacement purposes and that, together with any earnings that are reinvested in modern property, plant and equipment, provides jobs, a high standard of living and national security in case of emergency.

Peacetime Per Cent Income of Sales
vs. Per Cent of Capacity Operated

(Years arranged in order of per cent of capacity operated)

Year of Operation	Per Cent of Capacity Operated	Per Cent Income of Sales	Year of Operation	Per Cent of Capacity Operated	Per Cent Income of Sales
AFTER WORLD WAR II			1909	77.8	17.9
1947	96.7	6.0	1919	77.0	6.8
1948	93.8	5.2	1904	72.8	9.3
1949	82.5	7.2	1924	72.2	9.2
1946	72.9	5.9	1937	71.9	9.2
AVERAGE	86.5	6.1	1922	70.9	4.9
			1911	70.5	12.8
BEFORE WORLD WAR II			AVERAGE	74.7	10.8
90% to 100%					
1906	100.6	20.3	60% to 70%		
1902	97.2	21.3	1930	67.2	12.6
1905	93.2	16.8	1936	63.4	6.4
1929	90.4	18.0	1914	62.3	5.7
1913	90.1	14.5	1939	61.0	4.9
AVERAGE	94.3	18.2	AVERAGE	63.5	7.4
80% to 90%					
1912	89.8	10.2	40% to 60%		
1923	89.1	9.9	1908	50.3	13.8
1926	89.1	10.8	1921	48.3	5.0
1907	88.6	20.7	1935	40.7	0.2
1920	86.2	8.5	AVERAGE	46.4	6.3
1915	85.2	14.5			
1928	84.6	11.4	Under 40%		
1940	82.5	9.5	1931	37.5	2.4
1903	81.8	13.9	1938	36.4	− 1.3
1925	81.7	8.9	1934	31.7	− 5.1
AVERAGE	85.9	11.8	1933	29.4	− 9.7
			1932	17.7	−24.7
70% to 80%			AVERAGE	30.5	− 7.7
1927	79.8	9.2			
1910	79.5	17.8	AVERAGE BEFORE WORLD WAR II	70.8	8.8

1950 ANNUAL REPORT

$50 Million Additional Pension Funding for Past Service Costs

$53 Million Jump in Regular Contribution

Employee Insurance Costs Rise $10.5 Million

222

Employe benefits

U. S. Steel's cost of pensions, social security taxes, insurance and other employe benefits in 1950 compared with 1949 as follows:

Pension costs	1950	1949
Non-contributory part of Pension Plan		
Funding of current service cost.......$	56,273,653	$ 3,465,039
Funding of portion of past service cost.	50,000,000	—
Contributory part of Pension Plan........	2,707,552	3,664,885
Total for pensions	108,981,205	7,129,924
Social security taxes...	24,017,465	18,198,462
Insurance costs........	11,047,532	567,272
Payments to industry welfare and retirement funds for other employe benefits	16,804,125	13,592,725
Total cost of benefits .....$	160,850,327	$39,488,383

The material increases in 1950 in pension and insurance costs resulted from basic revisions in previously existing plans. These revisions became effective in 1950, following

14

stockholders' approval on February 27, 1950, pursuant to the agreements concluded on November 11, 1949, between certain subsidiaries of U. S. Steel and the United Steelworkers of America (CIO).

Under the U. S. Steel Pension Plan in effect during 1950, pensions were granted to 4,024 retiring employes. At the end of the year there were 14,445 former employes receiving pensions.

Under the U. S. Steel insurance plans, beneficiaries of 1,425 employes received death benefits of approximately $5.5 million in 1950. Other benefits of approximately $7.0 million also were paid to employes or their families under the insurance plans. At the end of the year about 252,000 employes were covered under U. S. Steel insurance plans.

1954 ANNUAL REPORT

Capital Expenditures Crucial

Depreciation Held to be Source of Funds

Construction Price Rise 160% Since 1940

Taxation of Capital Occurring

New Tax Changes Not Enough

Financial Summary
•
DEPRECIATION EXPEDIENTS

The money that industry spends for plant and equipment is important to a high level of employment. Not only does this money result in employment of those who produce the facilities, but once the facilities are installed they provide the continuing jobs of operating them. Stop such capital expenditures and not only is creation of new jobs cut off, but existing jobs are imperiled as existing facilities become worn out or obsolete and are not replaced. The factors impairing or encouraging capital expenditures for facilities are of vital importance.

Sources of Funds

One of the principal sources of funds spent for facilities is the money recovered through the wear and exhaustion cost of existing facilities — often called depreciation. This depreciation in any period represents that portion of the capital originally expended which is used up in the production of products in such period. Depreciation is properly regarded as a cost that is deductible in determining taxable income. Inadequate depreciation is a direct threat to capital expenditures and to employment.

With regard to the adequacy of depreciation we are faced with a disturbing fact: Since World War II, depreciation amounts as ordinarily calculated and recognized in tax laws have been quite insufficient to buy new facilities as fast as existing ones have been wearing out or becoming obsolete. These amounts have failed to perform their vital revolving-fund function of maintaining the supply and modernness of the tools of production.

The reason is this: The total number of dollars that can be recovered in depreciation over the life of a given facility is limited to the number of dollars originally expended for the facility. But the buying power of the dollar has not remained at all stable. According to the *Engineering News-Record*, it now takes $2.60 to buy as much construction as could be purchased for $1.00 in 1940. The buying power of the dollar during the years since 1940 has shrunk to 40 per cent of what it was. The depreciation dollars recovered today, based on the dollars spent many years ago for facilities, are simply not enough dollars to replace those facilities — not enough dollars to equal the buying power originally expended for those facilities.

The other principal source of funds, aside from borrowing or from selling stock, that corporations have to modernize or purchase tools of

production is income reinvested. If depreciation does not recover enough buying power, the income "after taxes" may have to be drawn upon to make up the difference if expenditures for facilities are to be sufficient to maintain the aggregate tool-life of the concern.

This is unfair and unfortunate because it results in the taxation of capital. Thus, if depreciation cost is understated in current buying power, then income is correspondingly overstated. If the income tax rate is 50 per cent then two additional dollars must be secured from customers to have one additional dollar after taxes to spend on facilities. This is tax absorption of the circulating flow of capital funds required to maintain the supply and modernness of the nation's tools of production.

Accelerated Amortization

During World War II and the Korean conflict, inflation undermined the buying power of depreciation dollars, while price controls and high taxation limited the availability of reinvestment funds. The problem of funds for facilities became acute. To avert disaster there was legislation to provide, not that ordinary depreciation amounts could be adjusted to take into account the shrinking buying power of the dollar, but that portions of the cost of new facilities certified as necessary to the national defense could, instead of being spread over the expected useful life of the facility, be absorbed as "accelerated amortization" within the sixty months following completion of the facility, such accelerated amortization being deductible in determining income subject to taxation.

The effect of this provision was to permit the business taxpayer greater wear and exhaustion allowances in the early years of a facility's life, with the greater amount of cash recovered through such allowances being currently available to meet the higher cost of needed facility

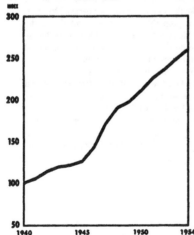

CONSTRUCTION COST INDEX

1940 = 100

Source: Engineering News-Record

228

24

replacements. For example, assume that 60 per cent of the cost of a 25-year life facility was subject to amortization and the balance to regular depreciation at 4 per cent per year. The recovery of the original expenditure through amortization and regular depreciation is 68 per cent thereof in the initial sixty-month period or the first 20 per cent of its life.

There can be no doubt that this provision was most helpful in stimulating national defense construction. The opportunity to recover capital expended on new facilities more quickly without eroding taxation produced a remarkable response. For example, business expenditures (excluding agricultural businesses) for plant and equipment totaled $83 billion during the four years, 1947-1950, which preceded the expansion made necessary by the Korean conflict. In the four following years (with the 1954 amount being partly estimated) the corresponding total was $107 billion — an increase of $24 billion. During the latter four years certificates of necessity covering approximately $30 billion were issued. By the end of 1954 actual expenditures on these certified projects approximated

$22 billion. Expenditures on certified projects thus were almost the same as the increase in the four-year expenditures over the 1947-1950 total.

Although accelerated amortization has thus proved effective, it must equally be recognized as a temporary expedient. For many companies the addition of amortization on new facilities to so-called regular depreciation on old facilities may approximate, temporarily, a truer total of wear and exhaustion on all facilities based on current dollar values. But it automatically guarantees something of a future crisis.

Thus U. S. Steel has recently constructed the Fairless Works. Parts of the cost are being amortized over 5-year periods. U. S. Steel has many other facilities on which there is no accelerated amortization. The amortization on Fairless Works partially offsets the inadequate depreciation allowed on other facilities, a situation which of course changes when the 5-year amortizations are completed.

New Methods of Accelerating Depreciation

Partly in recognition of prospective deficiency in depreciation when industry's accelerated amor-

CAPITAL EXPENDITURES
BY ALL BUSINESSES
(EXCLUDING AGRICULTURE)

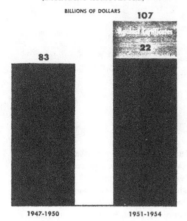

COMPARISON OF
CUMULATIVE DEPRECIATION
(FIRST 5 YEARS OF 25-YEAR LIFE)

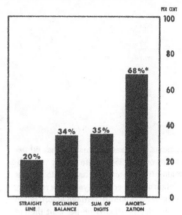

*Assumes 60% of cost subject to amortization

tization amounts "run out," the Revenue Act of 1954 provides two new optional methods whereby regular depreciation on new facilities may be accelerated. Both methods permit greater proportions of expenditures to be recovered in the earlier than in the later part of the facilities' lives. In the case of the 25-year life facility previously cited, 35 per cent of the dollars originally expended may be recovered in the first five years under the "sum-of-the-years' digits" method, and 34 per cent under the "declining-balance" method. These contrast with the previously noted 68 per cent under accelerated amortization during the same period.

For many companies the new provisions may serve for a time to lift total wear and exhaustion to an amount approximating true depreciation based on current dollars, provided serious further inflation is avoided. Although the 5-year recovery through depreciation under these methods is only about one-half of that under accelerated amortization in the examples given, the new methods may be applied to all expenditures for new facilities, whereas accelerated amortization is applicable only to those portions of new facilities that have been certified as necessary to national defense.

For other companies, however, the new provisions must for a period fall far short of yielding proper wear and exhaustion amounts. Such companies are like those in the steel, cement and railroad industries where relatively large amounts of capital have to be invested in costly long-term facilities. If additional depreciation is to be confined to new facilities, then larger amounts than have been provided under these two methods on such new facilities are required adequately to augment so-called regular depreciation on the relatively more numerous and older existing facilities.

Such a prospective depreciation dilemma is illustrated in the affairs of U. S. Steel. Total wear and exhaustion in 1954 was approximately $260 million. Of this amount about $140 million represented accelerated amortization and $120 million so-called regular depreciation. In future years necessary expenditures for replacing and modernizing facilities may range somewhere near the 1954 wear and exhaustion amount. Thus in a few years, when the accelerated amortization amounts arising out of present certificates will have substantially dropped out, there would then arise a large gap between wear and exhaustion totals and these necessary expenditures for facilities. The new sum-of-the-years' digits or declining-balance methods of depreciation will be inadequate for many years to fill this gap. It can be seen that even if there were to be as much as a 50 per cent increase in so-called regular depreciation it would still leave the total wear and exhaustion amount much smaller than such expenditures.

It is, of course, possible that before such a critical situation develops a fundamental solution of the problem of accounting for depreciation over periods of dollar instability may have been achieved and recognized in the tax laws or additional expedients may have been devised. Failing that, U. S. Steel and many other concerns will have to secure funds for capital expenditures from other sources if the supply and modernness of tools is to be maintained. If such funds come from income reinvested, then prices of products sold will have to be sufficient to cover the heavy taxation, as previously noted, of what is really depreciation but under tax law is considered taxable income.

The situation and prospect with respect to depreciation are such as to demand the most thoughtful consideration of business managements and of those responsible for determining accounting and tax policies.

231

1955 ANNUAL REPORT

No Disclosure of Current Market Value of Securities Held by Pension Trusts

Pension Fund Receipts Far Ahead of Payments

STATEMENT of ASSETS

	Dec. 31, 1955	Dec. 31, 1954
Investments, at cost or amortized cost (less than aggregate market or estimated fair value) *(details on page 40)*	$757,882,395	$628,120,092
Cash	2,664,179	2,589,041
Accrued interest and other receivables	5,162,444	4,218,319
Contributions receivable from employing companies in subsequent period	17,146,289	19,622,944
Payables	*145,489*	*908,080*
Assets	782,709,818	653,642,316
Reserves for investments	22,344,000	15,389,473
Assets, less reserves	$760,365,818	$638,252,843

235

STATEMENT of CHANGES DURING the YEAR

	Year 1955	Year 1954
Balance at beginning of year	$638,252,843	$534,206,415
Additions		
Receipts from employing companies	115,473,787	102,132,380
Receipts from participating employes	4,806,205	3,748,343
Income from investments	23,618,540	19,255,901
Gain on disposition of investments	2,839,556	2,587,399
	784,990,931	661,930,438
Deductions		
Pension payments	16,357,522	13,329,806
Refunds to withdrawing employes (including interest)	452,727	390,328
Administrative expenses	860,337	745,968
Transfers to reserves for investments	6,954,527	9,211,493
	24,625,113	23,677,595
Balance at end of year	$760,365,818	$638,252,843

To the Board of Directors of
United States Steel and Carnegie Pension Fund:

We have examined the above combined statements of the pension trusts administered as trustee by the United States Steel and Carnegie Pension Fund. Our examination was made in accordance with generally accepted auditing standards and included confirmation of the cash and investments owned at December 31, 1955 by certificates obtained from the depositaries and custodians, or by inspection, and such tests of the accounting records and such other auditing procedures as we considered necessary in the circumstances.

In our opinion, the above statements, together with the summary of investments shown on page 40, present fairly the combined assets of these pension trusts at December 31, 1955 and the changes therein during the year.

New York 5, N. Y.
February 28, 1956

Price Waterhouse & Co.

39

1958 ANNUAL REPORT

$496 Million Past Service Cost in 1950

Recession Causes Reversal of Prior Funding Practice

$61 Million Switched from Past Service Cost Contribution to Current Contribution

U. S. Steel Subject to Double the Average Effect of Business Swing

Corporate Incentive Undermined

Sharp Downward Trend of Profits

Shrinking Profits and Mounting Unemployment Tied Together

Dividends Only ½₀ of Wages

"Surplus" Misleads Many

$1,493 Million More Spent on New Tools of Production than Total of Depreciation for 1946–1958

$1,050 Million of That Caused by Inflation

Inflation Causes Deficiency in Depreciation

"Phantom Profit" Present

Income "Squeeze" Occurring

America and Russia Contrasted

Price Waterhouse Notes $47 Million Lack of Comparability in Net Income

and other employe benefits in the years 1958 and 1957 are shown on page 21.

Pension trusts

The sums shown in the table for the current service costs of pensions are determined by an independent actuary as the present value of that part of prospective future pensions to which present employes, as a group, may become entitled by reason of service rendered during the year.

The amount for past service cost applies against the actuarial cost of non-contributory pensions for service rendered prior to March 1, 1950, the effective date of the present plan. The cost which had not been funded at that date was then estimated at $496 million. For each year 1950 through 1957, U. S. Steel has funded the annual current service cost of pensions, including interest on past service cost, and in addition has paid the approximate maximum permitted by United States Treasury Department tax regulations against past service cost. Such additional payments totaled $297 million to December 31, 1957. In view of these earlier payments the Board of Directors, in the exercise of its discretion with respect to making financial provision for pension costs, determined that under business conditions and the reduced steel operating rate existing in 1958 no payments be made toward the funding of past service pension costs for the year, and also that $61 million of the $297 million so provided in past years be used to cover current service costs of non-contributory pensions for the first three quarters of the year. This determination

Cost of employe benefits

Sums provided by U. S. Steel to cover the cost of pensions, social security taxes, insurance

19

240

trustee, United States Steel and Carnegie Pension Fund (a non-profit Pennsylvania membership corporation), solely for the payment of benefits under the U. S. Steel pension plan, and were adequate at the respective dates to meet currently accruing pension costs incurred since the adoption of the present contributory and of the present non-contributory parts of the pension plan in 1940 and 1930, respectively, as well as to pay full pensions to all those then entitled to receive them.

Pension benefits

Under the U. S. Steel pension plan, pensions were granted during 1958 to 9,570 former employes, including 4,303 who retired in prior years and became entitled to pensions under the revisions to the pension rules that were effective November 1, 1957. At the end of the year there were 33,497 former employes or their co-pensioners receiving pensions as compared with 26,274 at the end of 1957. Pension benefits paid in 1958 were $30.7 million.

Group insurance benefits

Under the U. S. Steel group insurance plans, beneficiaries of active and retired employes received death benefits of about $13.0 million in 1958 and $13.1 million in 1957. At the year end approximately 227,000 active and retired employes were insured for about $1,479 million of life insurance. Accident, sickness,

provided additional cash to aid in carrying out facility additions and replacements. Provision was made for the funding of current service costs for the fourth quarter of the year. If provision for current service and past service pension costs had been made for the full year on the same basis as in 1957, the additional employment cost charged against income for the year 1958 would have amounted to approximately $97 million before the effect of income taxes and $46.6 million after such taxes.

There is no unfunded past service cost in connection with contributory pensions, since no service prior to the date of employe participation is involved in determining benefits.

The assets, less reserves, of the combined pension trusts were $1,103.0 million at December 31, 1958, and $1,051.1 million at December 31, 1957, as set forth in the statement appearing on page 39. These funds are held by the hospital, surgical, in-hospital medical and major medical benefits of $31.2 million were received during 1958 by employes or their families under the U. S. Steel insurance plans.

Cost of Employe Benefits	1958	1957
Pension costs		
Non-contributory part of pension plan		
Funding of current service cost (including interest on past service cost) — see below	$ 85,502,658	$ 93,660,184
Funding of portion of past service cost	–	38,000,000
Funding of past service cost in prior years used for current service cost (included in $85,502.658 above)	60,984,345	–
Total non-contributory pension costs	24,518,313	131,660,184
Contributory part of pension plan — current service cost	8,777,821	8,533,173
Total pension costs	33,296,134	140,193,357
Social security taxes	34,669,605	39,133,358
Insurance costs	26,291,921	30,210,632
Supplemental unemployment benefit costs	12,419,192	16,695,777
Savings fund costs	11,065,077	10,383,564
Payments to industry welfare and retirement funds and other employe benefit costs	26,250,103	28,502,306
Total cost	$143,992,032	$265,118,994

241

FINANCIAL SUMMARY
Profits - - their function

U. S. Steel and its management have long real-ized, as recorded in previous annual reports, that U. S. Steel — its employes and its stock-holders — can prosper only as its customers and the nation as a whole prosper. The combined good or ill fortune of its customers affects U. S. Steel in multiplied fashion. The percentage swings in U. S. Steel's business from one year to another are roughly double those of the Federal Reserve Board's index of industrial production.

Steel being cheap, durable and serviceable in so many ways is a principal material used in creating the nation's tools of production — plant, equipment, construction, transportation, and the like. Hence U. S. Steel's business responds especially to investment in new tools of produc-tion. U. S. Steel's direct interest in new produc-tive investment is but part of what is, or should be, a widespread national concern. For it is only as the nation's tools of production are kept

sufficient and efficient that the nation can either expect to enjoy economic progress with its rising standard of living, or hope to survive in a position of leadership in a troubled world.

Of relevance, too, in view of the unemploy-ment that exists, is the truism that the only way that a new self-sustaining productive job ever comes into existence is that savings are invested in tools of production. This creates the environ-ment in which men may go to work producing the marketable values to cover their continuing wage and the investors' profit.

In America people do not invest savings in job-creating tools of production unless they thereby expect to gain a profit in so doing or to diminish a loss otherwise to be incurred. The American competitive enterprise system is an acknowledged profit and loss system, the hope of profit being the incentive and the fear of loss being the spur. Since some two-thirds of all employment in America is furnished by corporations, it is of deep concern to observe how greatly over the years the corporate incentive has been undermined. This may be noted by comparing the compensation of employes in the nation with the corporate profit through which so great a part of the employment is maintained and new productive employment inspired.

The fact is that over the past decade there has been a sharp downward trend in the relative position of profit in the American economy. This trend has already cut the profit incentive approximately in half. Thus, as may be seen in the chart, corporate profits just before and shortly after World War II ranged from about 12 to 14 per cent of the nation's employe compensation. Since then the percentage has shrunk to about 7 per cent. Most employes realize that the only

true job security they have is that their employers can make profits and so continue to hire them. In terms of this measurement the margin for job security has been cut about in half.

Almost everybody "believes in" our competitive enterprise system. But many have misconceptions of its nature and function and so lend at least passive encouragement to those who would either bargain away, tax away or regulate away profits, all of which efforts have something to do with the undermining of the profit incentive which has taken place.

Profits and inflation

A principal pretense about profits, proffered primarily by labor union leaders, is that corporate profit rather than cost-push wage inflation is responsible for price inflation. This attitude ignores recorded facts. What the nation's prices must cover, if production is to continue, are the costs and profits of producing the goods and services that constitute the net national product. The principal official components of that product, as determined by the U. S. Department of Commerce, are: the compensation of employes, including employer contributions for social insurance and other employe benefits; taxes on business, including corporate income taxes; the income of unincorporated enterprises — proprietors; and the profits of corporations.

As portrayed in the chart on page 28, the net product increased, for example, from $221 billion in 1947 to an estimated $400 billion in 1958. Of the $179 billion increase, $125 billion was attributable to increase in employe compensation, $27 billion to increased taxes and $27 billion to increased income of unincorporated enterprises — proprietors — and miscellaneous items. There was no increase in the 1947 corporate profit component of $18 billion. To have

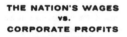

THE NATION'S WAGES
vs.
CORPORATE PROFITS
1940 and 1947-1958

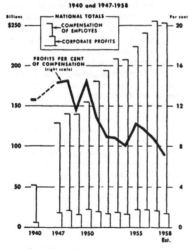

Source: U. S. Department of Commerce for both total compensation of employes (the nation's wages) and for corporate profit

26

kept pace with the rise in the combined other components since 1947, corporate profits in 1958 would have had to be about $34 billion, as contrasted with the all-time high in 1956 of $23 billion.

It is indeed curious reasoning which contends that rising prices are attributable to corporate profits – the only major component of net national product that did not increase – instead of to the wage and tax components which account for about 85 per cent of the increase.

A profitable economy is actually less susceptible to inflation than one in which profits are meager. Shrinking profits and mounting unemployment go together, invoking – as most recently witnessed in 1958 – inflation-threatening Federal deficits.

"Big" profits

Perhaps the most widespread misconception about profits is that a "big" profit, by whatever convenient measurement, is "unfair" and should therefore somehow be confiscated for other purposes – be they higher wages, bigger taxes or lower prices. But the fairness of a profit, or of a loss, is never to be determined from its arithmetic magnitude, but only in terms of the fairness of price, wage and other transactions of which it is the mere arithmetic consequence. In the American tradition fair dealings are those into which there enters no element of dictation, compulsion or intimidation. If they are honest and voluntary, they must be deemed fair and beneficial by the participants who otherwise are free not to undertake them – and so also must the profit or loss result be deemed fair.

Dividends

Among other misconceptions about profits is the notion that stockholders get all the profits of corporations. They do not. All the money that stockholders ever get from their corporations (except in the event of dissolution and distribution of assets) are the dividends declared to them. Dividends are a relatively small but exceedingly vital part of the nation's income. They are small – they average only about one-twentieth as much as the national compensation of employes, and the trend in this ratio over the past decade or more has been slightly downward. They are vital because on that slender thread of income to compensate those who have risked their savings to provide the tools of production depends the functioning of the American economy. They, like spark plugs in an automobile engine, are a tiny part of the whole mechanism, but one without which the whole mechanism fails. Abolish profits and dividends through taxation or otherwise and out of the ensuing chaos would inevitably arise some sort of socialistic dictatorship. In view of this it is as sadly surprising as it is socially foolish that corporate income paid in dividends should be double taxed – first as earned, and again when transferred to stockholders as dividends.

Income reinvested in business

Another fallacy is the belief held by some that the remaining part of income, which we designate "income reinvested in business," represents a stagnant pool of purchasing power that has been siphoned off from the economy and which, in the general interest, should somehow be forced back into circulation. It is a viewpoint sometimes urged as justification for bargaining, taxing or regulating away profits. But nothing could be further from the truth, and that the idea is given any public credence at all probably stems from accounting terminology which labels this remaining part as "undistributed profits" or "surplus." The people who compile the figures understand very well that "income reinvested in business" does not represent an accumulated pool of cash purchasing power. "Income reinvested" is a tag which, for convenience in keeping track of things, is put on part of the money which has come into, *flowed through*, and, for the most part, already passed out of the business as an expenditure for tools of production or other assets that are needed to operate the business.

Profits and cash flow

That there is no pool of purchasing power to be raided for any purpose can be readily demonstrated by the recorded facts of U. S. Steel. To establish this truth U. S. Steel has aggregated for the thirteen years, 1946-1958, the conventional items of its income statement (shown for individual years on page 31) and other items

relevant to the cash flow. The compilation, shown on page 24, discloses that although receipts from customers were $41,344 million, the increase in cash was only $20 million — and this despite the fact that $1,391 million was recorded as income reinvested. To have had even this little increase in cash U. S. Steel had to secure $750 million from the sale of its bonds, common stock and property. The simple fact is that income reinvested is a representation of purchasing power that has been expended rather than of purchasing power accumulated and available to be tapped.

The principal reason that income reinvested represents purchasing power already expended is that cash spent for new tools of production was $1,493 million more than the $2,473 million of wear and exhaustion of facilities — depreciation — recorded as cost. Of this excess, over $1,050 million was the extent to which recorded depreciation was deficient in recovering the buying power originally invested.

Uses of income reinvested

Corporate income reinvested, like dividends, constitutes a very small part of the nation's income flow; but, like dividends, it is an exceedingly vital part of that flow. It has numerous functions to perform.

In periods of inflation a first claim on income reinvested is to make good the deficiency in depreciation and so to preserve the enterprise. Under the tax code and presently accepted accounting principles the depreciation cost is based on the number of dollars originally paid — often long ago — for the depreciable asset. But as the buying power of the dollar declines, the depreciation amount becomes less and less adequate to cover the cost of equipment that must be purchased if the company is merely to "stay even." During inflation, depreciation recovers

246

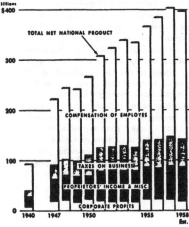

NET NATIONAL PRODUCT COMPONENTS

1940 and 1947-1958

Billions
$400

TOTAL NET NATIONAL PRODUCT

300

200

COMPENSATION OF EMPLOYES

100

TAXES ON BUSINESS

PROPRIETORS' INCOME & MISC

CORPORATE PROFITS

0   1940   1947   1950   1955   1958
Est.

Source: U.S. Department of Commerce

28

the dollars originally expended, but not the buying power represented by such dollars, and income reinvested is thus called upon to do part of the job that depreciation ought to do. The extent to which income is preempted to perform this "stay even" function has appropriately come to be called "phantom profit." In the case of U. S. Steel, as previously noted, the depreciation deficiency due to inflation over the years 1946-1958 amounted to over $1,050 million.

Not only is much of income reinvested thus necessary to maintain existing supplies of tools and the jobs that go with them, but income reinvested is also the most immediate, direct and traditional source of money to purchase additional tools of production. Such purchases not only provide the jobs of making the new tools but also the jobs of later operating them to increase the abundance of needed or wanted goods and services.

There are still other vital functions for income reinvested to perform. Additional money can neither be borrowed nor repaid unless income reinvested be present or prospective. Thus few will lend their money to a corporation except that it be a "going" corporation with income prospects to assure safety of principal and interest. And a corporation that once becomes indebted cannot pay off that debt except out of income earned or through sale of stock, which latter, in turn, is not possible without income prospects. Income reinvested is also the most immediate and direct source of increased working capital required not only by inflation but also to facilitate the functioning of an expanding productive economy.

He who would "squeeze" income reinvested to increase wages, taxes or other costs, or to reduce prices, would simultaneously be "squeezing out": (1) money needed to overcome depreciation deficiency and maintain existing tool

capacity and employment, (2) the employment supplied in making both replacement and additional tools, (3) the employment of more labor to operate the additional tools, (4) the new and better products that come from new and better tools, and (5) the most immediate and direct means that exist of financing and expanding industrial capacity, important in peacetime and essential in wartime.

Profits and freedom

There is a big difference between the American economy and the Russian economy. In the American economy productive effort, through the voluntary and competitive decisions of free men, is automatically and continuously devoted to meeting with maximum satisfaction the wants of *all* the people; in Russia production is by governmental compulsion directed toward satisfying the aspirations of its ruling class with mere subsistence for the people. But the American economy cannot function if there is interference with the voluntary and competitive markets by which the community bestows its rewards. These rewards are in terms of income or profits to those who most ably produce what the community wants at prices it is willing to pay, while those who serve to its lesser satisfaction receive lesser incomes or experience losses.

Our system rests on its provision of opportunity for free men to benefit themselves by saving and investing, but only if in so doing they serve the public's economic interest. If the benefits from so doing are removed, then progress must stop, unemployment arise and government compulsion replace the voluntary decisions of free men.

A profit and loss system can be practiced only by free men. They cannot sacrifice that system without sacrificing their freedom.

PRICE WATERHOUSE & CO.

56 PINE STREET
NEW YORK 5

February 24, 1959

To the Stockholders of
United States Steel Corporation:

248

As independent auditors elected at the annual meeting of stockholders of United States Steel Corporation held on May 5, 1958, we have examined the consolidated statement of financial position of United States Steel Corporation and subsidiaries at December 31, 1958 and the consolidated statement of income for the year 1958. Our examination was made in accordance with generally accepted auditing standards and accordingly included such tests of the accounting records and such other auditing procedures as we considered necessary in the circumstances.

Under the practice being followed by the Corporation in accounting for pension costs, the amounts charged to income annually have been equal to the amounts paid to the Trustee of its pension funds. With respect to non-contributory pensions, prior to 1958 such amounts included the annual current service costs (including interest on past service costs) and, in addition, the approximate maximum amount permitted by United States Treasury Department tax regulations for past service costs. Such additional payments for past service costs totaled $297 million to December 31, 1957. In view of these earlier payments, in 1958 the Board of Directors determined that, under the business conditions and the reduced steel operating rate existing during the first three quarters of the year, $61 million of the additional $297 million would be applied against current service costs for the first three quarters of 1958 and that no payment would be made for the year for past service costs; provision and payment have been made for current service costs for the fourth quarter. While the amount paid to the Trustee for 1958 for non-contributory pension costs is less than the related current service costs which accrued during the year, the aggregate of all amounts paid to the Trustee to date, for both current and past service costs, exceeds all current service costs accrued since the adoption of the plan in 1950. The assets held by the Trustee at December 31, 1958 were adequate to cover the estimated cost of all pensions for those then entitled to receive them.

As indicated in the preceding paragraph, the charges to income for non-contributory pension costs for 1958 were not comparable in amount with the charges for 1957, although the amounts for each year were equal to the amounts paid to the Trustee. If the Corporation had made payments to the Trustee and charged such amounts to income for 1958 on the same basis as for 1957, the additional pension costs charged against 1958 income would have amounted to approximately $97 million before the effect of income taxes and $46.6 million after such taxes.

In our opinion, with the foregoing explanation, the accompanying consolidated statement of financial position and related statement of income, together with the notes thereto, present fairly the position of United States Steel Corporation and subsidiaries at December 31, 1958 and the results of the year's operations, in conformity with generally accepted accounting principles applied on a basis consistent with that of the preceding year.

Price Waterhouse & Co.

1965 ANNUAL REPORT

U. S. Steel Chooses Deferral of Investment Credit
Past Service Costs Still Unfunded at $207 Million
New Policy for Past Service Costs
Interest Factors Adjusted

Financial Statements

JANUARY 1, 1966 MERGER

As explained on page 7 of this report, the January 1. 1966 merger of United States Steel Corporation, a New Jersey Corporation, into a wholly-owned Delaware subsidiary company involves the exchange of preferred stock for subordinated debentures and an increase in the par value of the outstanding common stock. The resultant changes in capitalization and costs applicable to future periods (before giving effect to any cash settlement in lieu of debentures or fractions thereof) were as follows:

	December 31, 1965	January 1, 1966 - After Merger	Increase Decrease
Long-term debt due after one year	$ 705.1	$1,335.6	$630.5
Preferred stock	360.3	—	360.3
Common stock	902.3	1,624.2	721.9⁽²⁾
Capital surplus	17.8	—	17.8
Income reinvested in business	2,362.3	1,424.0	(234.2⁽¹⁾ / 704.1)
Capitalization	$4,347.8	$4,383.8	$ 36.0
Less: Costs applicable to future periods			36.0
			$ —

(dollars in millions)

⑴ The $234.2 million excess of the aggregate market value of the preferred stock at the close of business on December 31, 1965 over its total par value was charged to Income Reinvested in Business and the difference between such market value and the aggregate principal amount of the Debentures authorized was reflected in Costs Applicable to Future Periods (unamortized debt discount).

⑵ The increase in par value of common stock from $16⅔ per share to $30 per share was transferred from Income Reinvested in Business in the amount of $704.1 million and from Capital Surplus in the amount of $17.8 million (included with the Reserve for Contingencies in the financial statements).

250

PRINCIPLES APPLIED IN CONSOLIDATION

Subsidiaries consolidated include all companies (with minor exceptions) of which a majority of the capital stock is owned by U. S. Steel or by any of its consolidated subsidiaries.

STOCK OPTION INCENTIVE PLANS

The Stock Option Incentive Plan approved by stockholders in 1964 and the Plan approved in 1951 authorized the option and sale of up to 1,500,000 shares and 2,600,000 shares of common stock, respectively, to key management employes, such shares of stock to be made available from authorized unissued or reacquired common stock at market price on the date the options are granted. An option may be exercised in whole at any time, or in part from time to time, during the option period. The option period begins on the date the option is granted and ends five years (1964 Plan) and ten years (1951 Plan) thereafter, except in cases of death, retirement or other earlier termination. No options to purchase stock were granted during 1965 under the 1964 Plan, and the granting of options under the 1951 Plan was terminated in 1964.

In 1965, no options were exercised under the 1964 Plan and 24 optionees purchased 8,150 shares at $48.00 per share under options granted under the 1951 Plan. At December 31. 1965, under the 1964 Plan, 225 optionees held options to purchase 462,350 shares at $55.50 per share for a total of $25.7 million and 1,036,550 shares were available for future options. Under the 1951 Plan. 111 optionees held options to purchase 147,025 shares at prices ranging from $55.00 to $82.00 per share for a total of $9.2 million.

SECURITIES SET ASIDE FOR PROPERTY ADDITIONS AND REPLACEMENTS

At December 31, 1965, completion of authorized additions to and replacements of facilities required an estimated further expenditure of $735 million and marketable securities set aside to cover in part such authorized expenditures totaled $655 million, the same as at the end of 1964.

WEAR AND EXHAUSTION OF FACILITIES

For the most part, wear and exhaustion of facilities is related to U. S. Steel's rate of operations within the guidelines established in 1962 by the Internal Revenue Service.

The investment tax credit provided for in the Revenue Act of 1962, as amended in 1964, amounted to $13.7 million in 1965 and $13.4 million in 1964 and was included in the provision for income taxes and established as a deferred investment credit to be amortized over the lives of the property acquired.

RESERVES FOR INSURANCE, CONTINGENCIES AND ACCIDENT AND HOSPITAL EXPENSES

U. S. Steel is, for the most part, a self-insurer of its assets against fire, windstorm, marine and related losses. The insurance reserve of $50 million is held available for absorbing possible losses of this character, and is considered adequate for this purpose.

The reserves for contingencies and accident and hospital expenses of $67.8 million, provided mainly in previous years by charges to operations, are held for exceptional unanticipated losses other than those covered by the insurance reserve.

PENSION FUNDING

Pension costs for 1965, as determined by an independent actuary based on various actuarial factors, were $34.6 million, and this amount was paid into pension trusts by U. S. Steel. At March 1, 1950, the effective date of the present non-contributory part of the pension plan, the actuarial cost of pensions for service rendered prior to that date which had not been funded was estimated at $496 million and as of December 31, 1964 approximately $207 million of this amount remained unfunded. In 1965, the basis of determining pension costs was changed to an actuarial method under which all costs, including previously unfunded past service costs, are funded over the future on a combined basis. Also, in the light of actual experience, interest factors were adjusted. The net effect during 1965 of the change in funding method and the adjustment of interest factors was to decrease U. S. Steel's pension costs for the year with a resultant increase in income of $3.8 million.

The combined assets of the contributory and non-contributory pension trusts were $1,717.5 million at December 31, 1965 (after write-off of the investment of $2.5 million in a Canadian finance company) and $1,659.7 million at December 31, 1964, as set forth in the statement appearing on page 30. These funds are held by the trustee, United States Steel and Carnegie Pension Fund (a non-profit Pennsylvania membership corporation), solely for the payment of benefits under the U. S. Steel pension plan, and were adequate at the respective dates to pay full pensions to all those then entitled to receive them as well as to meet currently accruing pension costs incurred since the adoption of the present contributory and of the present non-contributory parts of the pension plan in 1940 and 1950, respectively.

OTHER ITEMS

Products and Services Sold—Products and services sold includes interest, dividends and other income of $65.4 million in 1965 and $51.9 million in 1964. *Costs*—Wages and salaries totaled $1,655.7 million in 1965 of which $1,630.2 million was included in costs of products and services sold and the balance was charged to construction.

Products and services bought reflects the changes during the year in inventories and deferred costs. These items decreased during 1965 approximately $60 million.

If the total of wages and salaries and products and services bought in 1965 were reclassified as costs of products and services sold and general administrative and selling expenses, the amounts thereof would be $3,068.6 million and $186.4 million, respectively.

Maintenance and repairs of plant and equipment totaled $547.5 million in 1965.

Non-cancellable charters and leases covering ore ships, office space, and other properties with minimum rentals aggregating approximately $40 million per year were in effect at December 31, 1965, the major portion of which terminates within ten years. In 1965, expenditures on such charters and leases amounted to approximately $52 million.

251

PRICE WATERHOUSE & CO.

60 BROAD STREET

NEW YORK 10004

February 23, 1966

To the Stockholders of
United States Steel Corporation:

In our opinion, the accompanying Consolidated Statement of Financial Position and related Statement of Income present fairly the position of United States Steel Corporation and subsidiaries at December 31, 1965 and the results of operations for the year, in conformity with generally accepted accounting principles applied on a basis consistent with that of the preceding year. Our examination of these statements was made in accordance with generally accepted auditing standards and accordingly included such tests of the accounting records and such other auditing procedures as we considered necessary in the circumstances.

Price Waterhouse & Co.

1968 ANNUAL REPORT

$102 Million Drop in Depreciation
Income Significantly Increased
IRS Guidelines Procedures Dominant
Switch of Depreciation Methods
Investment Credit Policy Changed
Effect of Changes on Income Disclosed
Price Waterhouse Approves

Consolidated Statement of Income

	1968	1967
PRODUCTS AND SERVICES SOLD	$4,609,234,734	$4,067,227,425
COSTS		
Employment costs		
Wages and salaries	1,734,019,614	1,587,584,702
Employe benefits *(see page 18)*	321,897,182	284,061,968
	2,055,916,796	1,871,646,670
Products and services bought	1,766,144,174	1,431,838,466
Wear and exhaustion of facilities	253,114,609	354,705,686
Interest and other costs on long-term debt	67,043,333	54,394,067
State, local and miscellaneous taxes	113,340,273	106,162,955
Estimated United States and foreign taxes on income	100,000,000	76,000,000
Total	4,355,559,185	3,894,747,844
INCOME	253,675,549	172,479,581
Income Per Common Share	$4.69	$3.19
DIVIDENDS DECLARED		
On common stock *($2.40 per share)*	129,947,699	129,943,814
INCOME REINVESTED IN BUSINESS	$ 123,727,850	$ 42,535,767

256

PRINCIPLES APPLIED IN CONSOLIDATION
Subsidiaries consolidated include all companies (with minor exceptions) of which a majority of the capital stock is owned by U. S. Steel or by any of its consolidated subsidiaries.

STOCK OPTION INCENTIVE PLANS
The Stock Option Incentive Plan approved by stockholders in 1964 and the Plan approved in 1951 authorized the option and sale of up to 1.500,000 shares and 2.600,000 shares of common stock. respectively. to key management employes, such shares of stock to be made available from authorized unissued or reacquired common stock at market price on the date the options are granted. An option may be exercised in whole or in part from time to time. during the option period if no prior option is outstanding at a higher price. The option period begins on the date the option is granted and ends five years (1964 Plan) and ten years (1951 Plan) thereafter. except in cases of death, retirement or other earlier termination.

In 1968, options for 530,775 shares were granted to 230 employes at the then market price of $39.625 per share. During 1968, 4 optionees purchased 1,275 shares at $36.75 per share under options granted under the 1964 Plan.

At December 31, 1968, 325 optionees held options to purchase 1,468,625 shares at prices ranging from $36.75 to $82.00 per share for a total of $64.5 million and 35,100 shares were available for future options.

SECURITIES SET ASIDE FOR PROPERTY ADDITIONS AND REPLACEMENTS
At December 31, 1968, completion of authorized additions to and replacements of facilities required an estimated further expenditure of $1.110 million and marketable securities set aside to cover in part such authorized expenditures totaled $655 million. the same as at the end of 1967.

WEAR AND EXHAUSTION OF FACILITIES
For the most part, wear and exhaustion of facilities is related to U. S. Steel's rate of operations and is based on the guideline procedures established in 1962 by the Internal Revenue Service.

Effective for the year 1968. U. S. Steel. for financial reporting purposes, revised the lives of certain properties and changed from accelerated methods of computing depreciation to the straight-line method. The 1968 investment credit provided for in the income tax laws has been taken directly into income as a reduction in the provision for income taxes; the investment credit for 1967 and prior years continues to be allocated to future years; the amounts included in 1968 income totaled $38.6 million. After provision for deferred taxes on income. tne depreciation and investment credit changes resulted in increased income of $94.0 million.

RESERVES AND DEFERRED TAXES ON INCOME
U. S. Steel is. for the most part. a self-insurer of its assets against fire. windstorm. marine and related losses. The insurance reserve of $50 million is held available for absorbing possible losses of this character. and is considered adequate for this purpose.

The reserves for contingencies and accident and hospital expenses of $50.1 million. provided mainly in previous years by charges to operations. are held for exceptional unanticipated losses other than those covered by the insurance reserve.

PREFERRED STOCK
At the Annual Meeting held on May 6. 1968. stockholders of U. S. Steel voted to amend the Certificate of Incorporation to authorize the issuance of 20.000.000 shares of a new class of preferred stock, without par value. At December 31. 1968. none of this stock had been issued.

PENSION FUNDING
U. S. Steel's pension plan covers substantially all its employes. Pension costs are determined by an independent actuary, based upon various actuarial factors and an actuarial method under which both current and unfunded past service costs are funded over the future on a combined basis by payment into pension trusts. For 1968. the cost of pensions amounted to $70.2 million compared with $65.4 million in 1967.

The combined assets of the contributory and noncontributory pension trusts were $1.965.2 million at December 31, 1968 and $1,869.6 million at December 31. 1967, as set forth in the statement appearing on page 30. These funds are held by the trustee.

**Independent
Auditors' Report**

(Notes to Financial Statements continued)

United States Steel and Carnegie Pension Fund (a non-profit Pennsylvania membership corporation), solely for the payment of benefits under the U. S. Steel pension plan.

OTHER ITEMS

Other Investments — Other investments include long-term receivables of $84.1 million.

Production Payments — In December 1968, U. S. Steel sold proceeds of mineral production payments which represent an interest in a portion of future production of minerals. These transactions are reflected in operations over the lives of the contracts.

Products and Services Sold—Products and services sold includes interest, dividends and other income of $72.5 million in 1968 and $61.7 million in 1967.

Costs—Wages and salaries totaled $1,767.2 million in 1968 of which $1,734.0 million was included in costs of products and services sold and the balance was charged to construction.

Products and services bought reflects the changes during the year in inventories and deferred costs. These items decreased during 1968 approximately $32 million.

If the total of wages and salaries and products and services bought in 1968 were reclassified as costs of products and services sold and general administrative and selling expenses, the amounts thereof would be $3,295.8 million and $204.3 million, respectively.

Maintenance and repairs of plant and equipment totaled $639.5 million in 1968.

Non-cancellable charters and leases covering ore ships, office space, and other properties with minimum rentals aggregating approximately $38 million per year were in effect at December 31, 1968. the major portion of which terminates within ten years. In 1968, expenditures on such charters and leases amounted to approximately $46 million.

257

PRICE WATERHOUSE & CO.

60 BROAD STREET

NEW YORK 10004

February 25, 1969

To the Stockholders of

United States Steel Corporation:

In our opinion, the accompanying Consolidated Statement of Financial Position and related Statement of Income present fairly the position of United States Steel Corporation and subsidiaries at December 31, 1968 and the results of operations for the year, in conformity with generally accepted accounting principles. These principles were applied on a basis consistent with that of the preceding year, except for the changes, which we approve, in the methods of computing depreciation and accounting for the investment credit as described in the note. "Wear and Exhaustion of Facilities." Our examination of these statements was made in accordance with generally accepted auditing standards and accordingly included such tests of the accounting records and such other auditing procedures as we considered necessary in the circumstances.

Price Waterhouse Co.